Class, Culture, and Alienation

Class, Culture, and Alienation

A Study of Farmers and Farm Workers

William A. Rushing
Vanderbilt University

Lexington Books
D.C. Heath and Company
Lexington, Massachusetts
Toronto   London

To Claudia

Contents

viii

List of Tables

Preface

This book is about three of the oldest concepts in sociology: culture, class, and alienation. Culture, of course, is probably the central concept in sociology, and class and alienation constitute two of the most frequently researched and discussed ideas. The relationship between class status and alienation in particular has received considerable attention; indeed, it has been a central topic in sociology since the writings of Karl Marx.

Status deprivation and perceived denied opportunity are often regarded as the most important determinants of class differences, especially when alienation is viewed as the rejection of conventional norms and deviant behavior. Some sociologists, however, do not accept this formulation but argue that class differences in alienation and deviant behavior may stem not from feelings of class deprivation or perceived blocked opportunity, but from class differences in such factors as values, tradition, subcultures, life styles, cultural commitment, and so forth.

The disagreement may be more apparent than real. On the one hand, perceived class deprivation and denied opportunity may not contribute to differences between classes in alienation; the association between class and alienation may be independent of these two factors. On the other hand, however, the relationships of perceived deprivation and perceived opportunity to alienation may be independent of social class; they may exist at all levels of the class structure. It is generally agreed that status deprivation and especially denied opportunity are significant elements in the culture and social life of the United States. In this country, people strive hard for those things that separate them along class lines—education, income, good housing, and so forth—and the principle of equal opportunity may be the one most important aspect of the cultural ideology of the United States. Indeed, many court decisions and much legislative action have been and continue to be based on that principle. It is not unlikely, therefore, that the influence of this principle is not limited to the lower class alone. A major thesis of this book is that this is indeed the case. We suggest that the desire to achieve status and to have an equal opportunity are such important elements in the culture of the United States that, in combination with other elements of this culture, they exert an influence on alienation at all levels of the class structure. In short, they are cultural phenomena that transcend social classes. Consequently, theories which have emphasized the importance of perceived class deprivation and denied opportunity are more appropriately termed "cultural theories" than "class theories." They are specific to societies with cultures such as that which characterizes the United States.

Our hypothesis is that cultural emphasis on achieved status—rather than ascribed status—provides the specific cultural setting in which perceived class deprivation and denied opportunity are most likely to exert an influence in society. The book differs, therefore, from most other books on social class in that the central concern is with how certain effects generated by factors commonly associated with the class structure, i.e., perceived deprivation and denied opportunity, have similar effects for individuals in different locations in the class structure. By definition, members of the lower class differ from members of more advantaged strata, but forces generated by the class structure exist within a broad social and cultural environment which may determine how social class factors influence the behavior and attitudes of individuals within the class structure. The cultural setting may pervade the class structure to such an extent that the effects generated by components of social class blend with those of the broader culture to influence individuals throughout the class structure in similar ways.

The book differs in still another way from most social class studies, particularly those which have had the lower class or poverty stratum as their focus. The research on which our analysis is based includes data on one group—farm workers—that is an unequivocal lower-class group and a second group—farmers—that is an unequivocal middle- to upper-class group. Few class studies focus on a group from the *very bottom* of the class structure along with one from the middle to upper levels.

In addition, three distinct cultural groups are represented among the lower-class farm workers: English speaking anglo-Americans, bilingual Mexican-Americans, and non-English speaking Mexican-Americans. This permits the assessment of the interaction between class and cultural factors to a greater extent than most studies of social class and the lower class have allowed.

In writing a book of this nature one frequently has to choose between writing an ethnography of the groups on which the book is about or focusing on the testing of hypotheses derived from a theoretical base. There are advantages to both approaches. The former tells the reader more about the life style of the subjects of the research, the latter more about how the behavior and attitudes of the subjects conform to or deviate from theoretical propositions. This book takes the latter approach by investigating the role of perceived class deprivation and perceived denied opportunity in producing alienative attitudes and the differential role of class and cultural contexts in the generation of these attitudes.

Acknowledgments

This book has been several years in the writing and the author received help from a number of sources. Particular thanks go to the National Center for Urban and Industrial Health which supported the research on which the book is based. This book constitutes the final report for Public Health Service Grant No. UI 00230.

A number of individuals were especially helpful in the production of the book and the research on which it is based. Walter L. Slocum and F. Ivan Nye of Washington State University made helpful suggestions about the proposal for the study and provided advice concerning the field operations. Several research assistants from the Department of Sociology at Washington State University assisted in the field research; particular thanks go to Glenn Howze and Donald Tennant, now at the Tuskegee Institute and Oklahoma State University, respectively, who assisted with the field operations throughout the study. Vic Matthews, now at the University of Alberta, assisted with the early computer analysis, and Thomas James of Vanderbilt University did most of the computer analysis beyond the early stages. Harvey Williams of Vanderbilt was helpful with library research and a review of the literature.

A number of persons read different sections of the manuscript, in varying degrees of completion; their suggestions were always helpful, though not always judiciously heeded, I admit. I am especially grateful for the comments of Walter Slocum, Leo Rigsby of Vanderbilt University, and Phillip Hammond of the University of Arizona. Marianne Rigsby and Kay Rushing read the entire manuscript; I thank them for their suggestions and editorial advice. I also want to thank Donna Jordan and Cindy Miller for their typing assistance.

Most of all I want to thank by family—Kay, Todd, and Claudia—for their patience during the many hours I worked on the manuscript. Without their understanding the book would have been much harder to write and taken much longer to complete.

W.A.R.

Nashville, Tennessee
April 1972

Part I: Class and Cultural Contexts of Alienation

1 Perceived Deprivation, Opportunity, and Alienation: Class and Cultural Contexts

The idea of alienation has been central in sociology almost since the birth of the discipline, particularly in the writings of early sociologists such as Karl Marx, Emile Durkheim, Max Weber, and Georg Simmel, and it continues to be a prominent issue today. Robert Nisbet contends that alienation constitutes one of the most seminal ideas in the history of sociology.[1] And yet, sociologists have never agreed on a common meaning for the term. It has been viewed as the estrangement of individuals from the norms and social controls of society, as the inability of individuals to influence their situation in society, as a feeling of meaninglessness about life, and a general sense of social malaise. The conditions which have been postulated as leading to these various states also vary. Central to all formulations, however, is the postulate that the state of alienation, however formulated, stems from some condition of society. Although sociologists do not agree on what that precise condition is, two general approaches may be distinguished.

One approach views alienation as primarily the result of factors that are specific to certain groups in society, usually lower socioeconomic groups. For example, Marx viewed alienation largely in reference to the class structure. He considered conditions of work in the working class to be crucial, and argued that these conditions would generate feelings of alienation in this class.[2] Alienation, according to Marx, is one element among several that affect the development of class awareness among workers and eventually lead to their rebellion against dominant economic groups in society. The idea that the class structure is important in alienation has received considerable attention in research studies, which tend to show that regardless of the conceptualization and measure of alienation, it is greater in the lower class than in the middle and upper classes; it may be especially great in the poverty stratum.[3]

Another approach views alienation as the result of general cultural conditions of contemporary industrial society, as reflected in the works of Durkheim, Weber, and Simmel as well as others. Although different specific conditions are viewed as responsible for alienation such as bureaucratization for Weber and the erosion of societal consensus and social integration for Durkheim, the condition is general in society. The idea is stated as follows by Nisbet:

If in the Renaissance thought it was the myth of reasonable man which predominated; if in the eighteenth century, it was natural man; and in the nineteenth century, economic and political man, it is by no means unlikely that for our own age it is alienated or maladjusted man who will appear to later historians as the key figure of twentieth-century thought.[4]

3

Hence, alienation has been considered diffuse in society and not limited to specific groups, and is the result of conditions that are general throughout society.

This book reflects the influence of both approaches. We will be concerned with the relationships of two class-related factors to alienation: *perceived class deprivation* and *perceived denied opportunity*. Both have received considerable attention in research studies in their own right, and the latter in particular is often cited as contributing to class differences in alienation.[5] Although we will investigate this hypothesis, our primary concern is with *cultural* differences in the relationships of these two variables to alienation. We believe that such relationships exist only in combination with the cultural setting in which they operate, that is, they exist in some cultural groups but not in others. Moreover, unless there are major cultural differences between class groups, no differences in these relationships would be expected between social classes. Our specific concern, then, is not so much the way social class or culture influence level of alienation itself, but with the way either or both of these variables influence the *relationships* of perceived deprivation and opportunity to alienation. Our hypothesis, of course, is that culture is more important than class. Factors such as perceived deprivation and opportunity do not operate in a cultural vacuum; they are part of a complex of cultural variables and their influence on alienation will differ depending on the nature of these variables. Each plays a different dynamic role in different cultural settings. Thus, it is the complex of cultural elements associated with *achieved* status, in contrast to *ascribed* status, that is crucial. Perceived deprivation and denied opportunity interact with certain cultural conditions in their effects on alienation.

Design of the Study

Our analysis is based on what is probably the most impoverished occupational group in the United States—farm workers—and a middle- to upper-class group of farm owners and operators[6]; analysis of differences between these two groups provides the basis for class comparison. Samples of both groups are from the state of Washington. In addition, three distinctive cultural-ethnic groups are represented among farm workers: anglo-Americans, bilingual Mexican-Americans, and non-English speaking Mexican-Americans; comparisons between these three groups will permit us to investigate cultural differences within the lower class, and hence how lower-class experience is influenced by cultural background. Anglo-Americans are distinguished from the two groups of Mexican-Americans by cultural heritage and national origin, and the language difference among Mexican-Americans indicates a difference in cultural ties to Mexican society and a difference in cultural assimilation to the dominant culture of the United States. The class and cultural groups are listed in Table 1-1.

Table 1-1
Social Class and Cultural Group Affiliations of Farmers and Farm Workers in Washington State

Social Class	Cultural Group		
Middle (Farmers)	Anglo-Americans		
Lower (Farm Workers)	Anglo-Americans	Bilingual Mexican-Americans	Non-English Speaking Mexican-Americans

The analysis is incomplete, of course, since only one cultural group is represented within the middle class. However, comparisons between the two groups of anglo-Americans permit the examination of class differences for representatives of the dominant U.S. culture. And comparisons between the lower-class anglo-Americans and Mexican-Americans permit an assessment of how culture modifies the effects of poverty status; if cultural differences are not significant there should be no differences between the three cultural groups.

The Concept of Alienation

The theme of alienation appears, in one form or another, in the works of contemporary writers such as Merton, Erich Fromm, Erik Erikson, David Reisman, William H. Whyte, Jr., and C. Wright Mills, and before them, Marx, Durkheim, Sigmund Freud, Simmel, and Weber. As noted, there is no universally accepted definition of the concept. Different writers have written about alienation in terms of their varying perspectives on society, the individual, and the relationship between the two.[7] Before discussing specific meanings, however, a more general distinction should be made.

Alienation: Attribute of Social Structure
or the Individual?

Scholars disagree as to whether alienation is an attribute of social structure or culture, or an attribute of individuals. Daniel Bell,[8] following the emphasis in the later works of Marx, prefers the first conception; he sees alienation as a structural arrangement which characterizes the relationship between workers and owners (management), with workers being exploited by the owners. Moreover, alienation is viewed in terms of process, i.e., in historical perspective, because the structure of exploitation changes. To study alienation in this sense one must observe and analyze the relationship between groups (e.g., workers and farmers) over time and describe the conditions of exploitation that (presumably) increase with time. Other writers such as Melvin Seeman[9] follow statements in the earlier works of Marx[10] and focus on the subjective characteristics of individuals, that is, alienation refers to perceptions, expectations, or attitudes.[11]

The distinction is not always easy to grasp, and in some instances it may be spurious. The problem may be seen in the analogy of the "sick society." To some, "sick society" makes no sense except in terms of individuals; a "sick society" is simply a society which has a high proportion of members who are "sick." Hence, a "sick society" merely comprises many "sick" individuals. The same can be true of alienation; to call a society alienated may mean only that a large proportion of the population is alienated. Therefore, for those who view alienation as estrangement from oneself, an alienated society is an additive phenomenon; it makes little sense to speak of an alienated society except in terms of the proportion of individuals in that society who are estranged from themselves. However, some writers consider normlessness to be the central feature of alienation and the concept of a normless society need not refer to an additive quality of individuals. Thus, we can make a *societal* reference to conflicting conceptions and a lack of consensus about what the dominant norms of society should be.[12] For the *individual*, however, normlessness may mean preferring self-interest to the constraints of rule and law. Hence, in comparison to other societies, a high proportion of individuals in any one society may be normless even though most members of that society agree on what the dominant norms are.

Our concern in this book is with the individual. Although we will consider group differences in alienation, our interpretations will always be in terms of the individual conception rather than the group or societal conception. Group measures of alienation (e.g., measures by class status or cultural group) are the additive responses of individuals rather than measures of alienation in terms of group structure. For example, a higher degree of normlessness in one group as compared to another indicates only that there are more individuals who are normatively estranged, not that groups differ in the extent to which their members agree on what the dominant norms of society should be. We will, of course, consider the possible effect of group characteristics on alienation, e.g., the class position of farmers and farm workers, but our interpretation will be in terms of how such characteristics influence (or do not influence) the individual component of alienation.

Specific Meanings of Individual Alienation

The concept of alienation is usually traced back to the works of Marx, who was concerned with the relationship of the industrial worker to his work, and how the worker's separation from the means of production and the resulting condition of work affected this relationship. With the coming of the factory system, the means of production were increasingly appropriated as the capital-ist's private property, so that the worker had less and less power to affect decisions concerning his work environment. Consequently, he became alienated from his work, from the product of his work, from himself, from society, and from human nature.[13] Social scientists have not limited their investigation of alienation to work alienation and powerlessness, however. Other related con-cepts are normlessness, meaninglessness, value isolation, social isolation, self-estrangement, and anomia.[14]

This multiplicity of concepts creates problems, especially communication difficulties; it is not always clear what is meant by alienation (and, indeed, different authors may even mean different things when they refer to specific concepts such as normlessness, powerlessness, etc.). One solution is to consider the concept of alienation as multidimensional, with the different uses considered as aspects of the same general phenomenon. However, as Richard Schacht points out, there may be no apparent interrelations among various aspects, e.g., logically a person could be alienated from the norms of society but not be alienated from himself, and vice versa. There is also the question of whether all the uses and meanings mentioned can be logically linked to the same general phenomenon.[15]

Given this state of affairs, it might be best to start over and offer a new conceptualization of alienation even though this would involve problems, because any overall conceptualization will probably exclude meanings that are central to some specific formulations. We will instead build on an existing body of sociological literature by investigating some of the more prominent meanings.

Most sociologists would agree that alienation reflects something about the individual in relation to society and that the use of questionnaires can determine what this relation is. Three of the most prominent theoretical and empirical conceptions for which such questionnaires test are *powerlessness, normlessness*, and *anomia*, around which considerable bodies of theoretical and empirical literature have developed, much of which pertain to the influence of social class.

Powerlessness. One of the oldest debates among sociologists is whether members of the lower class feel more powerless than members of the middle and upper classes. Karl Marx and his followers have argued that they do; as noted, Marx felt that this resulted from the fact that members of the lower class (that is, industrial wage workers) have so little control over their work situation and work-related behavior. Others have extended the conception of powerlessness, formulating it in more general terms by not limiting it to working conditions in the lower class; rather, outcomes associated with political and general economic issue are seen as central.[16] There is evidence that such measures of powerlessness are inversely associated with social class.[17] Max Weber[18] and his followers, however, contend that powerlessness is more a function of bureaucratic trends in society than class position; such trends influence the middle and upper classes as well as the lower class.[19] For Marx and neo-marxists, alienation is largely class specific, whereas for Weber it is related to more general societal characteristics.

Normlessness. The concept of normlessness or normative alienation can be traced to the works of Durkheim, although our usage is more specifically influenced by Merton's formulation.[20] Durkheim emphasized the lack of normative regulation between different components of society[21] and contended that this lack was responsible for a certain type of suicide.[22] Durkheim called such a condition *anomie* (or normlessness) rather than alienation. Although sociologists do not agree on what Durkheim meant by an "anomic individual," we can say for our purposes that such a person is influenced by personal desires and appetites rather than normative controls—such as social norms, rules, and law; the individual "recognizes no other rules of conduct than what are founded on his private interests."[23] For example, the individual who falls in status, and is unable to adjust his aspirations and goals to his lower status is influenced more by the personal desires he assimilated by virtue of his previous status than by the norms associated with his new status. At the same time, the individual who experiences a rapid elevation in status may believe there are no social limits to what he can achieve; again, aspirations and goals may be determined by the inner desires of the individual rather than the controls and constraints of society.[24] Both kinds of individuals are considered "anomic," that is, they are alienated from normal societal controls and directives.

This conception is not unlike the image of the individual in utilitarian philosophy,[25] which was prominent in Durkheim's time. According to that body of thought, one's actions are determined by rational calculations of personal reward and punishment, not by the influence of social norms, law, and other societal controls.[26] Accordingly, when one makes decisions about individual actions the "center of attention begins to shift from moral to cognitive judgment."[27] Such an orientation may encourage one to forego allegiance to conceptions of universal moral principles, rules, and law for a calculation of personal advantage. We will call this attitude normlessness. It is central to the writings of Merton, who believes it is particularly high in the lower class.[28] Gouldner, however, feels normlessness is widespread in the culture of western and American society, which he calls the "utilitarian culture."[29]

Anomia. Although our major theoretical interest is in powerlessness and normlessness, the concept of anomia has been widely used in research studies, and is frequently referred to as a general index of alienation. We will include it in our analysis.

The term anomia was coined by Leo Srole, who constructed a series of questionnaire items for measuring it in a paper published in 1956.[30] Although Srole links his use of anomia to Durkheim's original conception of anomie, it is generally agreed that the former's definition is a measure of despair or hopelessness rather than a measure of Durkheim's conception of anomie.[31] Numerous investigations have shown that Srole's measure of anomia is inversely associated with socioeconomic status.[32] Some claim that the relationship is due to lower perceived opportunity in the lower class.[33] We want to know if this is true and, moreover, whether the relationships of perceived opportunity (and perceived deprivation) are associated with anomia under different cultural conditions.

To conclude, three of the most prominent uses of alienation in research and theoretical writings are powerlessness, normlessness, and anomia. Powerlessness refers to the individual's perceived inability to influence his fate in society; normlessness to the tendency to accord legitimacy to individual self-interest rather than to honesty and the norms, rules, and laws of society; whereas anomia refers to the individual's general sense of hopelessness, despair, and malaise about his situation in society. Each may be related to social class, as various authors have suggested, and cultural differences may also exist. Our primary interest, however, concerns the *contextual effects* of class and culture on the relationships of perceived deprivation and denied opportunity to these three conceptions of alienation.[34]

Relative Deprivation and Alienation

The Concept of Relative Deprivation

In our conceptualization we link the concepts of class perception, relative deprivation, and false consciousness. In so doing we must present some general definitions.

Deprivation is a general term which refers to the absence, withholding, or denial of something to an individual. It is useful, however, to distinguish between physical and social deprivation.

Physical deprivation refers to the absence of basic requirements for physical survival. This is a vague conception and perhaps can never be defined precisely, other than to specify that it must be measured in terms of physical misery caused by inadequate or nonexistent basic subsistence requirements. The sole criterion of physical deprivation is simply physical suffering. Although we could probably construct a scale of physical suffering, it would be difficult to apply it on a wide scale. In any case, we will have no occasion to use the term physical deprivation in this book.

Social deprivation differs from physical deprivation both in content and the basis for measurement. It is defined not by physical requirements but by social standards and "life chances," i.e., income, prestige, social power, educational and occupational opportunities, and other benefits that society considers important, as well as more basic advantages such as long life expectancy and good health. In terms of *measurement*, the degree of social deprivation characterizes one's life chances as high and low only in *relation to the life chances of others*. Marx and Engels put it this way: "Our desires and pleasures spring from society; we measure them, therefore, by society and not by the objects which serve for their satisfaction. Because they are of a social nature, they are of a relative nature."[35]

Thus, educational achievement, occupational opportunity, and prestige are important because society considers them to be important and they are high or low for one man only in relation to the educational achievement, occupational opportunity, and prestige of other men.

Let us note that there is an important difference between *absolute* deprivation and *relative* deprivation. No relationship between them need exist. An individual's level of absolute deprivation, e.g., his income, may improve substantially but there may be no change, or there may even be a decrease, in his level of relative deprivation. For example, in their discussion of the deprivation of industrial workers, Marx and Engels stated, "Although the enjoyment of the workers [may] have risen, the social satisfaction that they give has fallen in comparison with the increased enjoyments of the capitalists, which are inaccessible to the workers, . . . "[36] Elsewhere Marx stated, "When capital is increasing fast, wages may rise, but the profit of capital will rise much faster. The *material* position of the laborer has improved, but it is at the expense of his *social* position. *The social gulf which separates him from the capitalist has widened.*"[37] Also, "in proportion as capital accumulates, the lot of the laborer, *be his payment high or low*, must grow worse."[38] Clearly, Marx's conception of deprivation is a relative conception.[39]

There are two aspects of relative deprivation, objective and perceptual. Objective deprivation refers to how well off a person or group actually is relative to other persons or groups in terms of life chances. The perceptual aspect refers to how well off one *views* his position in relation to the positions of others. If the perception of one's position is not perfectly correlated with his actual position, the individual is, in Marx's terms, *falsely conscious*.[40] False consciousness is usually found among members of the working or lower class who do not perceive their situations to be as low as they are. Thus, to the extent that farm workers do not perceive their positions to be at the bottom of the class structure, they are falsely conscious of their class position. The concept, however, is equally applicable for persons higher in the class structure who perceive their positions to be *lower* than they actually are.

This formulation of relative deprivation differs somewhat from standard formulations in sociology and social psychology. Usually, relative deprivation refers to the individual's level of deprivation or satisfaction in comparison to members of some *specific* group with whom the individual may be engaged in face-to-face interaction on a regular basis. Such groups are the individual's comparative reference groups, and it is thus in reference to them that he assesses his standing with respect to some valued outcome such as income, promotion, or prestige.[41] According to our definition of relative deprivation, the entire class structure is the individual's reference group. We also define deprivation in terms of differences in life chances, which is how the class structure is usually defined. Consequently, we use the concepts of relative deprivation, class perception, and perceived or subjective deprivation interchangeably (when relative deprivation is used, it will be understood that our reference is to the *perceived* dimension). False consciousness is defined in terms of these concepts, and refers to the extent to which an individual's perceived deprivation corresponds to his relative ranking on life chances measured in objective terms.

Class and Cultural Contexts

Despite frequent statements to the contrary by various writers, it is not certain that the poor perceive themselves to be severely deprived, that is, to be at the bottom of the class structure.[42] We will be concerned with the possible social and cultural determinants of false consciousness (in the middle class no less than in the lower class), but it is the relationships between perceived deprivation and our measures of alienation that will receive most of our attention. Such a relationship has been suggested in various theoretical frameworks. Marx suggested that since social class is viewed as a determinant of relative deprivation as well as of alienation, a relationship between the latter two is implied. However, Marx did not explore the possibility of such a relationship independent of social class; certainly he did not conceive of this relationship among the middle and upper classes (that is, the *bourgeoisie*). The same is true of certain frameworks of normlessness and deviance. Although the authors of these frameworks contend that the rejection of conventional societal norms is greater in the lower class because feelings of status deprivation are higher in this class,[43] their theories are also class specific. They fail to consider the possibility that perceived class deprivation may be associated with deviance-normlessness in the middle and higher classes as well.

The most important aspects of the relationships between relative deprivation and our measures of alienation are class and cultural variations. Therefore, we will investigate the *contextual* effects of class and culture. We want to know whether these relationships vary between middle and lower class groups and between lower-class groups of different cultural status. We will suggest that the contextual effects of culture are greater than the effects of social class. Robert Blauner has observed that alienation is not just a product of industrial work, as Marx suggested, but is contingent upon the form of technology by which industrial work is carried out.[44] Thus, the technological context affects the relationship between industrial work and alienation. Similarly, the cultural context may be a significant factor in the relationship between perceived deprivation and alienation.

Opportunity Theory and Alienation

Robert K. Merton's theory of "social structure and anomie" may be the most well-known theory in sociology.[45] The specific focus of the theory is deviant behavior in the lower class of the United States, although the attitude which we have called normlessness, in which the calculation of personal interest is the primary agent of social control, is also central.[46] According to Merton's theory, we should expect normlessness to be higher for lower-class people because perceived blocked opportunity is higher in this class. Our hypothesis, however, is that the relationship between perceived opportunity and normlessness is as much a cultural as a class phenomenon, and is valid for anglo-American middle- to upper-middle class farmers as well as lower-class farm workers, although not for lower-class Mexican-American farm workers. A normlessness attitude is generated by the interaction of perceived opportunity and culture, not by perceived opportunity per se. In other words, the relationship between perceived blocked opportunity to achieve culturally induced aspirations and normlessness is culturally specific.

One study indicates that the relationship between blocked opportunity and deviant behavior may be specific to the situation. Glaser and Rice find that the relationship between the unemployment rate (as an index of blocked opportunity) and the crime rate over time varies with age; it is negative for young and old populations but positive for middle-age categories.[47] For example, the relationship is negative for persons under nineteen but positive for persons in the 25 to 34-year-old age range. Gibbs, using the same data, shows that the correlation between unemployment and crime rates for age groups varies with the status integration of the age group. Specifically, Gibbs' hypothesis is that the crime rate for an age group is not only a function of its unemployment rate, but also is influenced by the *cultural employment expectations* for members of that age group.[48] For example, persons under nineteen are not expected to be employed, and most of them are actually not in the employed labor force; consequently, we would not expect a positive correlation between unemployment and crime for persons in this age range. For this group, unemployment is not a barrier to the achievement of cultural goals that most members are likely to pursue. Cultural goals and social expectations are different for persons in, say, the 25 to 34-year-old category, for most of whom unemployment constitutes blocked opportunity.

Although cultural differences in the relationship postulated in Merton's central hypothesis have not been systematically investigated, the results of one study might be noted. In a cross-cultural study of 48 societies, Bacon, Child, and Barry find no relationship between the societal tendency to "emphasize the discrepancy between culturally induced aspirations and the possibility of achieving them" and the crime rate for society. They caution, however, that such a finding "does not deny the existence of such a relationship within our society."[49] In general terms, the relationship may be culturally specific, existing in some societies but not others. Americans who perceive that their opportunities to achieve goals which are approved by their culture are blocked may tend to have stronger normless attitudes than individuals who do not perceive their opportunities to be blocked. This may not be true in all societies. Indeed, Merton's theory is not formulated to apply to all societies, but is limited to those such as the United States. As we will note in Chapters 7 and 8, his theory applies primarily to societies in which the culture places strong emphasis on achieved status rather than ascribed status, that is, in which individuals are evaluated more on the basis of their performance and ability and less according to family background and social inheritance. Since anglo-American society is relatively more apt to emphasize achieved status and Mexican society relatively more apt to emphasize ascribed status, the correlation between perceived blocked opportunity and normlessness would be expected to be highest for anglo-Americans and lowest for non-English speaking Mexican-Americans.

In addition, perceived blocked opportunity may be associated with powerlessness and anomia as well as with normlessness. Considering the significance that is attributed to equal opportunity in American culture, perceived blocked opportunity may have a more general effect than Merton supposes. Although such blocked opportunity may be specific as to cultural context, it may also be associated with different aspects of alienation within that context.

Our emphasis on the cultural context of "opportunity theory" is contrary to the emphasis and interpretation of others. Mizruchi argues, for example, that blocked opportunity has a variable influence on alienation (actually anomia), depending on the *class* context. He believes that blocked opportunity contributes to alienation only in the lower class (in the middle class unrestrained aspiration is most crucial).[50] The sample of different cultural groups we have chosen to study will allow us to determine whether differences in the postulated relationships are greater between different classes of like culture than between different cultural groups with a common class status.

Conclusion

The study of class and cultural factors in alienation may be undertaken in two ways. One is to examine the relationships between social class and alienation and between cultural differences and alienation. The second is to examine the class and cultural contextual effects on the relationship between alienation and other conditions. We will be concerned with both approaches; we will examine the relationships between class and alienation and between culture and alienation as well as the class and cultural differences in the relationships between perceived class deprivation and alienation and between perceived opportunity and alienation. Our emphasis, however, will be on the latter approach. Our general hypothesis is that perceived deprivation and opportunity have effects that are general to American society, not limited solely to the lower class. Consequently, we expect cultural differences in the relationships of both perceived deprivation and opportunity to alienation to be greater than class differences. Our focus, therefore, is the cultural context.

Notes

1. Robert A. Nisbet, *The Sociological Tradition* (New York: Basic Books, Inc., 1966).

2. See Karl Marx, "Estranged Labor," in *Economic and Philosophic Manuscripts of 1844*, edited and with an Introduction by Kirk J. Struik (New York: International Publishers, 1964), pp. 106-19.

3. See Peter H. Rossi and Zahava D. Blum, "Class, Status, and Poverty," in Daniel P. Moynihan, ed., *On Understanding Poverty: Perspectives from the Social Sciences* (New York: Basic Books, Inc., 1968), Vol. I, p. 40.

4. Robert A. Nisbet, *The Quest for Community* (New York: Oxford University Press, 1953), p. 10.

5. Robert K. Merton, *Social Theory and Social Structure*, rev. ed. (New York: The Free Press, 1957), p. 147.

6. The class position of these two groups will be discussed in the next chapter.

7. See Melvin Seeman, "On the Meaning of Alienation," *American Sociological Review*, XXIV (December 1959), 783-91.

8. Daniel Bell, "Two Roads from Marx: The Themes of Alienation and Exploitation and Workers' Control in Socialist Thought," in *The End of Ideology*, rev. ed. (New York: The Free Press, 1962).

9. Seeman, op. cit.

10. Marx, loc. cit.

11. For an analysis of both the objective and subjective dimensions of alienation in the works of Marx, see Joachim Israel, *Alienation from Marx to Modern Sociology: A Macrosociological Perspective* (Boston: Allyn & Bacon, Inc., 1971).

12. For a similar interpretation, see J. Milton Yinger, *Toward a Field Theory of Behavior: Personality and Social Structure* (New York: McGraw-Hill Book Company, 1965), pp. 118-89.

13. Marx, op. cit. See also Richard Schact, *Alienation* (Garden City, N.Y.: Doubleday & Company, Inc., 1970), pp. 65-114.

14. Several uses are outlined in Seeman, op. cit.

15. Schacht, op. cit., pp. 174-75.

16. For examples, see: Dwight G. Dean, "Alienation: Its Meaning and Measurements," *American Sociological Review*, XXVI (October 1961), 753-58;

William Erbe, "Social Involvement and Political Activity: A Replication and Elaboration," *American Sociological Review*, XXIX (April 1964), 198-215; and Arthur G. Neal and Melvin Seeman, "Organization and Powerlessness: A Test of the Mediation Hypothesis," *American Sociological Review*, XXIX (April 1964), 216-26.

17. Ibid. (three references).

18. Hans H. Gerth and C. Wright Mills, *From Max Weber: Essays in Sociology* (New York: Oxford University Press, 1946), esp. pp. 50, 224-35; and Nisbet, *The Sociological Tradition,* op. cit., pp. 293-300.

19. See Mills' analysis of middle-class, white-collar workers in *White Collar* (New York: Oxford University Press, 1951).

20. Merton, op. cit., pp. 134-91.

21. Emile Durkheim, *The Division of Labor in Society* (New York: The Free Press, 1960), pp. 353-73.

22. Emile Durkheim, *Suicide: A Study in Sociology* (New York: The Free Press, 1951).

23. Ibid., p. 209. There are some who contend that conceptions of the individual in Durkheim are irrelevant, since Durkheim's concern is with societal states and conditions and not individual states and conditions. The issue is complicated, and need not deter us here but we should note that because societal states and conditions were Durkheim's concern he was not interested in *principle* in the individual. However, a reading of *Suicide* makes it clear that his formulation of societal conditions and states such as anomie and egoism, especially as they are relevant to suicide, are difficult to discuss without reference to individual states and conditions.

24. Ibid., pp. 209-10, and 248-49. Mizruchi uses this framework for his assessment of alienation in American life, particularly for class differences in the source of alienation. See Ephraim H. Mizruchi, *Success and Opportunity: Class Values and Anomie in American Life*, London: The Free Press, Collier-Macmillan Limited, 1964.

25. See Jeremy Bentham, *A Fragment on Government and An Introduction to the Principles of Morals and Legislation*, edited and with an Introduction by Wilfrid Harrison (Oxford: The Macmillan Co., 1948), esp. pp. 214-45; and John Stuart Mill, *Utilitarianism* (London: Longmans, Green and Co., 1901).

26. From this perspective, there is little difference between anomic and egoistic individuals in Durkheim's analysis. For both, ambitions and goals result from inner orientations and appetites, rather than social definitions. Egoism and anomie both represent a lack of restraint and regulation derived from societal controls.

27. Alvin W. Gouldner, *The Coming Crisis in Western Sociology* (New York: Basic Books, Inc., 1970), p. 66.

28. Merton, op. cit., p. 157.

29. Gouldner, op. cit., p. 61.

30. Leo Srole, "Social Integration and Certain Corollaries: An Exploratory Study," *American Sociological Review*, XXI (December 1956), 709-16.

31. Dorothy L. Meier and Wendell Bell, "Anomia and Differential Access to the Achievement of Life Goals," *American Sociological Review*, XXV (October 1960), 645-54; Edward L. McDill and Jeanne Clare Ridley, "Status, Anomia, Political Alienation, and Political Participation," *The American Journal of Sociology*, LXVIII (September 1966), 205-13; Russell Middleton, "Alienation, Race, and Education," *American Sociological Review*, XXVIII (December 1963), 973-77; and Gwynn Nettler, "A Comment on 'Anomy,' " *American Sociological Review*, XXX (October 1965), 762-63.

32. See the following: Srole, op. cit.; idem, "Anomie, Authoritarianism and Prejudice," *The American Journal of Sociology* LXII (July 1956), 63-67; Wendell Bell, "Anomie, Social Isolation and the Class Structure," *Sociometry*, XX (June 1957), 105-16; Meier and Bell, op. cit.; Mizruchi, op. cit.; Edward L. McDill, "Anomie, Authoritarianism, Prejudice, and Socioeconomic Status: An Attempt at Clarification," *Social Forces*, XXIX (March 1961), 239-45; Lewis M. Killian and Charles M. Grigg, "Urbanism, Race and Anomia," *The American Journal of Sociology*, LXVII (March 1962), 661-65; McDill and Ridley, op. cit.; and Joel L. Nelson, "Anomie: Comparison between the Old and the New Middle-Class," *The American Journal of Sociology*, LXXIV (September 1968), 184-92.

33. See Meier and Bell, op. cit.

34. For a discussion of the technique for examining contextual effects, see Herbert H. Hyman, *Survey Design and Analysis* (New York: The Free Press, 1956), pp. 276-311. Hyman calls this "specification."

35. Karl Marx and Frederich Engels, "Wage, Labor, and Capital," *Selected Works in Two Volumes* (Moscow: Foreign Languages Publishing House, 1955), Vol. I, p. 94 (cited in James C. Davies, "Toward a Theory of Revolution," *American Sociological Review*, XXVII [February 1962], 5).

36. Ibid.

37. Karl Marx, "Wage, Labor and Capital," in *Selected Works* (Moscow: Cooperative Publishing Society of Foreign Workers in the U.S.S.R., 1936), Vol. I, p. 273 (cited in Reinhard Bendix and Seymour Martin Lipset, "Karl Marx's Theory of Social Classes," in *Class, Status, and Power: Social Stratification in Comparative Perspective*, 2nd ed. [New York: The Free Press, 1966], p. 10). (Emphasis added.)

38. Karl Marx, *Capital* (New York: Modern Library, 1936), p. 709 (emphasis added).

39. James A. Geschwender, "Social Structure and the Negro Revolt: An Examination of Some Hypotheses," *Social Forces*, XLIII (December 1964), 249.

40. For a discussion of false consciousness in Marx, see Israel, op. cit., pp. 80-96. Israel points out that false consciousness has a number of dimensions, although our conception encompasses only one aspect.

41. Relative deprivation as a concept was first introduced in the sociological and social-psychological literature by Samuel A. Stouffer, et al. in *The American Soldier: Adjustment During Army Life* (Princeton, N.J.: Princeton University Press, 1949), Vol. I. The concept was given further theoretical formulation in the well-known analysis by Robert K. Merton and Alice S. Kitt, "Contribution to the Theory of Reference-Group Behavior," in Robert K. Merton and Paul F. Lazarsfeld, eds., *Continuities in Social Research* (New York: The Free Press, 1950), pp. 42-51. However, the idea of relative deprivation (not the term itself) goes back at least to Marx.

42. See, for examples, Dwight MacDonald, "Our Invisible Poor," in Louis A. Ferman, Joyce L. Kornbluh, and Alan Haber, eds., *Poverty in America* (Ann Arbor: University of Michigan Press, 1965), pp. 6-24; and Jack L. Roach, "Sociological Analysis and Poverty," *American Journal of Sociology*, LXXI (July 1956), 68-75.

43. Cf. Albert K. Cohen, *Delinquent Boys* (New York: The Free Press, 1955).

44. Robert Blauner, *Alienation and Freedom: The Factory Worker and His Industry* (Chicago: University of Chicago Press, 1964).

45. Merton, op. cit., pp. 131-94.

46. Ibid., p. 157. In addition, the theory also postulates class differences in goals and aspirations; we will investigate this issue in Chapter 9.

47. Daniel Glaser and Kent Rice, "Crime, Age, and Employment," *American Sociological Review*, XXIV (October 1959), 679-86.

48. Jack P. Gibbs, "Crime, Unemployment and Status Integration," *The British Journal of Criminology*, VI (January 1966), 49-58.

49. Margaret K. Bacon, Irvin L. Child, and Herbert Barry, III, "A Cross-Cultural Study of Correlates of Crime," *Journal of Abnormal and Social Psychology*, LXVI (May 1963), 300.

50. Mizruchi, op. cit.

2

The Study of Social Class and Poverty

During the past 40 years numerous studies of social class have been conducted by social scientists in a variety of U.S. communities and settings.[1] In the past several years, poverty—specifically the lower class—has received particular attention by sociologists.[2] At some risk of oversimplifying, such sociological studies can be classified as either "poverty studies" or "social class studies."[3]

The "poverty study" is based on a limited population that is assumed to be poverty stricken and may be further limited to the study of only a few subjects within such a population. The investigator may live and participate with the group in question for a period of time. The dominant technique involves anthropological field observation, and data consist of the observer's reports on the group's behavior as well as attitudes and values reflected in the behavior and verbalizations of individuals.[4]

The value of these studies is that they record in detail the problems, motivations, behavior, interactions, and life styles of individuals. They are limited, however, in that they may fail to view the study group in relation to the class structure, community, and broader culture that surround it. Instead, the behavior, attitudes, and values expressed are sometimes viewed as almost independent of the surrounding society, and as generated by conditions endemic to the lower class, such as a "culture of poverty," "lower-class subculture," "slum culture," etc., that separate the lower class from the rest of society (e.g., "middle-class culture").[5] The possibility that such behavior, attitudes, and values may be manifestations of broader cultural patterns that are adapted to a particular structural situation tends to be ignored.[6] And a methodological limitation is that nonpoverty groups are seldom included in the analysis. As a result, it is not always possible to know whether the observations, however rich in content, are specific to poverty groups because systematic comparisons between lower-class and middle- to upper-class groups are rarely conducted.[7] Moreover, these studies are frequently based on ethnic minorities, usually lower-class blacks, so that poverty (that is, class) status and ethnic status may be confounded; one wonders, therefore, to what extent characterizations of the poverty group in question are aspects of lower-class patterns or of ethnic-cultural patterns.[8] We have tried to overcome this problem by including three cultural groups in our study.

The other type of study is a "social class study" rather than a poverty study per se, since it is a comparison of persons from different levels of the class structure. Although many such studies are based on field observations made while the investigator(s) was living in the community, most make use of survey techniques wherein large numbers of individuals are interviewed or given questionnaries to complete.[9] Many of these studies have revealed the inequitable distribution of life chances in communities throughout the country, and socioeconomic differences in attitudes, beliefs, and behavior have been widely reported.[10]

This approach overcomes a major weakness of the poverty study in that observations of nonpoverty groups are available for comparison. Unfortunately, however, such studies have yielded very little information about the poverty stratum. They have generally failed to reveal the characteristics of the poor because the poor are rarely included in the research. Although these studies undeniably uncover differences in socioeconomic status, persons at the bottom of the class structure are usually not included in the analysis. Rossi and Blum, on the basis of their review of social class studies, conclude "that very few of the studies [have] paid close attention to [persons] on the very bottom of the stratification system" and that "systematic studies of the characteristics of the poor on an extensive basis are particularly lacking. . . ."[11] Typically, persons designated as "lower class" are lowest on certain socioeconomic characteristics (usually income, education, or occupation) among those individuals who are *included in the study*; hence, the "lower class" is frequently the lowest remnant remaining below a more or less arbitrary cut-off point used by the investigator to distinguish between different levels of socioeconomic status.[12] The lowest status group is usually not a stratum of persons from the bottom of the class structure but of persons from the *working* class instead.[13]

There is an interesting historical parallel between sociological research on the class structure and the public's image of the poor during the period in which so many social class studies were conducted. During the fifties the United States was thought to be "the affluent society"; socioeconomic differences were supposedly becoming less sharp and poverty was disappearing. But with the advent of the Kennedy and Johnson administrations that perspective changed. Poverty was suddenly discovered. It became apparent that 30 years after the Great Depression and the introduction of New Deal and welfare state programs, poverty had not been eliminated; indeed, for many of the poor, such as farm workers, these programs had little if any effect. It may be an overstatement to say that the most significant change during this period was a decrease in the *visibility* of the poor, not a decrease in their numbers. But overstatement or not, a poverty stratum suddenly became more visible to society in the sixties: the nonpoor became aware of the poor, in contrast to the dominant perception of the forties and fifties. And, as we have said, the tendency for society to ignore the poor, or at least to be relatively unaware of their existence, was paralleled by the sociologist's tendency not to study the poor.[14] Consequently, when sociologists also became interested in poverty as a field for theoretical and empirical study, they found that much of the data from previous research might be questionable when applied to persons who are truly from the lower class.[15] By focusing our analysis on a group that is unequivocally from the bottom of the American class structure, we have sought to overcome this problem.

Farm Workers in American Society

Like most poor people in the United States, very little is known about farm workers. They first came to the attention of social scientists and the general population with the publication of Nels Anderson's study of migrants *(Men on the Move)* during the Depression and John Steinbeck's fictional account *(The Grapes of Wrath)* of the Okies' trek to California during the same period.[16] Both works depict the migrants as people who were on the move because of severe breakdowns in the economy: coal miners whose mines had shut down, lumber mill workers who became stranded as lumber resources were depleted, sharecroppers who were forced off the land or who could no longer eke out a living on it, and bankrupt farmers who had lost their land because of drought or other natural conditions. The picture is one of men and their families on the road in dilapidated trucks and broken-down cars in search of something new. To these migrants, farm work is only a transition to something better, a temporary way of life, but it is also back-breaking work under the hot sun for meager pay, of economic exploitation, poverty, malnutrition, and ignorance, and illness, disease, and death. The picture is particularly stark in Steinbeck's novel.

This interpretation appears to be both true and false of the farm worker today. The conditions of work and life seem to have changed little, and many features of Steinbeck's descriptions of the Okies are also present in recent journalists accounts by such authors as Steve Allen, Truman Moore, Louisa Shotwell, and Dale Wright.[17] Wright's account is especially revealing since it is based on his personal experience as a farm worker on the Atlantic Seaboard. Television documentaries are consistent with journalistic accounts; the most famous of these is "Harvest of Shame," which was produced in 1960 for CBS by the former chief of the United States Information Agency, Edward R. Murrow. In this film, farm workers are pictured as an uneducated mass, isolated from the mainstream of American society, constantly going from place to place—driving old cars, herded in trucks, or riding in rickety buses—earning meager pay for hard work, and living in the same squalid conditions in which the farm workers of the thirties lived.

In contrast, documentary accounts of farm workers today show them to be more permanently fixed in society. They do not bear the burden of sudden financial disaster or dislocations in the economy, for farm work and its accompanying migration seem to have become a way of life which changes little from year to year. There is no past or future; everything blends into the present. Farm work is no longer thought to be a transition to a better life; it is all there is. Dale Wright illustrates this in his description of a farm worker, James Jackson:

For James Jackson, farm labor, on the season, at hundreds of nameless, indistinguishable wide places along various highways—both north and south—and collecting his meager pay at the end of the week, [is] the sum total of his existence. That [is] his only dimension. He knows nothing of what lay beyond the horizon of a vegetable field.[18]

No one really knows how many farm workers there are in the United States. The 1960 census reported 1,095,987 male farm workers,[19] but this figure does not include migrants who are on the move, in labor camps, or in isolated areas not canvassed by census takers. *Braceroes*, "wetbacks," and other foreign workers are also excluded.[20] Despite their numbers, however, farm workers have been the object of very little attention by social scientists. For example, in a review of social class in rural society, Walter L. Slocum cites no reference to research studies of farm workers.[21] Until recently, Anderson's study remained the primary source of sociological documentation.[22] For the most part, descriptions of farm workers have remained largely in the hands of novelists and journalists, or demographers who have enumerated the economic, educational, and ethnic characteristics of farm workers.[23]

Socioeconomic Factors

Existing evidence makes it clear that farm workers are at the bottom of the American class structure. On the basis of the 1960 census, the median personal income for male farm workers was $1,191; this is lower than any other occupation except bootblacks and only about one-third of the median income for all nonfarming and nonmining *un*skilled male laborers. (In Washington state, farm workers have the lowest median income of all workers except the 695 male private household workers.) These figures do not include many migrants whose income may be even lower. The median education for all U.S. male farm workers in 1960 was only 7.9 years, the lowest for any major occupation; thus, over half the resident farm workers have less than an eighth-grade education.[24] The education level of migrants is probably even lower: surveys from several areas indicate that as many as 70% of migrant farm workers over 45 years of age may not have more than a fourth-grade education.[25] Since low education reinforces low income status, most farm workers are unable to do anything else. Moreover, the low status of farm workers is reflected not only in their low income and educational status but in their substandard housing and medical care, and their social isolation.

Housing and living conditions of many farm workers can only be described as squalid. Many labor camps are simply unfit for human living: the supply of fresh water may be insufficient—one outlet may be available for an entire camp, and toilet facilities, sewage and refuse disposal, bathing and laundry facilities, and insect and rodent control are often inadequate or nonexistent.[26] One labor camp was described as having

[a] vile outdoor privy, a kerosene stove in a community kitchen, a naked waterpump, rising out of the dust before one of the shanties, dripping its waste into a stagnant pool. Flies and mosquitoes buzzed hungrily about the place, and garbage and other litter were scattered all around. The structures were elevated a foot or so off the ground, either to let rain water run underneath or to provide a convenient place to throw garbage. . . . Intermingled with the smell of [chickens and goats nearby], garbage and decay, was the offensive odor of human waste. The old outhouse . . . was tipped askew. Its door hung ajar. . . . The unmistakable rankness of rotted food mixed with the other odors hung over the camp in a shroud of foul stench.[27]

The quarters of farm workers are described as one- and two-room units in which entire families live, often with one bed to a family. Farm workers are reported to live in tents, haylofts, tarpaper shacks, chicken sheds, and even duck coops.[28] A bankrupt duck breeder converted his coops into housing for farm workers. "He divided the flimsy wood-siding coops into one-, two- and three-room units, . . . and moved people right in behind the ducks."[29] Some farm workers are literally living like animals.

Farm workers experience a high death rate from job-related accidents: they constituted nearly one-fourth of all workers killed on the job (the rate of fatal accidents in agriculture is higher than all other industries except the extractive and construction industries).[30] The infant mortality rate, which some authorities consider one of the best indices of health in a population,[31] is almost double the national average for migrant farm workers.[32] Because of migrancy and poor housing, migrants are apt to be exposed to unsanitary living conditions and communicable diseases, to which their poorer general health makes them more susceptible. To the extent that medical care is received at all, it is obtained from different persons in different places and so reflects little continuity; one result is that children may never receive immunization shots, or may receive duplicate shots.[33]

Behind these impersonal statistics and general patterns, some grim examples unfold: a person with active tuberculosis working in the field[34]; a physician finding "a dead mother with six children lying in the same bed, all covered with blood from the hemorrhage of a dying tubercular mother"[35]; three children found in a "stifling car"—one with raw flesh on the lower part of his body from diarrhea, another with a burning fever, and the third unconscious and nearly dead—while their parents were working in a nearby cherry orchard.[36] Although these examples are extreme, the high infant mortality rate together with the prevalence of illness and general unsanitary conditions as described by journalists indicate that the problems of health, illness, and medical care are widespread. As is true with regard to income, education, and housing, farm workers would appear to be at the bottom of American society.

A theme which pervades popular and journalistic accounts concerns the physical and social isolation of farm workers from the rest of society. They enter communities, do their work, and leave unknown to most permanent residents. Their labor camps and housing are usually near the crops, in the countryside and in out-of-the-way places, but sometimes they are located almost under the noses of the more affluent. Highway 99 in California, which stretches from the Sacramento Valley in the north to the Imperial Valley in the south, has been called "the longest slum in the world." The slum, however, is invisible to those who travel the highway, for "the farm workers' shacks and shanties which border it are set back from the highway, out of sight of the tourist blithly speeding from one vacation attraction to another."[37] In a systematic analysis, Dorothy Nelkin reports that the life of farm workers rarely takes them beyond their labor camps and, therefore, seldom brings them into contact with permanent members of a community.[38] These factors contribute to the invisibility of farm workers in American society; since most Americans rarely see them, most do not even know they exist.

Who, then, are the farm workers? Many are members of ethnic minorities, especially blacks and Mexican-Americans. Others are anglo-Americans—"poor whites." Some are residents of the states in which they work; others are migrants mainly from states in the South and Southwest who work in three national geographic "streams": Atlantic Coast Stream, Mid-Continent Stream, and Pacific Stream.[39] But regardless of ethnic status, residence status, or "stream," farm workers embody a microcosm of factors that are considered characteristic of the lower class: they earn little money for performing physically gruelling work, they are poorly educated, they are unemployed much of the year, they have little job security, they have a high infant mortality rate, and they are segregated from the rest of society. Indeed, for all of these characteristics, it is probably fair to say that they suffer the most extreme conditions in the United States. Their position at the bottom of the class structure can hardly be questioned. On the basis of a study of several migrant farm worker families Robert Coles concludes that "in general what most migrants share is more than occasional exposure to poor housing, bad sanitation, a diet poor in vitamins and protein, inadequate medical care, continual movement—and consequent lack of firm association with any particular community—a very limited income, and a lack of eligibility for a number of privileges many of us either take for granted or consider 'rights,'—the vote, a telephone, a library card, unemployment or welfare benefits, minimum wage protection."[40] A personnel director of an industrial farm on the eastern seaboard is more blunt: "When spring comes, whoever they are, they're people who are the hungriest. Who else want to work that hard for that little money."[41]

As noted previously, existing accounts would suggest that there has been little improvement in the level of living for farm workers over the past 30 or 40 years. Nevertheless, Herman P. Miller has shown that for the United States as a whole, the proportion of families whose income is $3,000 or less, measured in 1962 dollar equivalents, dropped from approximately 50% of the population in 1929 to about 20% in 1964; hence, the standard of living has risen for most of the poor.[42] Two general reasons account for the farm workers' continued low position: the nature of farm work and the position of farm workers in the agricultural economy; and the relationship between farm workers and the rest of society, particularly as this involves the workers' access to political power.

Farm Work and the Agricultural Economy

Pay is low for farm work because the skills required are manual and hence in ample supply. The availability of a large number of farm workers is assured because there are so many pools from which farm labor can be recruited. In addition to those who work more or less permanently in the fields (when work is available), vacationers, retired persons, and students, as well as hoboes, drunks and "day-haul"[43] workers may enter farm work during peak harvest seasons, the times of greatest demand. In addition, the use of *braceroes*, "wetbacks," Puerto Ricans, and natives of the West Indies has usually assured an ample supply of farm labor in the United States.[44] This large and various labor pool not only depresses the wage scale, but makes unionization and successful strike activity difficult. Allen cites a number of instances in which foreign workers have been used to break strikes.[45]

But the ineffectiveness of strike activity is not necessarily contingent upon the use of foreign workers. For example, during the 1965 fruit harvest season in the state of Washington there was a shortage of labor, apparently due to the closing of the *bracero* program and the introduction of higher wage legislation in California. This shortage gave Washington workers a potential power advantage and the opportunity to introduce collective bargaining; indeed, efforts at unionization had already begun in the state by the Industrial Workers of the World (IWW). However, the governor called a press conference, attended by apple industry representatives from Yakima and Wenatchee, during which he urged vacationers, retired persons, and other Washington residents to participate in the fruit harvest; and industry representatives related how much fruit pickers could expect to make. An account of the conference, which was picketed by four members of the IWW who demanded higher hourly wage rates and higher piece rates for fruit pickers, was published in newspapers throughout the state. Although we do not know how many persons heeded the governor's request, during the harvest season the author met several retired couples and vacationers in harvest areas who had come specifically to pick fruit, and the IWW picketing achieved no apparent success. Some fruit (mostly pears) went unharvested that year, but that was due to the labor shortage, not striking workers.

There are other aspects of the farm worker's position in the system of production that depresses his living conditions.[46] Much of the problem revolves around "crew chiefs" or "crew leaders," who contract with a grower to "deliver" farm workers at stipulated prices. Sometimes the contract is made with a field boss, who is a middleman between the grower and the crew leader. The grower or field boss pays the crew leader who in turn pays the workers, but the crew leader gets a percentage of each worker's pay. The worker must agree to the wages set by the grower and crew leader; he has no bargaining power. "It is the role of the crew leader to function as the agent of the employer, but there are no union shop stewards or business agents to represent the laborer and bargain on his behalf."[47] Obviously, the worker's position in the system of production is powerless, putting him at a disadvantage from the outset.

In addition, because the farm worker is uneducated as well as powerless, he may be cheated out of what he has actually earned. The crew leader may defraud the worker of his wages by making a deal with the field boss to pay the worker less than the grower has paid them for the worker's services, and pocket the difference. Or the worker may have no record of how many hours he has worked, or if he is paid according to piece work for picking crops, the exact number of units he has picked. He must rely on the crew leader's word. And if he challenges the crew leader's "record," he may be fired or physically harmed. In some instances crew leaders have even been accused of pocketing Social Security tax and "union" dues from workers' pay.[48]

In addition, the seasonal character of farm work permits exploitation. Farm workers are unemployed and without income much of the year; in a study of farm workers in New York State, for example, Emmit F. Sharp and Olaf F. Larson report that interstate migrants worked only about 160 days the previous year.[49] Being without funds, farm workers are easy prey for crew leaders who entice them to travel to areas with the assurance that crops will be ready for harvesting upon arrival. After riding several days in a bus or truck, workers may arrive only to be told that crops will not be ripe for several days, or weeks. With no money and sometimes in debt to the crew leader for travel or loans, the worker has no alternative but to remain until the harvest is ready. In the meantime he frequently goes in debt for his housing and food, for which he may be charged highly inflated prices. Consequently, he may have little left when the harvesting is finished and have no alternative but to sign on with another crew and travel to another setting, only to repeat the experience.[50] Such conditions have led journalist Dale Wright to conclude that the conditions of life and work for farm workers in the United States amount to "economic slavery—indeed, conditions only a step or two removed from peonage. . . ."[51]

Relationship of Farm Workers to Society

A second general reason for the farm workers' plight stems from the relationship between them and the rest of society. Farm workers have been ignored, forgotten (if they were ever remembered), and rejected by society. And, despite the fact that the workers' function in society—to provide much of what we eat each day—is obviously quite important, they have been *specifically excluded* from legislation designed to aid other elements of society. In 1933 the so-called Wagner Act was passed, which gave industrial workers the legal right to bargain collectively; farm workers were excluded. Indeed, most of the programs identified with the New Deal of the Roosevelt administration and other federal welfare state legislation have excluded farm workers. This includes coverage on minimum wage, workman's compensation, unemployment compensation, social security, and child labor practices. State legislatures have also ignored and excluded farm workers. For example, in 1965 only eight states protected farm workers with compulsory workman's compensation—despite the high accident rate in agriculture—and only Hawaii provided them with unemployment compensation.

Such protective programs were designed to cushion the impact of poverty and financial crises and to provide a standard of living and human dignity below which no American should fall. But there has been no such standard for farm workers. In addition, because of state residence restrictions, migrant workers, who are frequently those most in need, may be denied welfare assistance.[52] Thus, many of the mechanisms which ease the suffering for other lower-class groups are not available to farm workers. Their rejection by society and its elected representatives appears to be virtually complete. A few years ago Senator Harrison A. Williams of New Jersey could state:

Almost three decades ago we gave ourselves the basic standards of minimum security: minimum wages, unemployment insurance and workmen's compensation, the right to bargain collectively, adequate provisions against child labor. All of these things we gave ourselves. But we refused to give them to the American farm workers. [Consequently, he] has lived out his life, ignored, forgotten, and left behind by progress.[53]

Industrial sweat shops have been eliminated, but "blue-sky sweatshops"[54] have not. Thus, the standard of living for farm workers has improved little both absolutely and relatively since the thirties.

Nevertheless, several changes have been made in the past several years which may improve the situation. In 1955 farm workers were first covered by Social Security (Old-age and Survivors' Insurance). We might note, however, that farm workers were supposedly covered by Social Security at the time crew leaders were accused of pocketing workers' Social Security deductions.[55] In any event it is questionable how much benefit farm workers will actually derive from Social Security. One reason is that since their mortality rate is higher than most groups, many will not live to receive any of the old-age assistance that they have paid for. In addition, given their low level of education, one can only wonder to what extent farm workers and their survivors understand their rights under the Social Security program. Sharp and Larson found, for example, that only two out of 455 farm workers they questioned were aware of all the benefits provided by the program.[56]

Legislation designed to regulate crew leaders has also been passed. The Crew Leader Registration Act requires crew leaders of more than ten interstate migrants to register with the Department of Labor. Certification can be refused or revoked for giving false information concerning work conditions and pay or for breaking agreements made with workers. It is difficult to ascertain to what extent such laws are actually being complied with and enforced. Before this act was passed, the laws that did exist were, according to Wright, "chronically, purposefully ignored, frequently with the knowledge and approval of farmer-employers and just as frequently with the tacit permissiveness of the authorities charged with their administration and enforcement."[57]

Finally, in 1967 federal minimum wage legislation for farm workers was passed. The beneficial effect of this legislation is also questionable, since so many conditions are written into the legislation that probably less than one-third of all workers are actually covered.[58] Moreover, the minimum wage established in the legislation was set at $1.00 for the first year, $1.15 for the second, and $1.30 for the third. Even the latter figure does not allow for a decent wage; at this rate, a person who worked a 40-hour week for 52 weeks would have an annual gross of $2,704. Considering that farm workers work considerably less than 52 weeks a year, the minimum wage legislation may have very little practical effect overall.

Much of the blame for the farm workers' situation is laid to farmers and their agribusiness organizations. Farmers have opposed protective legislation for farm workers through the lobbying activities of their organizations and passage of recent legislation, minimum though it is, has thus been in the face of opposition from growers and their organizations.[59] From the fields to the halls of Congress, the power of farm workers has been insignificant in comparison to the power of the growers.

Still, legislation was passed during the sixties, so we can say that some change has occurred, although the effectiveness of most of this legislation remains to be demonstrated. Most of the laws have not been in existence long enough for a fair assessment of their effectiveness. Perhaps they reflect chiefly the increased public awareness of farm workers and the conditions under which they live and work, which in turn has been largely due to the work of journalists and television documentary film makers. Also, the unionization efforts of farm workers (especially Cesar Chavez and the California grape-pickers) have made news across the nation and thus focused national attention on the economic and living conditions of this group. Nevertheless, farm workers continue to constitute a significant component of what Michael Harrington has called "the other America." Everyone must agree that they continue to exist at the bottom of the American class structure.[60]

The Present Study

As we have said, the present study differs from other accounts of farm workers in that it systematically explores certain perceptions and attitudes of farm workers—perceived deprivation, perceived opportunity, goals and aspirations, and alienation—and compares them with the perceptions and attitudes of a middle- to upper-middle class group of farmers. That farm workers are at the bottom of the class structure is clear, and their lack of opportunity is not debatable. Yet we do not know to what extent they perceive themselves to be deprived or as being denied opportunities that others take for granted. Also, their goals and aspirations may be quite different from those that middle-class journalists and sociologists sometimes impute to them; goals and aspirations may be quite modest and, indeed, adjusted to the realities of their situation. Moreover, considering the structure of the farm workers' lives, there is every reason to believe that they are alienated from society, but this has not been demonstrated. A comparison of farm workers with farmers will help us confirm or deny these suppositions.

The fact that farm workers are so far down in the class structure makes them a particularly strategic lower-class group for studying with regard to these issues, about which sociologists have been concerned for some time. The usual assumptions are that poor persons do perceive themselves as deprived and as having few opportunities, are more alienated, and—which is somewhat more controversial—have goals and aspirations that are similar to persons from higher class levels. Farm workers are probably not truly representative of all lower-class groups in the United States, but they do constitute a significant segment of this stratum; of the 4,488,666 male unskilled workers reported in the 1960 census, approximately one-fourth (1,095,987) were farm workers.[61] To the extent that formulations about lower-class persons in the United States are generally true, they should certainly hold for this group since they constitute the largest single component of the unskilled stratum. Moreover, since only one occupation is represented among farm workers (as it is among the farmers), variation within the lower class stemming from occupational differences is eliminated. This is an advantage our study has over other studies in which a variety of occupations are represented in different class groups.

However, simply because farm workers are so low in the class structure cultural differences may be difficult to detect; indeed, class effects may be so overriding that cultural differences may have little or no influence. Because of this, tests for the influence of cultural differences in the relationships of perceived deprivation and denied opportunity to alienation may be conservative.

The Samples

The samples studied consist of 1,029 farm workers from six counties in east and central Washington and 240 farm owners and operators from one county in east

Washington. The farmers are a probability sample but the farm workers are not. However, the farm workers are predominantly full-time farm workers in Washington: 67% report that farm work is their "only" job, and for another 20% it is their "primary job"; only 22% report having received job or occupational training of any kind; and 84% report that they plan to continue working at farm work.[62] As we will note in the next chapter, the isolated position in the community of our sample and their living conditions are similar to observations described above.

Only male family heads were interviewed but both residents and migrants were included (a resident had to have lived in Washington for at least six months before the interview). The number of farm workers interviewed by residence and cultural status is as shown in Table 2-1.

Note that most anglo-American migrants are from West Coast states, 69% being from Arizona, California, or Oregon. Eighty-two% of the bilingual workers are from Texas, as are 76% of the non-English speaking migrants. Another 14% of the latter report that Mexico is their home.

Although our study differs from most other studies of farm workers, because we include residents as well as migrants, our findings reveal few differences between the two groups. Consequently, they will not usually be differentiated in the analysis.

Data and Data Analysis

The data and conclusion are limited by the particular data collection procedures that were used. Most data are based on interviews. Systematic observations were not conducted; observers did not work in the fields and orchards, and they did not live with farmers or farm workers. However, interviewers did visit labor camps and other areas where farm workers were concentrated, and residential patterns were noted; moreover, because interviews were conducted in the respondents' living quarters interviewers obtained first-hand impressions of the life situations of many respondents. For the most part, however, detailed and systematic observations of behavior, life styles, and interaction patterns were not conducted since description of the subculture and social organization that are

Table 2-1
Farm Workers Interviewed, by Residence and Cultural Status[a]

	Residents	Migrants
Anglo-Americans	282	259
Bilinguals	192	109
Non-English speakers	72	115

[a]For a detailed discussion of the sample and sampling procedures, see Appendix A.

specific to farm work was not our objective.[63] Nor was it to identify and describe the range of cultural differences between the three subgroups of farm workers.[64] Rather, we sought to determine how factors commonly identified as aspects of the class structure (e.g., relative deprivation and perceived opportunity) have differential effects for individuals originating from different cultural backgrounds. That is, we wanted to identify differences in how members of different cultural groups respond to the same conditions.

We assume, of course, that anglo-American, bilingual Mexican-American, and non-English speaking Mexican-American farm workers represent distinct cultural groups. Anglo-Americans are understood to be the most assimilated in the dominant culture of the United States, with bilinguals next, and non-English speakers least.[65] In our conceptualization of cultural differences between the three groups we rely strongly on John Gillin's distinctions between the culture of the United States and those of Latin America, including Mexico.[66] Although Gillin does not use the terms, he draws sharp contrasts between the two cultures in the emphasis placed on achieved status and ascribed status. The former he finds to be relatively more dominant in the United States, the latter more dominant in cultures such as that of Mexico. We believe this cultural difference is significantly related to the relationships of perceived deprivation and opportunity to alienation.

Methodologically, our data analysis consists largely of the specification by class and culture of certain relationships that would be expected to exist on the basis of theory and empirical research.[67] That is, we will not only examine differences between class and cultural groups for specific attributes (e.g., alienation), but will also examine differences between groups in the *relationships* between various attributes (e.g., perceived opportunity and alienation). In the process, we hope to be able to show how the poor and nonpoor from like cultural backgrounds are both similar and different. More generally, we hope to discover just how culture and class structure interact. The relationship between two variables may be the same for groups who are different in class but similar in culture, but be different for groups from the same class but different cultures. Although forces generated by the class structure differentiate between poor and nonpoor individuals and groups such as farmers and farm workers, broader cultural patterns may influence several levels of the class structure and thus shape the way individuals and groups respond to certain of those forces. These patterns may interact with components of the class structure in such a way that certain responses of the poor and nonpoor, anglo-American farm workers and farmers, are similar regardless of how different these groups may be in other respects.

Conclusion

Most approaches to the study of poverty, the lower class, and the class structure have been primarily concerned with the differences between social classes and between the poor and nonpoor. This is part of a long tradition of sociological research whereby numerous studies have shown that an individual's behavior and attitudes are apt to be associated with his socioeconomic status. Indeed, some studies have shown that socioeconomic factors may be more important than cultural differences. For example, in a study of attitudes about modernism in the United States, Mexico, and Brazil, Joseph A. Kahl reports that although attitudes differed within cultures depending on socioeconomic status, there were no significant differences between individuals from different cultures whose socioeconomic status was similar.[68]

This emphasis on differences between social classes reflects the sociologist's tendency to view societies in terms of social differentiation, that is, to study how various parts of society (groups, races, classes, etc.) differ. This perspective may lead to and is extended by conceptions such as "lower-class subculture" and "poverty subculture"; the lower class is viewed as differentiated not only in economic, behavioral, and attitudinal characteristics, but in values and norms as well. Some researchers maintain that such subcultures transcend broader cultures and exist in any society where poverty is found.[69]

Although it is obvious that the poor are different from other groups, studies derived from this observation are often incomplete: only differences are revealed in the descriptions. But the poor and nonpoor, the lower class and middle class, if they are from the same society, also have many things in common. Quite simply, they share many aspects of American culture such as similarities in language, beliefs, folklore, and opinions. Resemblances may go deeper and affect phenomena usually assumed to be products of the class structure, such as class perception, perceived opportunity, alienation, and the relationships between them. The belief and value systems of the broader culture may influence forces of the class structure so as to produce consequences that are similar regardless of location in the class structure. In certain respects, then, lower-class anglo-American farm workers are expected to resemble middle-class farmers more than Mexican-American farm workers because anglo-American farmers and farm workers are more integrated in the dominant culture of the United States than are the two groups of Mexican-American workers. Comparisons between these groups should reflect this fact.

There are two forms of cultural homogeneity. Individuals and groups may be homogeneous with respect to the acquisition of various attributes such as values, beliefs, and attitudes—i.e., culture. Or they may be homogeneous with respect to the relationships between the various attributes. The former tells us something about the attributes of a culture, whereas the latter tells us what some of the cultural dynamics are. We will be concerned with both, but primarily with the latter.

Notes

1. For a summary of a number of these studies, see Kurt Mayer and Walter Buckley, *Class and Society* (New York: Random House, 1970). Many of these

studies are limited because persons from the very bottom of the class structure are excluded from them, a point we shall discuss below.

2. Studies of, perspectives on, and characteristics attributed to the poor are presented in a number of anthologies. See the following: Margaret S. Gordon, ed., *Poverty in America* (San Francisco: Chandler Publishing Company, 1965); Louis A. Ferman, Joyce L. Kornbluh, and Alan Haber, eds., *Poverty in America* (Ann Arbor: University of Michigan Press, 1956); Robert E. Will and Harold G. Vatter, eds., *Poverty in Affluence* (New York: Harcourt Brace Jovanovich, 1965); Herman P. Miller, ed., *Poverty American Style* (Belmont, Calif.: Wadsworth, 1966). See also Frank Riessman, Jerome Cohen, and Arthur Pearl, eds., *Mental Health of the Poor: New Treatment Approaches for Low Income People* (New York: The Free Press, 1964).

3. Rossi and Blum make a similar distinction. See Peter H. Rossi and Zahava D. Blum, "Class, Status, and Poverty," in Daniel P. Moynihan, ed., *On Understanding Poverty: Perspectives from the Social Sciences* (New York: Basic Books, Inc., 1968), Vol. I, p. 40.

4. Examples would include: Allison Davis, "The Motivation of the Underprivileged Worker," in William H. Whyte, ed., *Industry and Society* (New York: McGraw-Hill Book Company, 1946); Walter B. Miller, "Lower Class Culture as a Generating Milieu of Gang Delinquency," *The Journal of Social Issues*, XIV (September 1958), 5-14; Charles Keil, *Urban Blues* (Chicago: The University of Chicago Press, 1966); Oscar Lewis, *La Vida: A Puerto Rican Family in the Culture of Poverty—San Juan and New York* (New York: Random House, Inc., 1966); and Elliot Liebow, *Tally's Corner: A Study of Streetcorner Men* (Boston: Little, Brown & Company, 1967).

5. The conclusion drawn appears to be related to the methodology used. Thus, Lewis states that, "To understand the culture of the poor it is necessary to live with them, to learn their language and customs, and to identify with their problems and aspirations. The anthropologist trained in the methods of direct observation and participation, is well prepared for this job. . . ." Oscar Lewis, *Five Families: Mexican Case Studies in the Culture of Poverty* (New York: Basic Books, Inc., 1959), p. 16 (emphasis added).

6. See Charles A. Valentine, *Culture and Poverty* (Chicago: The University of Chicago Press, 1967).

7. In addition, it is hard to know what *specific* factors contribute to (or at least are correlated with) certain types of behavior. For example, Walter Miller contends that a cultural concern with "toughness" characterizes the lower class and leads to deviant behavior (op. cit.). It has not been demonstrated, however, that the lower-class individuals who adopt a "toughness" orientation are more apt to be deviant than those who do not. Moreover, such analyses may be precluded because of the small number of individuals being studied.

8. For a discussion, see Valentine, op. cit., esp. p. 127.

9. This is not to say that survey techniques have not been used in what we have called "poverty studies." David Caplovitz's superb study of the poor in Harlem is an exception; see his *The Poor Pay More* (New York: The Free Press,

1967). It is of some significance to note, however, that Caplovitz's major concern is the relationship of the poor to the dominant institutions of society, specifically various institutions of the economic sector, rather than a description of the "culture of poverty."

10. For a review, see Mayer and Buckley, op. cit.

11. Rossi and Blum, op. cit., p. 37.

12. At times class differences are based on the distinction between manual and nonmanual workers, which may well be the one best distinction between class levels. See Peter M. Blau, "Occupational Bias and Mobility," *American Sociological Review*, XXII (August 1957), 392-99. The use of such gross groupings, however, conceals differences within them such as that between poverty and nonpoverty strata within the manual category.

13. See Jack L. Roach, "Sociological Analysis of Poverty," *American Journal of Sociology*, LXXI (July 1965), 68-75. See also Rossi and Blum, op. cit., pp. 37-38.

14. This in itself is an interesting phenomenon from the perspective of the sociology of knowledge.

15. See Rossi and Blum, op. cit., p. 38.

16. Nels Anderson, *Men on the Move* (Chicago: The University of Chicago Press, 1940); and John Steinbeck, *The Grapes of Wrath* (New York: The Viking Press, 1939).

17. Steve Allen, *Ground Is Our Table* (Garden City, N.Y.: Doubleday & Company, Inc., 1966); Truman Moore, *The Slaves We Rent* (New York: Random House, Inc., 1965); Louisa R. Shotwell, *The Harvesters: The Story of the Migrant People* (Garden City, N.Y.: Doubleday & Company, Inc., 1961); and Dale Wright, *They Harvest Despair: The Migrant Farm Worker* (Boston: Beacon Press, 1965).

18. Ibid. (Wright), p. 76.

19. U.S. Bureau of the Census, *U.S. Census of Population: 1960. Subject Reports. Occupational Characteristics.* Final Report PC (2)-7A (Washington, D.C.: U.S. Government Printing Office, 1963), Table 1, pp. 1-10.

20. *Braceroes* are Mexicans who enter the United States on a contractual basis to perform farm work. Originated in the early forties in response to a shortage of manpower, this procedure was formalized by Public Law 78 in 1951, during the Korean War. This law, which requires that growers provide minimum standards of food and housing as well as the guarantee of a certain number of days of work, was strongly supported by the Mexican government because of the exploitation that existed prior to its enactment. (Incidentally, no such guarantees were provided for domestic workers!) The law was repealed in 1967. "Wetbacks" are Mexicans who illegally enter the United States to engage in farm work (and are often deported). For a discussion and analysis of *braceroes* and wetbacks in American agriculture, see Ernesto Galarza, *Merchants of Labor: The Mexican Bracero Story* (Charlotte, N.C.: McNally and Loftin, Publishers, 1964).

21. Walter L. Slocum, *Agricultural Sociology* (New York: Harper & Row, 1962), pp. 342-43. Only four pages in the entire text are devoted to farm workers (pp. 323-25, 327-28), and virtually no research studies are cited.

22. Recent studies include: Robert Cole, "The Lives of Migrant Families," *American Journal of Psychiatry*, CXXII (September 1965), 271-85; William Friedland, "Labor Waste in New York: Rural Exploitation and Migrant Workers," *Transaction* (February 1969), 58-63; Dorothy Nelkin, "Response to Marginality: The Case of Migrant Farm Workers," *British Journal of Sociology*, XXXVI (December 1969), 375-89; and idem, "Unpredictability and Life Style in a Migrant Labor Camp," *Social Problems*, XVII (Spring 1970), 473-87.

23. See Emmit F. Sharp and Olaf F. Larson, *Migratory Farm Workers in the Atlantic Coast Stream: II. Education of New York Workers and Their Children, 1953 and 1957* (Ithaca: Cornell University Agricultural Experimental Station Bulletin 949, May, 1960); U.S. Department of Agriculture, Economic and Statistical Analysis Division, *Economic, Social, and Demographic Characteristics of Spanish-American Wage Workers on U.S. Farms* (Washington, D.C.: Economic Research Service, Agricultural Report, No. 27, 1963).

24. Nationwide figures are from U.S. Bureau of the Census, op. cit.; figures for Washington are from U.S. Bureau of the Census, *U.S. Census of Population: 1960. Detailed Characteristics. Washington.* Final Report PC(1)-49D (Washington, D.C.: U.S. Government Printing Office, 1962), Table 124, pp. 325-26.

25. Sharp and Larson, op. cit.; Colorado State Department of Education, *A Social Profile of Agriculture Migratory People in Colorado* (1959); United States Department of Agriculture. "Migratory Farm Workers in the Atlantic Coast Stream" (1955), Circular No. 966; and United States Department of Agriculture, Agricultural Research Service in cooperation with Texas Agricultural Experiment Station, *Migratory Farm Workers in the Mid-Continent Streams*, Production Research Report 41 (1960).

26. See Earl L. Koos, *They Follow the Sun* (Jacksonville: Bureau of Maternal and Child Health, Florida State Board of Health, 1957); and United States Department of Health, Education and Welfare, Social Security Administration, Children's Bureau, *Children in Migrant Families* (Washington, D.C.: U.S. Government Printing Office, 1960).

27. Wright, op. cit., pp. 84-85.

28. Allen, op. cit., p. 41.

29. Wright, op. cit., p. 113.

30. Subcommittee on Migratory Labor, Committee on Labor and Public Welfare, United States Senate, *The Migratory Farm Problem in the United States*, Report No. 109 (Washington, D.C.: U.S. Government Printing Office, 1961), pp. 14, 21.

31. David D. Rutstein, *The Coming Revolution in Medicine* (Cambridge, Mass.: The M.I.T. Press, 1967), p. 11.

32. Subcommittee on Migratory Labor, op. cit.

33. Shotwell, op. cit., p. 145. Shotwell states: "Working in half a dozen states in the course of a season means no continuity of either health records or health services" (ibid.).

34. See Wright, op. cit., Chapter 1, "Flecks of Red in the Dirt."

35. Allen, op. cit., p. 29.

36. Ibid., p. 27.

37. Ibid., p. 41.

38. Nelkin, "Unpredictability . . . ," op. cit., esp. p. 478. See also, U.S. Dept. of HEW, *Children in Migrant Families*, op. cit.; and Truman Moore, "Shacktown U.S.A.: Migrant Farm Labor," in Herman P. Miller, ed., *Poverty American Style* (Belmont, Calif.: Wadsworth, 1966).

39. The Atlantic Coast Stream runs from Florida up the Eastern Seaboard to New York State; migrants may work their way from Florida to New York State and then return, following the harvest seasons. The Mid-Continent Stream runs from Texas north, and supplies farm labor for vegetable fields in the midwest, especially in Illinois, Indiana, Michigan, Minnesota, Ohio, and Wisconsin. The Pacific Coast Stream runs from southwest Texas, Arizona, and New Mexico west and northwest, and supplies vegetable and fruit harvesters for California, Colorado, Idaho, Oregon, and Washington. The different crops and variations in seasons in the several states permits migrants to begin work in the southern part of the latter region and work their way north for the fruit harvests of Washington in late summer and early fall.

40. Coles, op. cit., 272-73.

41. Shotwell, op. cit., p. 39.

42. Herman P. Miller, *Rich Man, Poor Man* (New York: Thomas Y. Crowell Co., 1964).

43. "Day-haul" laborers are workers brought to the fields from the city for the day and then returned.

44. Several writers claim that growers have used foreign labor (and resisted the repeal of Public Law 78 which allowed Mexican nationals to enter the country on a contract basis) in an effort to keep wages low, not because there was a shortage of domestic farm workers. See Shotwell, op. cit., pp. 59-82. See also Allen, op. cit., pp. 51-67; and Galarza, op. cit., esp. pp. 214-18.

45. Ibid. (Galarza), pp. 111-12.

46. The discussion of the next three paragraphs draws heavily on Wright, op. cit.

47. Ibid., pp. 110-11.

48. Ibid., pp. 117-18.

49. Sharp and Larson, op. cit.

50. The farm worker's plight in this situation is revealed in the following remarks of a farm worker after arriving at a location only to be told that harvesting could not begin for several more days. "We got ourselves mixed up with another lyin', son-of-a-bitch crew boss . . . an' ain't nothin we can do about

it. We're a long way from nowhere out here in these fields an' we're gonna be owin' that bastard for eatin' an' sleepin' long 'fo' these 'matoes an' cabbages is ready to pick. . . . We didn't have nothin' when we got here. Well, we ain' gonna have nothin' when we leave neither." Wright, op. cit., p. 45.

51. Ibid., p. 107.

52. Recent court decisions suggest that this may be in the process of changing.

53. Wright, op. cit., pp. 150-51, and Foreword, p. 1.

54. Allen, op. cit., p. 41.

55. Wright, op. cit., p. 118.

56. Sharp and Larson, op. cit.; see also Shotwell, op. cit., pp. 119-21.

57. Wright, op. cit., p. 111.

58. U.S. Subcommittee on Migratory Labor, Committee on Labor and Public Welfare, *The Migratory Farm Labor Problem in the United States* (Washington, D.C.: U.S. Government Printing Office, March 15, 1967), p. 6.

59. For a discussion about Public Law 78, see Shotwell, op. cit., pp. 59-69.

60. However, farm workers may be part of the lower class which Miller classifies as "hard core"—who are characterized by prolonged unemployment, irregular employment, and low income—in contrast to the "secure" lower class. S.M. Miller, "The American Lower Classes: A Typological Approach," in Frank Riessman, Jerome Cohen, and Arthur Pearl, eds., *Mental Health of the Poor: New Treatment Approaches for Low Income People* (New York: The Free Press, 1964), pp. 139-54.

61. *U.S. Census of Population, Subject Reports*, op. cit. As noted, no one really knows how many farm workers there are, although one report claims a total of 5,723,000 farm workers in 1960. See Slocum, op. cit., p. 327.

62. The question on job training was: "Have you had vocational or job training of any kind—training that prepares you for a specific job—for example, plumber, barber, carpenter, mechanic, machinist, etc.?" In many instances farm workers interpreted the question as including low-level skills such as truck and tractor driving. Consequently, the 22% who claim to have had job or occupational training is an exaggeration.

63. Studies of this type include Friedland, op. cit., and Nelkin, "Unpredictability . . . ," op. cit.

64. Until recently few studies of Mexican-Americans had been conducted. See Celia Heller, *Mexican-American Youth: Forgotten at the Cross-roads* (New York: Random House, Inc., 1968), p. 4. However, see both the older and the subsequent newer studies which generally assume that there is a distinctive Mexican-American subculture: Ruth Tuck, *Not with the Fist: Mexican-Americans in a Southwest City* (New York: Harcourt, Brace and Company, 1946); George C. Baker, "Social Functions of Language in a Mexican-American Community," *Acta Americana*, IV (July-September 1947), 188-92; William Altus, "The American Mexican: The Survival of a Culture," *Journal of Social*

Psychology, XXIX (April 1949), 211-20; Leonard Broom and Eshref Shevsky, "Mexicans in the United States: A Problem in Social Differentiation," *Sociology and Social Research*, XXXVI (January-February 1952), 150-68; Lyle Saunders, *Cultural Differences and Medical Care* (New York: Russell Sage Foundation, 1954); Margaret Clark, *Health in the Mexican-American Culture* (Berkeley: University of California Press, 1959); Clark S. Knowlton, "The Spanish American in New Mexico," *Sociology and Social Research*, XLV (July 1961), 448-54; idem, "Patron-Peon Pattern among the Spanish Americans of New Mexico," *Social Forces,* XLI (October 1962), 12-17; Arthur J. Rubel, *Across the Tracks: Mexican-Americans in a Texas City* (Austin: University of Texas Press, 1966); Leo Grebler, Joan W. Moore, and Ralph C. Guzman et. al., *The Mexican-American People: The Nation's Second Largest Minority* (New York: The Free Press-Macmillan, 1970); Joan W. Moore, *Mexican Americans* (Englewood Cliffs, N.J.: Prentice-Hall, Inc., 1970); John M. Burma, ed., *Mexican-Americans in the United States* (Cambridge, Mass.: Schenkman Publishing Company, Inc., 1970), esp. John M. Burma, "A Comparison of the Mexican-American Subculture with the Oscar Lewis Culture of Poverty Model," pp. 17-28, and Horacio Ulibarri, "Social and Attitudinal Characteristics of Spanish-Speaking Migrant and Ex-Migrant Workers in the Southwest," pp. 361-70. Joan Moore contends that there are three subcultures or "culture areas": "classic colonialism" (New Mexico), "conflict colonialism" (Texas), and "economic colonialism" (California); see her "Colonialism: The Case of the Mexican Americans," *Social Problems*, XVII (Spring 1970), 463-72.

65. For an assessment of differences between farm workers in assimilation, see Appendix B.

66. See John Gillin, "Ethos Components in Modern Latin American Culture," in Dwight B. Heath and Richard N. Adams, eds., *Contemporary Cultures and Societies of Latin America* (New York: Random House, Inc., 1965), pp. 503-16.

67. For a discussion of specification, see Herbert H. Hyman, *Survey Design and Analysis* (New York: The Free Press, 1956), pp. 276-311.

68. Joseph A. Kahl, *The Measurement of Modernism: A Study of Values in Brazil and Mexico* (Austin: The University of Texas Press, 1968).

69. See Lewis, *La Vida,* op. cit., pp. xiii-lii. Emphasis on the differentiation of the poor may encourage social scientists to think of the poor as the "new aborigines" to be studied as "natives" who are somehow different from those who study them. See Bernard Beck, "Bedbugs, Stench, Dampness, and Immorality: A Review Essay on Recent Literature about Poverty," *Social Problems*, XV (Summer 1967), 101-14.

Part II: Relative Deprivation and Alienation

3

Class, Community, and Relative Deprivation

In the next four chapters we will be concerned with the class, community, and cultural determinants of relative deprivation, and with class and cultural differences in the relationship between relative deprivation and alienation. In the present chapter, we will examine the influence of class and community positions on relative deprivation. Studies have shown that perceived class position (or class identification) is inversely related to actual position in the class structure, but the correlation is far from perfect because class perception is not always accurate. We want to know if class perception is related to community position as well as to class status, and with whether community position may contribute to the distortion in class perception. In order to reduce the influence of cultural differences, the analysis will be limited to a comparison of anglo-American farm workers and farmers. Comparisons of cultural groups will be presented in Chapter 6.

Social Class

Despite the wide use of the concept of social class, it has no universally accepted definition among either the lay public or social scientists. However, two conceptions are prominent. One definition is in terms of *production functions*, the other in terms of *consumption patterns*. The former is emphasized in the writings of Karl Marx; it views position in the system of production as the primary criterion of social class. The other is more common, both in research studies and among the general public, and views aggregates of individuals who are similar with respect to socioeconomic attributes such as income, educational achievement, and prestige, or some combination of these, as constituting a social class. We will consider farmers and farm workers in terms of both conceptions.

Production Functions

According to Marx, a social class is any "aggregate of persons who perform the same function in the organization of production."[1] Therefore, he considered freedman and slave, lord and serf, guild-master and journeyman as members of different social classes in different historical periods. The two major classes in a capitalist society he called the bourgeoisie (capitalists) and the proletariat (wage laborers); the former possess all the capital and hence control the means of production whereas the latter are propertyless and have little or no control over production.

Actually Marx had two conceptions of class—a class *of* itself and a class *for* itself. He thought that until members of the proletariat become aware of their real economic and political situation vis-à-vis capitalists and acquire a sense of identity with other members of the proletariat, they are "falsely conscious" and remain a class unto themselves but not for themselves. They are, in other words, a *statistical aggregate*, not an organized group or true class. When workers assess their position with regard to capitalists realistically, are conscious of their common position, interact with each other, develop class solidarity, and form political organizations to achieve collective economic and political goals, then the aggregate class is transformed from a class *of* itself to an organized group that is a class *for* itself. Marx felt, however, that only the latter, a class for itself, constituted a true social class.[2]

If we apply this reasoning to farmers and farm workers, it is clear that the two groups constitute classes of themselves, since each consists of individuals with common functional positions in the economy, and with one group owning the means of production and the other merely providing labor. Farmers also conform rather closely to Marx's conception of a class for itself: farmers seem to identify with each other, join common organizations within which they interact, and organize to achieve common economic and political objectives.[3] However, farm workers seem to constitute less a class for itself than a class of itself.[4] Consequently, in our usage we will use "class" to refer to social classes in the aggregate as well as organized forms.

Consumption Patterns

As noted, the more general conception of social class is that of consumption patterns rather than functional position in the system of production. The two functional positions vary considerably in their consumption patterns.

Income. Respondents were asked to report their annual family income for the preceding year (1965). Median total family income for workers ($3,223) is less than one-third that of the farmers' median income ($10,212) (the average income per family member is $3,140 for workers vs. $865 for farmers). In recent years the poverty level for family income has been variously set at $2,000, $3,000, and $4,000; 26% of all farm workers earn under $2,000, 47% earn under $3,000, and 66% earn under $4,000. Less than 5% of farmers earn under $4,000.

Education. The median education for workers (6.7 years) is almost half that of farmers (12.0 years). Thus, 62% of all farm workers have not gone beyond the eighth grade, compared to only 17% of farmers.[5]

Housing. Although no categories of housing were recorded, it was clear that the housing of most workers was inferior and in many instances deplorable, whereas the housing of most farmers ranged from comfortable to luxurious. The residences of workers, which included public and private labor camps, motels, and apartment houses, were usually dirty, dilapidated, and, as often as not, with only communal running water and toilet facilities. These living quarters were usually very crowded; entire families lived in one- and two-room shacks, most of which were poorly heated and ventilated, making them uncomfortably cold or hot. The housing of most farm workers was similar to that portrayed in journalistic accounts and television documentaries.[6]

Medical Care. Although we obtained no measurement of the actual amount of medical care needed or received, respondents were asked if: (1) they thought anyone in their family needed medical care during the previous year but did not receive it; (2) they thought a family member currently needed medical care but was not receiving it; and (3) they would have spent more on medical care the previous year if they had earned more money. With each affirmative response being scored 1 and each negative response scored 0, the possible range of scores is from 0 to 3. The median for farmers was found to be 0.44 whereas that of farm workers was 1.33.

Fathers' Occupation. Clearly, farmers are in the upper to middle level of the class structure and farm workers are at the bottom. Moreover, most farmers and farm workers were born into the same level of the class structure that they currently occupy. Among farmers, 87% reported that their fathers were farmers while only 4% reported that their fathers were farm workers. In contrast, 46% of the fathers of farm workers were farm workers and another 9% were unskilled laborers. An additional 26% of workers said their fathers were farmers. Probably many of the latter were share-croppers, tenant farmers, and individuals who farmed on the margin, especially considering the respondents' low level of formal education, which depends to a considerable extent on fathers' income status. Therefore, we can conclude that farm workers come predominantly from a lower-class background; few appear to have dropped in status from that of their fathers. Most are not only at the bottom of the class structure but have always been there.[7]

Poverty: A Structural Formulation

A number of writers have approached poverty in cultural terms—i.e., "the subculture of poverty" or "lower-class subculture."[8] These conceptions imply that poverty groups have more in common than their objective deprivation; they are also similar in values, beliefs, and norms, which may give rise to habit patterns that reinforce and lead to further deprivation. Consequently, in order to raise the standard of living among the poor, the "subculture" of the poor (values, attitudes, habit patterns) must also be changed. Our results suggest, however, that poverty can be defined in terms of objective or situational conditions alone. Such conditions reveal, of course, that objective deprivation in the lower class, at least among farm workers, can not be fully described in terms of any one element, such as low income or low education, but consists of several factors. This situation reflects an important principle of social stratification, that of cumulative disadvantage (and advantage). To repeat, lower-class or poverty status is not reflected in any one characteristic but in a series of characteristics, such as low income, low education, inferior housing, a background of poverty, and so forth.[9]

Our point here is not that situational and subcultural aspects of poverty are not reciprocally related. They may well be. But, as we have said, there are a number of situational factors (low income, low education, etc.) that are themselves mutually dependent and which differentiate the poor from the nonpoor. Lipset and Bendix state:

Occupational and social status are to an important extent self-perpetuating. They are associated with many factors which make it difficult for individuals to modify their status. Position in the social structure is usually associated with a certain level of income, education, family structure, community reputation, and so forth. These become a part of a vicious circle in which each factor acts on the other in such a way as to preserve the social structure in its present form, as well as the individual family's position in that structure.

In addition, the tendency for status to be ascribed (rather than achieved) is part of the overall picture:

. . . the poverty, lack of education, absence of personal "contacts," lack of planning, and failure to explore fully the available job opportunities that characterize the [poor] are handed down from generation to generation. . . . This cumulation of . . . disadvantages is evident . . . in the choice of the first job. . . . Those in the lower socioeconomic groups tend to take "the only job they know about" at the time they enter the labor market. . . . Thus, the cumulation of disadvantages (or of advantages) affects the individual's entry into the labor market as well as his later opportunities for [upward] mobility.[10]

Thus, the structure of poverty consists of a series of disadvantages. And although this pattern is characteristic of other poverty groups, it is especially descriptive of farm workers.[11]

It does not automatically follow, however, that the objective experience of deprivation is perfectly mirrored in the subjective experience of individuals. Although farm workers may be extremely deprived, they may feel no more deprived than farmers, i.e., they may be falsely conscious of their position in the class structure.

Social Class and False Consciousness

False consciousness refers to an inaccurate perception of one's position in the social structure. To the extent that one's image of his position is consistent with characteristics of that position, one's position is accurate and he is conscious of his position. Although the term has been used to refer to one's awareness of the true nature of society and the overall social structure,[12] its use is usually limited to awareness of class position. Marx felt that workers are falsely conscious of their position if they are unaware of the level of their deprivation (relative to capitalists), are not a class for itself, and continue to believe in the prevailing cultural ideology, which is, after all, the rationalization of the dominant (capitalist) class.[13] Our usage is more restricted since we are concerned only with one's perception of rank in the class structure. False consciousness is therefore a subjective or social-psychological dimension of socioeconomic deprivation; we would expect it to be much higher for farm workers than for farmers. Furthermore, since farm workers are virtually at the bottom of the class structure and are characterized by a number of social and economic disadvantages, it is easy to determine whether they are falsely conscious. Quite simply, if they do not view themselves as more deprived than virtually all other persons in society—that is, if they do not view themselves as being at the bottom of the class structure—they are falsely conscious.

Farmers and farm workers were asked to compare themselves with all other members of society (the U.S.) in the following areas: income, education, housing, medical care, and good employment; all are important aspects of life chances in America. Response alternatives were as follows:

Almost everyone is better off than you [5].
Over half of the people are better off than you [4].
Most people are in about the same condition as you [3].
You are better off than over half the people [2].
You are better off than almost everyone [1].[14]

Responses are scored 1 to 5 (with 5 being the highest degree of deprivation) and are added to obtain an overall score. The theoretical range is 5 to 25, with the actual range being 8 to 25 (seven respondents, all workers, endorsed the first alternative all five times).[15]

Since the questions require one to compare himself with others, the total score is a measure of relative deprivation (degree of perceived deprivation in comparison to others). At the same time, because the respondent compares himself on attributes that are themselves criteria which largely define the class structure (at least for consumption patterns), the score is also a measure of perceived class position. And for farm workers especially (since they are comparatively worse off than almost anyone else), the score is a measure of false consciousness as well.

On all five items farm workers are more deprived than farmers at the .001 level of statistical significance; average total scores are 14.06 for farmers and 17.63 for farm workers. In addition, degree of perceived deprivation systematically increases as income increases for both classes (see Table 3-1).

Since farm workers are at the bottom of the class structure, if their perceived position corresponded to their objective position, their score should be 25 on the deprivation scale. Interestingly, even farm workers with less than $2,000 annual income do not place themselves this low. Thus, most workers think a substantial segment of the population is worse off than they are. Even those with the lowest income, on the average, do not believe that "over half of the people are better off than" they are.[16]

Two patterns can be seen in these scores. One is that workers assess their situations in accordance with the objective facts. They view themselves as worse off than farmers in life chances, and perceived deprivation tends to increase as income decreases. Hence, their perceptions relative to farmers are realistic. However, since most farm workers view a large proportion of the population as being at least as badly off as they are, they imagine a world that does not exist. Consequently, the perception of their position relative to the rest of society is not realistic. We can say that most farm workers are falsely conscious of their position in the class structure.[17]

Considering the farmers' income levels, their perceived deprivation is too high. Therefore, both classes are characterized by two patterns of class perception, although deviation from reality is too low for one group and too high for the other. For neither class is class perception completely accurate.

Table 3-1

Average Perceived Deprivation[a] Score by Income, for Farmers and Farm Workers

	Lowest Income Group	Second Lowest Income Group	Second Highest Income Group	Highest Income Group
	0-$6,000	$ 6,001-$10,000	$10,001-$16,000	Over $16,000
Farmers	15.09	14.21	14.02	13.10
	(35)[b]	(59)	(49)	(58)
	0-$2,000	$ 2,001-$ 4,000	$ 4,001-$ 6,000	Over $ 6,000
Farm Workers	18.33	17.43	16.74	15.03
	(91)	(181)	(124)	(59)

[a]Combined perceived relative standing in the United States on income, education, housing, medical care, and good employment.
[b]Figures in parentheses are N.

Community Position and Relative Deprivation

Poverty groups are frequently characterized as living in isolation from the rest of society and as largely invisible to society. Although people may recognize that the poor exist, such recognition is frequently based on knowledge about income distribution rather than direct contact with the poor; the nonpoor usually do not know who the poor really are or where they live. Except in statistics, therefore, the poor almost do not exist; they are isolated from the rest of society.[18] This may be a factor in the pattern of false consciousness because isolation can influence poor people's perception of the rest of society just as it influences how the poor are perceived by society. The more isolated a poor person, the less apt he is to have contact with persons who are better off than he; and consequently he may view himself as being higher in the class structure than he really is.

Journalistic and impressionistic writings describe the same pattern of isolation for farm workers that has been attributed to other poverty groups: they are portrayed as physically segregated and nonparticipating in community affairs.[19] Results of our analysis reaffirm the existence of this isolation.

Residential Patterns

In describing the residential patterns of farm workers in the six counties studied it is necessary first to describe some of the procedural problems encountered in locating the workers. The original plan was to choose subjects at random from labor camps and farms. Investigation revealed, however, that no master list of labor camps existed and farmers might oppose sampling on their farms due to publicity that farm workers had been and were still receiving in the mass media.[20] However, we soon found that farm workers in all counties could easily be found wherever run-down, dilapidated housing existed as well as in labor camps, cheap motels, and shacks on back roads that were advertised as "cabins." After these residential patterns were identified, locating most groups of workers was relatively easy; most communities are small and most workers lived in segregated areas.

There are some residential differences within groups of workers, however. Migrants were living in buildings which almost exclusively housed temporary agricultural workers, including private and public labor camps, run-down motels, clusters of inexpensive and deteriorating cabins, apartment houses, and trailer camps. Many of these structures were located on the outskirts of town, usually away from the main flow of traffic, or in isolated areas on back roads. Mexican-Americans (residents and migrants) were especially easy to find because they lived in predominantly ghetto-like neighborhoods and in isolated communities. Anglo-American residents generally were more dispersed than the other groups because they were more apt to live in neighborhoods with nonfarm workers, although these neighborhoods were still predominantly low income areas.

Community Visibility

Low visibility of farm workers is reflected in several ways. Despite the fact that members of interviewing teams who were virtual strangers to the communities were able to identify the residential patterns of farm workers, as well as the fact that agriculture is a major industry in all counties so that there is some demand for farm workers all year (but strongest during the harvest season), community officials of the United States Employment Security Office and Office of Economic Opportunity provided little help in locating farm workers. Such officials usually knew about the existence of public labor camps and low-grade public housing built specifically for farm labor but they knew little else about residential patterns. When these officials were asked where farm workers might be located, typical comments were, "They have not arrived," or "They'll be coming in any day now," referring of course to migrants who were already living in the community (of whom we interviewed 483!). When asked where anglo-American workers might be located, especially residents, officials usually replied that there weren't any—they didn't even *exist*; as one put it, "You are ten years too late," referring to the replacement of anglo-American workers by Mexican-Americans. (As noted previously, 541 anglo-Americans, 282 of whom were residents, were interviewed!) Our conversations with similarly misinformed persons in bars, restaurants, and other public places indicated that farm workers were not very visible to the local population generally.

Part of the reason for low visibility is the residential patterns noted above. With the exception of some anglo-American residents, farm workers tend to live in residential areas occupied almost exclusively by farm workers, most of which are in out-of-the-way places—on the outskirts of town, on the back roads, and in run-down sections of communities where most people have little reason to visit. Even in small communities, housing occupied mostly by farm workers may be difficult to find since labor camps are concealed by fences, walls, trees, shrubbery, and other buildings. The statement that, "a tar paper curtain separates the migrant from the rest of America,"[21] appears accurate not only for farm workers but for many residents as well. As with other poverty groups, the community reaction to farm workers seems to be, "out of sight, out of mind."[22] Our experience in locating farm workers is exemplified in the following statement by Truman Moore: "You can drive from New York to California and never see a migrant camp. You have to know where to look."[23] We must also say that this holds true for the living quarters of resident farm workers as well.

Low residential visibility is probably reinforced by the workers' patterns of work and social life. Most workers are in the fields or orchards eight to fourteen hours a day, six days a week; there are usually grocery stores and taverns near their living quarters, making it unnecessary for them to go to other parts of the community.[24] Indeed, farm workers appear to be "isolated and unrelated to the communities in which they live. . . ."[25]

Social Participation

Community isolation and segregation are reflected in social participation patterns. Respondents were asked about their membership in clubs, churches, and other voluntary associations. Sixty-eight % of workers reported no membership, and another 22% reported only one (usually church).[26] In contrast, corresponding percentages for farmers were 4 and 13. Respondents were also asked about the occupation of their best friend. Fifty-seven % of farm workers report their one best friend is also a farm worker (77% of the farmers report that their best friend is a farmer).[27] Such findings are consistent with the picture of community isolation and invisibility of farm workers: they are not likely to participate in community activities and their primary contacts are with persons who are, like themselves, isolated and poor.

Mental Hospital Admissions

Finally, the community exclusion of farm workers is reflected in mental hospital rates. One index of community exclusion is the ratio of involuntary to voluntary hospitalization rates to state mental hospitals.[28] The rationale for this index derives from the coercive nature of involuntary hospitalization, which is believed to be high for groups that are rejected by and isolated in society. A comparison of involuntary-voluntary ratios between farm workers and other major occupational groups in the state of Washington reveals that the ratio of involuntary to voluntary commitments for farm workers (4.11) is more than twice as large as the next highest category (1.97) for nonfarm and nonmining laborers.[29] Therefore, hospital admissions findings agree with our general observation that farm workers have been rejected by society and the government as well as observations on their community isolation.

We have seen that regardless of the criterion observed, then, farm workers are differentiated from the rest of society and community; they live on the very fringes. This may be a factor in their low scores on relative deprivation. Because they have little contact with persons whose status is higher than their own, the real range of class differences may not be visible to them. And since most of their contacts are with persons of like status, they may be aware only of persons whose life situations are as bad or worse than their own. Interviewers noted, for example, that farm workers frequently volunteered that they knew they were "in bad shape" and "worse off than a lot of people," but knew others (persons "back home," for migrants) who were worse off than they. Because workers are isolated from affluent members of the community, they may assume that many people live as they do, and their image of society and their place in it is shaped accordingly.

Farmers, however, may perceive themselves to be less well off than they actually are. One reason is that they are so integrated in their class level in the community that they are unaware of the many persons who are much worse off than they.

Toward the end of the interview for each subject, the life chance items were asked once again (see p. 45). This time, however, respondents were asked to compare themselves with all persons in their "home community." Although they are isolated from society (by virtue of their isolation from the community), farm workers probably do realize that there are many other persons in the society as a whole who are worse off, but they look upon only a small proportion of community residents as being worse off. Paradoxically, that aspect of the overall class structure (that is, the community class structure) that is closest to them may not be very visible to them. If this is true, their responses to the deprivation scale should be lower when community is the frame of reference than when society is. Table 3-2 presents scores for the two scales for income and residence categories. In seven of eight comparisons, scores are lower when community is the frame of reference. Position in community appears to influence class perceptions, and on the basis of these results, it contributes to false consciousness: the farm workers' perceptions of their place in the community class structure is higher than the perception of their place in the class structure for society as a whole.[30]

Table 3-2
Average Perceived Deprivation with Society and Community as Frames of Reference,[a] by Residence and Income for Farm Workers

	$2,000 and below	$2,001-$4,000	$4,001-$6,000	Over $6,000
Residents				
Society	18.11 (49)[b]	16.10 (92)	16.36 (92)	15.59 (33)
Community	17.41 (48)	16.57 (91)	15.91 (78)	14.31 (32)
Migrants				
Society	18.59 (42)	18.66 (99)	17.04 (45)	14.31 (26)
Community	17.09 (41)	16.78 (95)	16.05 (45)	13.37 (28)

[a]Combined perceived relative standing in the United States and community of residence on income, education, housing, medical care, and good employment.
[b]Figures in parentheses are N.

At the same time, however, the influence of community location does not override the influence of socioeconomic status. Most farm workers still perceive themselves to be more deprived than farmers, and differences among farm workers are associated with differences in income. In ten out of twelve comparisons between adjacent income groups in Table 3-2, the lower income group has the higher score. Thus, although results indicate that community position influences one's perception of his location in the class structure, class structure continues to exert an effect, although the effect is not as great (scores are not as low) as might be expected considering the farm workers' low position in the class structure. Despite the difference between scores for the two scales, then, the presence of *two* patterns in the lower class is reflected in each: the tendency to be aware of one's true class position as well as the tendency to falsely perceive oneself as being considerably better off than one actually is.

Results for farmers, however, show that relative deprivation is slightly *higher* when farmers compare themselves with other persons in their community than when the entire society is the frame of reference; average scores are 14.50 versus 14.06. A score of 15.00 indicates that "most people" in the community are seen to be in about the same condition as oneself. Thus, on the average, farmers believe that their socioeconomic position is only slightly higher than that of most others in the community.[31] The same is true even for those earning over $16,000, since their score is 13.5. Results suggest that farmers are so integrated in their class level that many people who are considerably below them in class status are unknown to them. If so, community comparisons appear to have an effect on farmers that is opposite to their effect on farm workers.

For both groups two patterns emerge. First, the tendency for class perception to be associated with class position exists, and second, the lower-status group perceives its position to be higher than it is and the higher-status group perceives its position to be lower than it is. The influence of greater community isolation on farm workers and greater community integration (in the middle-class sector) for farmers is reflected by the fact that the difference between average scores of farmers and farm workers on the relative deprivation scale is less when community is the frame of reference than when society is; there is a difference of 1.77 between the scores when community is the frame of reference but 2.95 when society is the frame of reference. Although farm workers have a higher score in each case, the difference is less when comparisons are made in terms of the community class structure. It appears, therefore, that community isolation-integration may be a significant factor in the false consciousness of both the lower and middle to upper class, although it has opposite effects for the two groups.

Conclusion

The results described in the foregoing discussion are generally consistent with the hypothesis that class perceptions are associated with actual class position.

But they also reveal two patterns of class perception—one realistic and the other unrealistic—and the presence of both patterns among the middle- to upper-class farmers as well as among lower-class farm workers. In addition, findings suggest that community position is a significant factor in the distorted pattern we have described. The physical and social separation of the poor and nonpoor tends to raise the level of deprivation among the nonpoor and to lower it among the poor. Thus, those "on top" in rural society are not satisfied with their positions because they perceive, unrealistically, that many others are better off than they are, whereas those "on the bottom" imagine many to be worse off.

Such perceptions probably contribute to a stable class structure. Farmers think of themselves as unrealistically low, and as a result, may be less apt to sympathize with movements and policies that are designed to redistribute life chances. The lower-class farm workers, however, view their life chances relative to others as unrealistically high, which may lead to few, weak, or modest demands for a redistribution of life chances. Findings on the degree of satisfaction among farmers and farm workers are relevant here. Respondents were asked if they were satisfied with the income (farmers) or wages (farm workers) they were receiving. A larger proportion of farmers than workers expressed dissatisfaction (87% to 73%). When workers were asked how much they felt they should make by the hour, the median response was $2.05; their reported median income per hour is $1.70. This difference does not represent an extreme "demand" or dissatisfaction.[32]

These findings are consistent with the conclusions of Simmons and Rosenberg, who also found that objective and subjective class placement (upper, middle, working, and lower) were imperfectly correlated. They state, "This failure to realize or admit the full extent of one's deprivation would be expected to help counteract pressures toward class conflict."[33] This tendency, along with the failure of the more advantaged strata to realize or admit the full extent of their advantages, would be expected to help preserve the class structure in its present form.

The paradox is compounded by another. When the perceptions of persons on the bottom do become more realistic or more in line with their objective class position, such as seems to be the case for many blacks today in the United States,[34] the resulting actions may be disruptive, revolutionary, and violent. From the perspective of "those on top," such persons may seem reckless, senseless, suicidal, or *unrealistic.*[35]

We know that in any society life chances are not distributed equally throughout the population and will probably never be. Also, as a result some degree of class tension is likely to be inevitable in any society. Extreme inequities in life chances exist in the United States, but despite this disparity, historically the amount and intensity of class conflict have been low. One possible explanation is the influence of the idea of achieved status, the belief that status should be based on performance and ability rather than social inheritance. Consequently, it is always *possible* for low-status persons to rise in the class structure and for high-status persons to fall. Research on intergenerational mobility does not reveal extensive mobility in the United States, however;[36] for example, as we have seen in this chapter, most farmers and farm workers have about the same status as their parents. This is understandable in light of the principle of cumulative advantage (disadvantage): because disadvantage in one area is dependent on and contributes to disadvantage in another, efforts at improving one's situation in one area may be counteracted by forces holding one back in other areas. And, of course, this helps the more advantaged strata to preserve their status. Nevertheless, achieved status exists as a cultural principle, that is, large numbers of the population believe it operates. As a result class tensions and conflict may be reduced.

Even so, results of this chapter suggest that false consciousness may also be a significant factor in preserving the status quo. Its operation is not limited to the lower class, however, for the tendency for higher-status persons to perceive their position as unrealistically low exists along with the tendency for lower-status persons to perceive their class position as unrealistically high. Together the two trends contribute to a stable class structure.

If our reasoning about the effect of community isolation among the poor is correct, and if violent actions are largely the result of relative deprivation as some contend,[37] then tension between blacks (and other minority groups) and the more affluent sector of society can be expected. As minorities become increasingly integrated in society, more higher-status persons become visible to them so that their assessment of their position in the class structure becomes more accurate. Consequently, community tension and violence may be short-run consequences we will have to suffer for a society in which barriers separating the poor from the nonpoor are removed.[38]

Notes

1. Reinhard Bendix and Seymour Martin Lipset, "Karl Marx's Theory of Social Classes," in Reinhard Bendix and Seymour Martin Lipset, eds., *Class, Status, and Power: Social Stratification in Comparative Perspective*, 2nd ed. (New York: The Free Press, 1966), p. 7.

2. In commenting on the peasants of France, Marx stated: "In so far as millions of families live under economic conditions of existence that separate their mode of life, their interests, and their culture from those of the other classes and put them in hostile opposition to the latter, they form a class. In so far as there is merely a local interconnection among these small-holding peasants and the identity of their interests begets no community, no national bond, and no political organization among them, they do not form a class." *The Eighteenth Brumaire of Louis Bonaparte*, in Lewis S. Feuer, ed., *Marx and Engels: Basic*

Writings on Politics and Philosophy (Garden City, N.Y.: Doubleday & Company, Inc., 1959), pp. 338-89. Actually, Marx used several criteria of social class at different points in his many writings. See Bertell Ollman, "Marx's Use of 'Class,'" *American Journal of Sociology*, LXXIII (March 1968), 573-80. The distinction between a class "of" and "for" itself is a particularly general one, however.

3. R. Joseph Monsen, Jr., and Mark W. Cannon, *The Makers of Public Policy: American Power Groups and Their Ideologies* (New York: McGraw-Hill Book Company, 1965), pp. 96-132.

4. In a pretest interview one worker commented that he wanted most of all that farm workers "stick together," referring to the problem of the low degree of common identity and organized effort in the pursuit of common economic goals. The recent success of unionization efforts among California farm workers suggests that the situation may be changing.

5. One consequence of low education is probably evidenced in the following results. Farm workers were asked ten factual questions dealing with the legal rights of farm workers in Washington, several of which dealt with their contractual rights with farmers. Since each question had two alternatives— "right" or "wrong"—by chance a worker should have gotten five questions correct. The average for all resident farm workers was 5.05! Although we can make no comparison (that is, farmers were not asked comparable questions and we have no data for industrial workers), we can say that farm workers are basically ignorant of the rights they do have. Their knowledge of legal constraints on persons (that is, farmers) who have so much control over their fate is no better than chance. And in this respect there are no significant differences between cultural groups among workers. Dale Wright's description, which can apply to resident farm workers as well as migrants, is apt: "The migratory agricultural worker has been hidden away in that clump of trees for so many years, for so many generations, that he often doesn't know he has certain rights and privileges in the American System. Who can expect the sweating, hardworking, underpaid, exploited, always-on-the move laborer to demand the rights and privileges due him in a free society when he doesn't even know they exist? Historically, he has not found a place in the system; he has not been able to find his way out of the trees." *They Harvest Despair: The Story of Migrant Workers* (Boston: Beacon Press, 1965), pp. 157-58.

6. Two of the best documentaries are the television films, "Harvest of Shame" (CBS) and "Bitter Harvest" (KING of Seattle, Washington). This is not to say that all the workers' housing was equally inferior. Some resident farm workers lived in housing that, although below middle-class standards, was roomier, cleaner and in better repair than the housing of other workers, particularly migrants. And some migrants lived in house trailers that, although not spacious, were adequate for two people and even with children better than most other housing. Such exceptions suggest that housing for farm laborers in

this part of Washington has improved over the past 30 years; moreover, there was no evidence of families living in automobiles, lean-tos, or makeshift tents. See Carl F. Reuss and Paul H. Landis, *Migratory Farm Labor and the HOP Industry on the Pacific Coast*, Agricultural Experiment Station Bulletin No. 363 (Pullman, Wash.: Washington State University, 1937).

7. Even though birth into a poor family of origin does not totally account for the fact that an individual is poor, it does increase the likelihood. And it is probably not the poverty status of one's family of origin per se that contributes to an individual's subsequent poverty status, but the fact that the status of one's family of origin influences the educational experiences and occupational training apt to have been received. Because a connection exists, then, between poverty status in family of origin and family of procreation does not preclude the influence of other factors such as ethnicity and race. See Otis D. Duncan, "Inheritance of Poverty or Inheritance of Race?" in Daniel P. Moynihan, ed., *On Understanding Poverty: Perspectives from the Social Sciences* (New York: Basic Books, Inc., 1968), Vol. I. For a review of the relationship between ascribed status and welfare, see Norman S. Weissberg, "On Intergenerational Welfare Dependency: A Critical Review," *Social Problems*, XVIII (Fall 1970), 257-74.

8. For a critical assessment of the conceptual and empirical status of these conceptions, see Charles A. Valentine, *Culture and Poverty* (Chicago: The University of Chicago Press, 1967).

9. See Thomas Gladwin, *Poverty U.S.A.* (Boston: Little, Brown, & Company, 1967), pp. 76-77.

10. Seymour M. Lipset and Reinhard Bendix, *Social Mobility in Industrial Society* (Berkeley: The University of California Press, 1959), p. 199.

11. In addition, as we noted in chapter 2, there are the elements of limited power deriving from the position of farm work in the agricultural economy and the relationship of farm workers to the rest of society, particularly the political institutions.

12. See Charles A. Reich, *The Greening of America* (New York: Random House, Inc., 1970).

13. See C. Wright Mills, *The Marxists* (New York: Dell Publishing Company, Inc., 1962), pp. 81-95, esp. 87-88. For an outstanding treatment of Marx's conception of false consciousness, see Joachim Israel, *Alienation from Marx to Modern Society: A Macrosociological Analysis* (Boston: Allyn & Bacon, Inc., 1971), pp. 80-96.

14. Just before presenting these questions to the respondent, the interviewer stated that he wanted to ask "some questions about where you think you stand in the United States on some specific things, such as income, medical care, education, etc. For example, I want to know how you think you compare with all other people in the U.S. in income. I want you to answer in one of five ways." The five alternative responses were then presented to the respondent followed by the five questions, e.g., "How do you compare in income?"

15. Scalogram analysis using the Goodenough technique reveals a coefficient of reproducability (Rep) of .83. Although this is not high, the *Gammas* between item score and total scale score range from .67 to .92. In addition, item analysis reveals that the disciminatory power *(DP)* for the seven items, which ranges between 1.16 and 1.45, are all well above the minimum level of 0.50 recommended by Goode and Hatt (William J. Goode and Paul K. Hatt, *Methods in Social Research* [New York: McGraw-Hill Book Company, 1952], p. 276).

16. The score of slightly more than 18.00 for this group (see Table 3-1), when divided by the number of questions (5), gives a score of slightly less than 4.00. A score of 4 is given for the item, "Over half of the people are better off than you."

17. This may partially explain why militancy and unionization have been so weak within this class. Of course, structural factors are involved, such as the farmers' political power, the dispersion of farm workers, the migratory status of many workers, and the sheer number of groups from which farm workers are recruited. It is possible, too, that at least some of these factors partially account for the worker's distorted perception. In any case, militancy stems not so much from a group's objective deprivation as from its members' perception that their life chances are fewer than those of others. This psychological state is probably a necessary condition for unions to flourish as well as the militant and revolutionary-like actions exhibited by some black Americans. This state does not appear to exist among many farm workers.

18. Michael Harrington writes: "The millions who are poor in the United States tend to become increasingly invisible. . . . I discovered this personally in a curious way. After I wrote my first article on poverty in America, I had all the statistics down on paper. I had proved to my satisfaction that there were around 50,000,000 poor in this country. Yet, I realized I did not believe my own figures. The poor existed in the Government reports; they were percentages and numbers in long, close columns, but they were not part of my experience. I could prove that the other America existed, but I had never been there." *The Other America: Poverty in the United States* (New York: The Macmillan Company, 1964), pp. 1-8, quotes at pp. 2-3. See also Dwight MacDonald, "Our Invisible Poor," in Louis A. Ferman, Joyce L. Kornbluh, and Alan Haber, eds., *Poverty in America* (Ann Arbor: University of Michigan Press, 1965), pp. 6-24; and Ben H. Bagdikian, *In the Midst of Plenty* (Boston: Beacon Press, 1964), pp. 1-9. However, considering the national attention given to poverty in recent years (e.g., the "War on Poverty" programs), the public is much more aware that poverty does exist, even if most people don't know precisely where it exists or who is affected; poverty remains largely invisible in the sense that most persons never have direct contact with it and observe it first-hand.

19. See p. 24 above.

20. Much of the publicity stemmed from the newly enacted Office of Economic Opportunity programs. However, the living conditions of farm

workers have been the topic of discussion and the target of programs for several action groups in the state.

21. Truman Moore, *The Slaves We Rent* (New York: Random House, Inc., 1965), p. 132.

22. Bagdikian, op. cit.

23. Moore, loc. cit.

24. Dorothy Nelkin observes that in New York State migrant labor camps, few workers enter the surrounding communities and that "most activities take place within the physical setting of the camp." "Unpredictability and Life Style in a Migrant Labor Camp," *Social Problems*, XVII (Spring 1970), 478.

25. United States Department of Health, Education and Welfare, Social Security Administration, Children's Bureau, *Children in Migrant Families* (Washington, D.C.: U.S. Government Printing Office, 1960).

26. Findings are consistent with other studies of associational membership among the poor. For a review of the evidence, see Russell L. Curtis, Jr. and Louis A. Zurcher, Jr., "Voluntary Associations and the Social Integration of the Poor," *Social Problems*, XVIII (Winter 1971), 339-57.

27. These findings are not particularly surprising, since the tendency for friendship patterns to follow status lines is general. (See the review in Paul F. Secord and Carl W. Backman, *Social Psychology* [New York: McGraw-Hill Book Company, 1964], pp. 244-45.) However, the proportions of workers and farmers whose best friend is also a farm worker or farmer, respectively, appear to be unusually high; friendship patterns for other occupations may not be so high. Our findings may be compared with studies of printers and police officers. In reporting the occupations of their *three* best friends, both groups report that 35% are from their own occupations. See Seymour M. Lipset, Martin H. Trow, and James S. Coleman, *Union Democracy* (New York: Anchor Books, 1962), p. 123; and Jerome H. Skolnick, *Justice Without Trial: Law Enforcement in Democratic Society* (New York: John Wiley & Sons, Inc., 1967), p. 52. In a study in Scotland, it was found that 50%, 57%, and 66% of police officers from county, burgh, and city forces, respectively, reported more than three "personal friendships with other police officers." MIchael P. Banton *The Policeman in the Community* (New York: Basic Books, Inc., 1964), p. 248. Considering the fact that our question asks about only the respondent's *one* best friend, findings suggest that farmers and farm workers may be isolated from the rest of society to a much greater extent than printers and police officers.

28. See Arnold S. Linsky, "Who Shall be Excluded: The Influence of Personal Attributes and Community Reaction to the Mentally Ill," *Social Psychiatry*, V (July 1970), 166-71; and William A. Rushing, "Individual Resources, Societal Reaction, and Hospital Commitment," *American Journal of Sociology*, LXXVII (November 1971), 511-26.

29. A detailed analysis is presented in ibid. (Rushing).

30. Farm workers fare just as poorly in comparisons in their home communi-

ties as they do in society as a whole. In comparison to farm worker median family income of $3,233, the 1960 median incomes for all families in the six counties studied included were: $7,288, $6,077, $5,926, $5,850, $5,674, and $5,152. The median family income for the U.S. population as a whole was $5,660. U.S. Bureau of the Census. *U.S. Census of Population, 1960. General Social and Economic Characteristics*, Washington, Final Report PC(1)-49C (Washington, D.C.: U.S. Government Printing Office, 1962); and idem, *U.S. Census of Population, 1960*. Vol. I, *Characteristics of the Population*. Part I, *United States Summary* (Washington, D.C.: U.S. Government Printing Office, 1964), p. 225.

31. That most farmers are considerably better off is indicated by the fact that the 1960 median family income for the county from which farmers were sampled was $5,799, considerably below the $10,200 figure for farmers. County figures are from *U.S. Census of Population, General Social and Economic Characteristics*, ibid.

32. This is not to say, of course, that the desired level will not rise once the present desired level has been reached.

33. Roberta G. Simmons and Morris Rosenberg, "Functions of Children's Perceptions of the Stratification System," *American Sociological Review*, XXXVI (April 1971), 235-49, quote at p. 245.

34. See Bayard Rustin, "A Way Out of the Exploding Ghetto," *New York Times Magazine*, XXIV (August 13, 1967).

35. These terms were often directed at rebellious and riotous blacks during the late sixties. Such comments seem to be less frequent now.

36. Lipset and Bendix, op. cit.

37. See James A. Geschwender, "Social Structure and the Negro Revolt: An Examination of Some Hypotheses," *Social Forces*, XLIII (December 1964), 248-56; idem, "Explorations in the Theory of Social Movements and Revolutions," *Social Forces*, XLVII (December 1968), 127-35; and Carl F. Grindstaff, "The Negro, Urbanization, and Relative Deprivation in the Deep South," *Social Problems*, XV (Winter 1968), 342-452.

38. It is noteworthy that the black riots and "rebellions" in the United States began when racial integration was receiving its strongest support from the courts and the federal government, and was being strongly advocated by a sizable proportion of the population for the first time in the country's history. Because greater attention was being given to integration, the blacks' points of comparison may have shifted from other blacks, which a segregated society encourages, to the members of the more privileged white society, which an integrated society encourages. Thus, if militant efforts, including unionization, depend to a large degree on the correspondence between objective conditions and subjective awareness of those conditions, militant movements among farm workers may be weak as long as they remain isolated from the rest of society.

Class Position, Relative Deprivation, and Powerlessness

In this chapter we will investigate the effects of class status and relative deprivation on powerlessness. Class differences in life chances reported in the previous chapter are especially relevant to this investigation. Individuals with low income, limited occupational skills, inferior education, and so forth, have relatively little power to improve themselves. We have seen, however, that one's class position is imperfectly mirrored in one's perceptions. Thus, farm workers may perceive themselves as having more power than they in fact have.

We will also want to know to what extent perceived deprivation is associated with feelings of powerlessness. Perceived status deprivation may be more responsible for feelings of powerlessness than class status itself; how one views his life chances in comparison to the life chances of others may be more important than the actual level of life chances itself. We will want to know if the relationship between perceived deprivation and powerlessness exists among farmers as well as farm workers. If it exists only among the latter, then results should indicate that the effects of perceived deprivation are specific to the lower class. But if it exists within both classes, results would show that the effects of perceived deprivation transcend social classes and stem from factors that are common to both classes, such as a common culture. As in Chapter 3, in order to reduce the influence of cultural differences, we will limit our analysis to anglo-American farmers and farm workers.

For Marx, alienation arises from a complicated relationship between social class and powerlessness which involves a number of elements. Three essential factors generate alienation: private property, wages, and division of labor.[1] Because capitalists own the means of production (i.e., factories and technology), the worker's position of power is eroded. As a result, labor is placed on a wage basis and workers are controlled by the wage and not by the activity itself; they work only for the wage and not because of the intrinsic value of work: "labor does not appear as an end in itself but as the servant of the wage."[2] With regard to the division of labor, Marx distinguishes between manual and intellectual functions of work. With the coming of the factory system, intellectual functions become concentrated in the hands of capitalists and manual functions in the hands of wage labor. But this division removes all decision-making power from the worker and concentrates it in the hands of the capitalist. As a consequence of these three factors, then, the faculties of "knowledge, judgment and will" are no longer needed by the worker. They "are now required only for the workshop as a whole. Intelligence in production expands in one direction, because it vanishes in many others. What is lost by the detail laborers, is concentrated in the capital that employs them."[3] With "knowledge, judgment, and will" about the work process being denied them, workers become mere "appendages to the machine," and they are powerless to influence their work environment.

According to Marx, then, class differences in power position lead to differences in perceived, felt, or subjective power. The hypothesis has been extended by Haggstrom, who states that power differences between middle- and lower-class positions determine differences in "internal personality characteristics"[5] such that lower-class persons feel that they have less power than those above them. (Haggstrom further contends that the psychological characteristics that are often assumed to be associated with being poor [e.g., short-term planning, hostility, and a restricted range of interests] are due to feelings of powerlessness rather than other class characteristics such as income.[6])

Studies confirm that powerlessness and socioeconomic status are inversely related.[7] However, these relationships are not very close, as is reflected in low correlation coefficients,[8] and the differences between "classes" (e.g., manual vs. nonmanual workers) have been quite small.[9] Also, since age may be related to powerlessness,[10] findings from some studies are questionable because age is not controlled. And, apart from these factors, results may be irrelevant to the Marxian hypothesis since they are based on "class" groupings that are heterogeneous with respect to occupational status and economic function (e.g., manual vs. nonmanual workers).[11] As noted previously, for Marx a necessary condition for a social class is the existence of an aggregate of persons who are homogeneous as to production function. By limiting our analysis to two positions in one system of production, and analyzing the differences in powerlessness as we minimize the effects of age, income level, and perceived deprivation, we can overcome some of the difficulties of other studies.[12] However, before we compare farmers and farm workers in perceived power, we must present a more detailed discussion of the differences between the two in terms of the *structure* of power.

Social Class, Power, and the Agricultural Production System

Marx's description of the differences in power between factory owners and workers is especially applicable to differences between many farmers and farm workers. Indeed, his description may be more accurate for agricultural systems than for urban factory systems.

Contrary to Marx's predictions, the economic conditions of factory workers have continued to improve rather than worsen, largely through peaceful means and the power of labor unions, and political parties have emerged which protect the workers' economic interests. The functions of most owners have been assumed by industrial managers, who are themselves employees of absentee owners. Moreover, the relationship between management and workers is increasingly mediated by bureaucratic organizations (i.e., factory and union administration); collective bargaining takes place within this framework so that conflicts are usually settled by negotiation, diplomacy, and compromise, according to law and rules of procedure, not merely the interests of the owners.

The agricultural economy has also moved toward absentee ownership, managerial operations, and bureaucratic administration, although a far larger proportion of farms than industrial plants are still individually or family owned. Also, like factory workers, agricultural workers are divorced from the means of production. Unlike factory workers, however, as we noted in Chapter 2, until recently agricultural workers have had no strong unions to protect their interests, and only sporadic attempts at unionization have been made in Washington and most other states prior to 1967 (only 10% of the workers in this study belong to a union of any kind). And contrary to factory workers, agricultural workers have had almost no voice in economic decisions which affect them. They have had virtually no opportunity to exercise "knowledge, judgment, and will" in the production process.

Farmers, however, have strong organizations in the Farm Bureau, Farmers Union, and Grange, in addition to numerous cooperatives and local agrieconomic organizations (almost 90% of the farmers in this study are members of such organization).[13] These political pressure groups, as well as the rural overrepresentation in Congress and state legislatures, assure that the farmers' economic interests will be protected (e.g., by legislation to guarantee price supports for crops). Of course, the farmers' power is decreasing with reapportionment, and the ideological disputes between the three major farm organizations may continue to undermine the farmers' position of power.[14] Nevertheless, in comparison to farm workers the farmers have great power. Workers have virtually no representation in Congress and their interests have not been protected by federal legislation in areas such as collective bargaining and the minimum wage; most state legislatures have virtually ignored them. In addition, the fact that many farm workers are migrants, are dispersed, and are recruited from a number of labor pools makes organization difficult and the realization of power almost impossible.[15] The farm worker has, according to Dale Wright,

none of the wherewithal that is necessary to wrest from employers or political organizations the living, working, and educational facilities that would take him out of the abyss into which he has been forced by the society around him. He [is] a classic example of powerlessness.[16]

Alienation (powerlessness) among farm workers is especially reflected by their economic helplessness. To Marx, alienation is a condition wherein one's economic actions are "an alien power, standing over and against [the worker], instead of being ruled by him."[17] Certainly the conditions described by journalists, which we reviewed in Chapter 2, indicate that the farm worker's economic actions are indeed ruled by a system over which he has no control, and which is not oriented to his interests. The farm worker is treated much like Marx believed the industrial worker would be: he is exploited, overworked, and dealt with as a commodity to be bought and sold who has no intrinsic worth as an individual human being. We recall Dale Wright's remarks that the farm worker works under conditions of "economic slavery" (see p. 26 above). Wright also states that he is "cheated, overworked, underpaid and exploited for work honestly done. He is dealt with as a commodity, a chattel, a piece of impersonal machinery necessary in the harvest of crops."[18]

Many of the social and economic constraints under which farm workers live are evident from the analysis in the previous chapter. Most workers are constrained to take low paying jobs because they have no educational or occupational skills. Many are functionally illiterate. Naturally, because of their low income, limited occupational skills, etc., these workers can do little to assist themselves. Thomas Gladwin states:

the crucial characteristics of poverty: lack of money, discrimination, and lack of social and occupational skills . . . each . . . has a share in robbing the poor of power. . . . The economics of poverty are . . . a straitjacket which, like the straitjacket on a mental patient . . . restrains movement. . . . [Hence,] powerlessness is an almost inevitable consequence of poverty.[19]

Farm workers, and poor persons generally, even those who are motivated to improve themselves educationally and occupationally, may be caught in a vicious circle that robs them of any power to change their economic situations; they must continue to work at jobs which do not allow them an income surplus and freedom to pursue education and training that would in turn permit them to obtain better jobs.

In addition, the farm workers do not work regular schedules; one day they may work long hours, the next none at all. And when one job ends they must look elsewhere for another; they are controlled by weather conditions and the agricultural harvest cycle. Such constraints were expressed as follows by a farm worker testifying before the President's Commission on Rural Poverty: "I have felt the need of an education, but because of my job, I have no set hours. There are days that I must work 10 or 12 hours. Consequently, I cannot fit myself to a schedule for school."[20]

In summary, not only do farm workers have little economic-political collective power or power based on social contacts with other members of the community, but the nature of their occupation is such that in many respects the individual's occupational activity is to him "an unfree activity"—Marx's condition of alienation. As we have said, farm workers have little power over when and where they will work, and the alternatives to farm work are few or nonexistent. Because such a large proportion were reared in farm work most know no other way of life[21], are severely constrained by the nature of their situations and their backgrounds, and would appear to be powerless to change their mode of existence. Indeed, their occupational and work activities would appear to be quite "unfree."

Powerlessness

Interestingly, despite the different nature of their work situations, farm workers may feel no more powerless than the farmers. Let us remember that the individual's perspective of his situation, rather than the actual structure of that situation, determines whether he thinks he can do anything to improve things. For example, Seeman defines powerlessness as the "expectancy or probability held by the individual that his own behavior cannot determine the occurrence of outcomes, or reinforcements, he seeks."[22] For Marx, of course, work outcomes are important, but we feel that powerlessness need not be restricted to work outcomes. It may be conceived as a much broader phenomenon, such as the individual's general insignificance vis-à-vis a bureaucratic society, as suggested in the writings of Max Weber.[23]

In our analysis powerlessness is not limited to work outcomes, as for Marx, and is more narrowly defined than in Weber's conception, although it is consistent with Seeman's general definition. We emphasize the individual's perceived ability to influence his outcomes, especially the economic outcomes. Our definition is based on yes or no responses to the following six questions:

1. Do you think that persons like yourself can improve their economic position?
2. Some people say that almost anyone in our country can improve his standard of living if he is willing to work hard. Do you think that this is true?
3. Would you say that persons like yourself have less say-so in how the government is run than most other people?
4. Do you think that there is much that you can do about most of the important problems that you face today?
5. Do you feel that too often you have to take the pay offered (by the farmer) (for your crop) without any opportunity of bargaining (with him) (for the price)?
6. Is there much that you can do as an individual to increase your income?

The possible range in total scores is 0 to 6, with 6 representing the highest degree of powerlessness. A score of 6 would be achieved if respondents replied "no" to all questions except the third and fifth questions.[24] Psychologists and sociologists have known for some time that certain individuals have a tendency to give consistently "yes" or "no" answers to questions regardless of the question asked. Consequently, if a person has a tendency to respond "yes" to questions and if "yes" answers are considered powerlessness responses (scored as one), he is more apt to score higher on the powerlessness scale than a person who has a tendency to respond "no," even if there were no actual difference between them in perceived power. The problem of acquiescence (the tendency to "yeasay") is especially problematical when responses of persons from different social classes are compared since acquiescence is believed to be stronger for persons from the lower class than for persons from higher strata. To guard against this problem we have worded questions so that a "no" answer is a powerlessness response for four of six questions. Consequently, a high score among farm workers cannot be attributed to the tendency to acquiesce. Two questions (the third and fifth) are "reverse scored," that is, a "yes" response is scored as one. This compensates to some degree for those individuals who tend automatically to respond negatively to questions.[25]

Although the questions are broader in scope than Marx's conception in that they are not limited to work outcomes, and even here they deal only with economic outcomes,[26] they do permit a test of the hypothesis that differences in power associated with different positions in the system of production lead to differences in subjective response.[27]

Findings

Although the average powerlessness score for farm workers is higher than that for farmers, 2.59 (N = 539) vs. 2.45 (N = 240), respectively, the difference is quite small and not statistically significant. It is possible, however, that age, income, and perceived deprivation are related to powerlessness and hence obscure the magnitude of the true differences.

Results (based on Chi-square analysis) show that all three of these variables are significantly related to powerlessness within both groups.[28] Controlling these factors, however, does not modify our conclusion that farm workers do not have higher powerlessness scores than farmers.

One difficulty arises because of the small overlap in the income distributions for the two groups; consequently, we will ignore very low worker incomes and very high farmer incomes and limit our comparisons to respondents in two ranges: less than $6,001 and $6,001-$10,000 (the $6,001-$10,000 category includes 31 workers who reported incomes in excess of $8,000, which is quite extraordinary, but they are included in this category for coding purposes because "above $8,000" is the highest coding category for farm workers). Average powerlessness scores, by income, age, and relative deprivation are given in Table 4-1. Inspection shows that farmers have *higher* powerlessness scores than workers in seven out of eight comparisons, contrary to our supposition of an inverse relationship between powerlessness and degree of power associated with position in the system of production. Note that for all within-class comparisons the powerlessness score is higher for those whose relative deprivation is high; in seven out of eight comparisons the score is higher for the lower

Table 4-1

Average Powerlessness Scores for Farmers and Farm Workers, by Income, Perceived Deprivation, and Age

	Under $6,001	$6,001-$10,000[a]
Under Age 45		
Farmers, high deprivation[b]	4.33 (3)[c]	3.28 (7)
Workers, high deprivation	2.61 (105)	2.11 (9)
Farmers, low deprivation[b]	2.62 (8)	1.78 (18)
Workers, low deprivation	2.05 (86)	1.46 (28)
Age 45 and Over		
Farmers, high deprivation	3.55 (9)	2.65 (17)
Workers, high deprivation	3.31 (134)	2.83 (6)
Farmers, low deprivation	2.70 (17)	2.35 (20)
Workers, low deprivation	2.08 (71)	2.11 (18)

[a]For farm workers, all persons with incomes above $6,000.

[b]High deprivation is 15 and above on the perceived deprivation scale; low deprivation is below 15 (community frame of reference).

[c]Figures in parentheses are N.

income group, and in six out of eight comparisons it is higher for persons over 45.[29]

Since powerlessness is related to two dimensions of socioeconomic status (income and perceived deprivation) but not to the one dimension (position in system of production) with which objective differences in power are so clearly associated, our results raise the question of whether the relationship between socioeconomic status and powerlessness observed in other studies is due to differences in actual position power.[30] In any case, our findings indicate that power based on class position is not necessarily related to perceived power although this does not mean that objective position power has no effects on perceived power, for such effects may be counteracted by other processes. Several factors may be involved.

Occupational Constraints and Bureaucracy

One major factor may be the occupational constraints which surround both farmers and farm workers. Let us note that although the powerlessness questionnaire items focus on perceived ability to influence outcomes, they do not refer to one's ability to influence a change in occupational position. They thus refer to control over microscopic outcomes rather than macroscopic or global outcomes; they are limited to the outcomes within the context of one role (occupation). Given the alternatives of both farmers and farm workers to influence outcomes within these contexts—that is, outcomes that are *associated with the different positions*, particularly economic outcomes—there may indeed be little difference between them. Although desired economic outcomes differ for the two classes (see Chapter 7), occupational constraints on the achievement of these outcomes may be just as great for farmers as for farm workers. Perhaps the farm worker can often (but certainly not always) influence desired economic outcomes by his own actions; for example, he may influence his employment status by relocating when jobs are no longer available in his current location. The farmer may find it difficult to raise his already higher standard of living, especially when it is contingent on weather conditions and a market over which he has no individual control. Still it is probable that given the farm workers' low income, limited education, and almost nonexistent occupational skills, constraints generated by the nature of their occupation per se are greater than those generated for farmers.

However, externally generated constraints of another kind are probably greater for farmers. According to Max Weber, the growth of bureaucracy—the central characteristic of western society—causes the individual to feel he is without power. Weber saw the modern role of man—of whatever class—as "being almost totally governed, managed, dealt with custodially, in ever-widening areas of life and, more crucially, in ever smaller and more personal details."[31] Therefore, "the great question [of the times] is, . . . what can we oppose to this machinery in order to keep a portion of mankind free from this parceling-out of the soul, from this supreme mastery of the bureaucratic way of life?"[32] Thus, it is bureaucracy and not wages or private property, consequences of social class, that deprives modern men of freedom and control over their fate. Bureaucracy is to Weber what social class is to Marx.

Since individuals of all social classes are insignificant in the face of this trend, the psychological impact of bureaucracy is just as great for the bourgeoisie as for the proletariat. Indeed, the process affects politicians, scientists, professors, civil servants, and soldiers as well as industrial factory workers.[33] The most influential factor, therefore, is not class or position in the system of production, but how directly and to what extent the individual is subject to bureaucratic constraints (e.g., regulations, qualifications, "red tape," etc.). There are more government regulations which directly constrain the farmer in his day-to-day operations than constrain the farm worker. It is revealing, therefore, that in response to the open-ended question regarding their fears and worries for the future,[34] 17% (33 respondents) of the farmers mentioned government control, interference, or oppression; in addition, 10% cited the fear of losing personal freedoms or a lack of control over some aspect of their lives (usually farming operations). Not one farm worker voiced such fears.[35]

We have noted that farmers are more integrated into society and possess considerably more power than workers. Perhaps this is due to the fact that one's ability to perceive the constraints of society, especially a bureaucratic society, increases as one's involvement in society increases. (Note, too, that by supporting their organizations and organized pressure groups, farmers contribute more to the bureaucratic character of society than workers.)

Reference-Group Processes

We have observed a relationship for both farmers and farm workers between perceived relative deprivation and powerlessness. Perception of one's relative standing in the community in life chances may also reflect one's perceived standing in his ability to influence outcomes that are deemed important. We have seen that farm workers are only loosely integrated into the communities in which they live and work, and that their reference points for assessing their situations may be different from those of farmers. Consequently, their *comparative* reference groups may be of lower status than those of farmers, which may give them a sense of relatively greater power than they objectively have.

More important perhaps are norm-sending processes of *normative* reference groups,[36] which are the source of much of the farmer's power. Since that power is collective, forces which control his fate, especially the policies of the federal bureaucracy, are influenced largely through his organizations. But collective power does not necessarily give one a sense that *he* has power. Indeed, much of the propaganda generated—the norms that are set—by farm organizations, as well as the mass media generally, contends that farmers are constrained far too much by policies of the federal government. Thus, even when his organizations are strong, the farmer may feel helpless because these same organizations which represent him propagandize about his helplessness. Let us note that farmers may accept as true much of the publicity which focuses on them, especially that promulgated by farm and political organizations, and their subsequent responses to these issues probably reinforces the conceptions that are generated. By contrast, farm workers have no strong economic-political organizations or political representatives. Consequently, the worker may not feel dependent on some external force which exerts a positive influence on his fate, and certainly he has no strong organizations to propagandize about how helpless he is. Moreover, because of their low literacy level most farm workers are probably unaware of the sympathetic publicity the media publish about them; consequently, their weak objective power position may not become psychologically salient. As a result, farm workers may think that their life chances are primarily dependent on their own efforts, rather than those of organized groups. The norm-sending process may thus be an important intervening variable to consider in the hypothesis that organizations serve as a bulwark against powerlessness.[37]

Conclusion

It is possible that all of the above factors (and others) are involved in the absence of any significant difference between farmers and farm workers in perception of power. But whatever the explanation, it is clear that differences in power associated with social and economic *position* do not automatically produce differences in perceived powerlessness. Even the view that the world is hostile or indifferent to one's interests may not distinguish the poor from the nonpoor. In response to the question, "Do you think most people in the United States care what happens to farmers (farm workers)?" 39% of *each* class gave an affirmative reply. Hence, perception of society as hostile to or at least indifferent to one's interest is equal in the two classes. Farmers feel that they have no more power than farm workers to do anything about those forces to enhance their economic well-being. There is no evidence, therefore, that agrees with the assertion of at least one sociologist that, "The world of the lower class [in comparison to that of the middle class] appears hostile and threatening, and [members of the lower class] feel weak and powerless in the face of stronger forces."[38] There appears to be no correspondence between the structure of one's power, at least as determined by position in the system of production, and one's perception of his power—at least in the economic context.

It is essential to keep the distinction between *collective* power and *individually perceived* power in mind. It is clear that the collective power of farmers is far greater than that of farm workers. Our results suggest, therefore, that the efforts of those who are attempting to organize the poor may not succeed in promoting a feeling among lower-class individuals that they can control their personal economic fate. This is not to say that such efforts should be terminated, or that they may not have other important consequences. Organization of the poor may modify the redistribution of power, and the economic well-being of persons now poor may be enhanced accordingly. But whether this will lead to an improvement in the poor individual's belief that he can control his personal economic outcomes is another matter. Indeed, our data indicate that the poor person's image in this respect may be no worse than that of the nonpoor. Of course, our findings for farmers and farm workers may not be applicable to other groups. It is sometimes assumed that recent greater organization among American blacks has led to major changes in black self-esteem,[39] although evidence on this point is far from conclusive. But even if the assertion is true, our results indicate that such organizing efforts may not modify feelings of powerlessness in all poverty groups.

In any case, there appears to be no relationship between our two rural classes and powerlessness. To this extent our data do not support the hypothesis that different positions in the system of production lead to differences in alienation (powerlessness).[40]

Relative Deprivation, False Consciousness and Powerlessness

Although our results do not seem to support a central Marxian hypothesis, they are not altogether inconsistent with the Marxian framework. At least in one context, Marx proposed that class differences in alienation might disappear, presumably because class differences in the conditions of work might disappear.[41] We have suggested that farmers and farm workers are similar with respect to certain conditions: both are subjected to important occupational restraints, although the primary sources of those constraints differ.[42] This similarity between classes in conditions of work appears to have been an incidental thought to Marx, however, and certainly it does not constitute a major thrust in his statements on alienation.

But our results may be consistent with Marx in another respect. Relative deprivation is an important factor for Marx, and is postulated as being greater in the proletariat than in the bourgeoisie. Although to this writer's knowledge Marx never addressed the point, he implies that relative deprivation and alienation are associated. Both are elements of the general state of the working class. To the extent that the individual is falsely aware of his position, he is less apt to be alienated than if he is conscious of his position. We may note from Table 4-1 that in all four comparisons among farm workers, with income and age controlled, the farm workers who are high on perceived deprivation have higher powerlessness scores than those who are low. A summary measure of the relationship can be obtained by computing a Gamma coefficient between perceived deprivation and powerlessness. Gamma is an appropriate statistic for measuring the degree to which two variables are correlated when the variables are in ordinal form, that is, when persons in different categories have higher or lower values with respect to each of the variables in question. In this instance, farm workers are divided into low and high categories on perceived deprivation, depending on whether they score 15 or above on the perceived deprivation scale. Also, respondents are categorized low, medium, or high on powerlessness, with these categories corresponding to scores of 0-1, 2-3, and 4-6. The Gamma is .47.[43] Thus, as perceived class deprivation increases among farm workers, or as false consciousness decreases, alienation increases. To this extent results are consistent with an implication from Marx's theory of the working class. The presence of false consciousness among farm workers apparently inhibits feelings of powerlessness.

Let us note that results are virtually the same for farmers. In Table 4-1, with income and age controlled, powerlessness is higher for farmers whose perceived deprivation is high, rather than low, in all four instances. The Gamma between the two variables is .59.[44] Among farmers, false consciousness is indicated by a *high* rather than a low deprivation score; class perception is consistent with actual class position only when farmers view their deprivation of life chances in relation to others as low. Therefore, if false consciousness and powerlessness are generally related, the relationship between our measure of relative deprivation and powerlessness should be negative for farmers. And, since the relationship is the same for farmers as for farm workers, false consciousness among farmers enhances—rather than inhibits—feelings of powerlessness. Even among farmers who earn more than $10,000, the high deprived group has a higher powerlessness score than the low deprived group; the respective means are 2.70 (N = 27) and 2.11 (N = 84).[45] Apparently, therefore, perceived relative deprivation per se rather than class position or the accuracy of class perception is the most significant factor in powerlessness.

Conclusion

Although farmers are more integrated into society and do possess considerably more power than workers, they do not view themselves as having greater power than the farm workers. Perhaps they feel the constraints of our bureaucratic society as their involvement in that society increases. Or it may be that integration is associated with reference-group processes which influence one's perception of societal constraints. But whatever the explanation, it is clear that differences in power associated with position in the system of production and the individual's perception of having power are not necessarily related. It is also clear that poverty does not necessarily cause one to have a greater sense of being without power, at least as we have measured it.

More important in producing feelings of powerlessness is the perception of how one compares with others in life chances, that is, one's perception of his position in the class structure. The relationship, however, is not contingent upon the *accuracy* or *falseness* of class perceptions, since it is true for farmers as well as farm workers.

Notes

1. For a discussion of these three factors, see Joachim Israel, *Alienation from Marx to Modern Sociology: A Macrosociological Analysis* (Boston: Allyn & Bacon, Inc., 1971).

2. Karl Marx, *Economic and Philosophic Manuscripts of 1844*, edited and with an Introduction by Dirk J. Struik, Margin Mulligan, trans. (New York: International Publishers, 1964), p. 117.

3. Karl Marx, *Capital* (New York: The Modern Library, 1936), p. 396.

4. This interpretation of Marx's conception of alienation is influenced by Melvin Seeman's analysis in "On the Meaning of Alienation," *American Sociological Review*, XXIV (December 1959), 783-91.

5. Warren C. Haggstrom, "The Power of the Poor," in Frank Reissman, Jerome Cohen, and Arthur Pearl, eds., *Mental Health of the Poor* (New York: The Free Press, 1964), pp. 214-15.

6. Ibid.

7. Dwight G. Dean, "Alienation: Its Meaning and Measurement," *American Sociological Review*, XXVI (October 1961), 753-58; William Erbe, "Social Involvement and Political Activity: A Replication and Elaboration," *American Sociological Review*, XXIX (April 1964), 198-215; and Arthur G. Neal and Melvin Seeman, "Organization and Powerlessness: A Test of the Mediation Hypothesis," *American Sociological Review*, XXIX (April 1964), 216-26. See also Russell Middleton, "Alienation, Race, and Education," *American Sociological Review*, XXVIII (December 1963), 973-77.

8. Ibid. (Dean), p. 757.

9. Neal and Seeman, op. cit., p. 221.

10. Dean, op. cit., p. 757.

11. Neal and Seeman, op. cit.

12. Even so, our two groups are to Marx's conception of social class the relevance of might be questioned. In particular, farm workers consist largely of persons who Marx considered to be the lumpenroletariat—people "living on the crumbs of society, people without a definite trade, vagabonds, people without tie or home." Karl Marx, "The Class Struggles in France, 1848-1850," in Lewis S. Feuer, ed., *Marx and Engels: Basic Writings on Politics and Philosophy* (Garden City, N.Y.: Doubleday & Company, Inc., 1959), p. 298. This class is "sharply differentiated from the industrial proletariat" (ibid.), which is the focus of Marx's analysis. However, the definition of proletariat—"the class of modern wage laborers who, having no means of production of their own, are reduced to selling their labor in order to live"—certainly applies to farm workers. Karl Marx and Frederich Engels, "Manifesto of the Communist Party," in Feuer, ibid., p. 7, n. 1. A difficulty here is that several criteria of social class are present in Marx's writings. See Bertell Ollman, "Marx's Use of 'Class,'" *American Journal of Sociology*, LXXIII (March 1968), 573-80. We do not claim that either of our groups comprises a class with regard to all criteria. However, since each consists of persons who are homogeneous with respect to function in a system of production in which one sells his labor and the other buys it, they conform more closely to important criteria of Marx than do "class" groups that have been used in other studies.

13. On the power of farm organizations, see R. Joseph Monson, Jr. and Mark W. Cannon, *The Makers of Public Policy: American Power Groups and Their Ideologies* (New York: McGraw-Hill Book Company, 1965), pp. 96, 132.

14. Ibid.

15. The California grapepickers' effort to mobilize a *public* boycott on grapes is a testimony of their weak power; they must turn to a third party to uitlize its power in their behalf because they have so little power themselves.

16. Dale Wright, *They Harvest Despair: The Migrant Farm Workers* (Boston: Beacon Press, 1965), p. 124.

17. Karl Marx, *Der Historische Materialismus, Die Fruhschriften* (Leipsig: S. Landshut and D.P. Mayer, 1932), II, 25 (quoted in Eric Fromm, *The Sane Society* [New York: Holt, Rinehart and Winston, 1955], p. 232). It is clear, then, that the alienation of labor was not viewed by Marx as stemming solely or even primarily from the workers' low income, in comparison to that of the capitalists. Indeed, even if income were equal, alienation could continue to exist among the capitalists no less than the workers: "[E]ven the *equality of wages* ... only transforms the relationship of the present-day worker to his labour into the relationship of *all* men to labour. Society is then conceived as an abstract capitalist." Karl Marx, *Economic and Philosophic Manuscripts of 1844*, op. cit., p. 118; second emphasis supplied. That is to say, it is the *conditions of work* rather than the money return on one's work that is the essential causal factor in alienation, although to be sure, differences in economic return and alienative conditions of work are also correlated.

18. Wright, op. cit., p. 110. Compare Marx's comments on "Alienated Labor," in *Economic and Philosophic Manuscripts of 1844*, ibid.

19. Thomas Gladwin, *Poverty, U.S.A.* (Boston: Little, Brown & Co., 1967), pp. 153, 103, 162.

20. The President's National Advisory Commission on Rural Poverty, *The People Left Behind* (Washington, D.C.: U.S. Government Printing Office, 1967), p. 8.

21. For 67% of anglo-American farm workers farm work is the only job and for another 17% it is the main job. Only 22% reported having received job training of any kind; as noted above (p. 30, n. 62), however, the interpretation workers gave to "job training" was quite liberal, so the 22% is probably an overestimate of the proportion who actually have marketable occupational skills.

22. Seeman, op. cit., p. 784.

23. Hans H. Gerth and C. Wright Mills, *From Max Weber: Essays in Sociology* (New York: Oxford University Press, 1946), esp. pp. 50, 224-35; and Robert N. Nisbet, *The Sociological Tradition* (New York: Basic Books, Inc., 1966), pp. 292-300. One may *agree* that the Weberian thesis is not really inconsistent with that of Marx, provided that bureaucracy is considered as the condition of work. As noted above (see note 17), the condition of work is the essential alienating condition for Marx. Nevertheless, in terms of *class* differences in the conditions of work, Marx and Weber differ in emphasis since Marx did not portray middle-class capitalists as being constrained by the conditions of work to the same extent that wage laborers were.

24. "No opinion" responses were classified as "no" responses except for the third and fifth questions, in which case they were considered to be "yes" answers. However, respondents were not aware that a "no opinion" category was available. If there was no response after a brief pause, the interviewer repeated

the question. Then after a short wait, if there was no answer, the interviewer circled "no opinion" and replied, "Okay, let's go to the next question." No responses averaged less than 4% for the six questions.

25. For a discussion of "response set," see Eugene J. Webb, Donald T. Campbell, Richard D. Schwartz, and Lee Sechrist, *Unobtrusive Measures: Nonreactive Research in the Social Sciences* (Chicago: Rand McNally and Company, 1966), pp. 19-21. We will discuss the problem of "response set" in some detail in reference to the results of the present study in the next chapter.

The coefficient of reproducibility (Rep), using the Goodenough technique (see Allan L. Edwards, *Techniques of Attitude Scale Construction* [New York: Appleton-Century-Crofts, Inc., 1957], pp. 184-88) is rather low (.81), but the Gammas between item score and total score are moderate to high in magnitude (.52, .63, .77, .82, and .85). Furthermore, item analysis indicates that all items discriminate well between high and low scorers; discriminatory power (DP) ranges between 0.98 and 1.73.

26. Alienation from work takes a variety of forms in Marx, including alienation from self, society, and human nature. See Karl Marx, *Economic and Philosophic Manuscripts of 1844*, op. cit., pp. 106-19. For an excellent review of Marx's conception of alienation, see Richard Schacht, *Alienation* (New York: Doubleday and Company, Inc., 1970), pp. 65-114.

27. Some might agree that this hypothesis is not directly relevant to Marx since a concern with the perceptual and attitudinal aspects of alienation was emphasized only in certain of Marx's earlier writings (e.g., *Economic and Philosophic Manuscripts of 1844*, op. cit.). In later writings, he focused on the structural aspects of alienation—specifically, the structure of the relationship between capitalists and workers. (See Daniel Bell, "Two Roads from Marx: The Themes of Alienation and Exploitation and Workers' Control in Socialist Thought," in *The End of Ideology*, rev. ed. [New York: The Free Press, 1962]). Israel, however, sees no discrepancy between the two approaches and argues that the structural focus is a continuation of Marx's earlier concern with subjective aspects (op. cit.). Schacht, however, would probably contend that we have not captured the essence of Marx's meaning in our measure (op. cit.). We agree that the inability to influence economic outcomes is not necessarily the crucial feature of alienation in Marx. Rather, alienation from human existence (in which work is an end in itself) is the most important factor. Still, the inability to influence economic outcomes is not irrelevant to Marx and is probably more accessible to reliable and valid measurement than are other aspects. In any case, the hypothesis as stated is not an implausible hypothesis regardless of whether it is found in the early or later works of Marx, or whether, in fact, Marx postulated it at all.

28. In this analysis, respondents are divided into "high" and "low" on the powerlessness scale, with a score of 3 and above considered to be high. For each group, there are two perceived deprivation categories (less than 15, and 15 and

above), two age categories (under 45 and 45 and above) and four income categories (0-$6,000, $6,001-$10,000, $10,001-$16,000, and over $16,000 for farmers; and 0-$2,000, $2,001-$4,000, $4,001-$6,000, and over $6,000 for farm workers).

29. In addition, control for dependence on farm work/farming has no influence on the results. As revealed by the answers to questions on job training and farm work as the only job, those respondents for whom farm work is the only job are significantly more powerless than those for whom it is not (2.79 [N = 361] vs. 1.98 [N = 176] [p < .01]), and the same results obtained between farm workers who have had no job training in comparison with those who have had some training (2.69 [N = 384] vs. 2.29 [N = 153] [p < .01]). The same trends were also obtained when comparable questions were asked of farmers, although neither relationship reaches statistical significance; for job training, scores are 2.52 (N = 180) and 2.02 (N = 50) and for the question on whether farming is the only job, scores are 2.57 (N = 167) and 2.17 (N = 71). Hence, the more dependent farmers/farm workers are on farming/farm work, the less is their perceived ability to influence their futures. At the same time, comparison of scores for farmers and farm workers shows that control for dependence on farm work/farming has no influence on the nature of the difference (or lack thereof) between farmers and farm workers.

30. Dean, op. cit., Erbe, op. cit., and Neal and Seeman, op. cit. We may note, however, that most other studies have focused on political outcomes whereas in our measure we have focused on economic outcomes. Organizations may have different effects on member perceptions of their individual power in the two areas.

31. Nisbet, op. cit., p. 295.

32. J.P. Mayer, *Max Weber and German Politics* (London: Faber and Faber Ltd., 1944), p. 12.

33. Gerth and Mills, op. cit., pp. 77-156, 240, 243, and 255-61.

34. See Chapter 7.

35. Farmers are probably ambivalent about federal controls. Insofar as government policy reduces the risks of farming (e.g., by guaranteeing a minimum price for wheat), most farmers probably want controls. Perhaps this "bureaucratic dilemma" is reflected in the comments of one farmer who, in discussing his wishes and hopes for the future, said he wanted a "secure, orderly future," but also expressed fear of a centralized government "and the leveling of all responsibilities and rewards." Ambivalence to bureacracy was noted by Weber. Although the evolution of bureaucracy deprive men of freedom, the "passion for bureaucracy" continues as though "we were deliberately to become men who need 'order' and nothing but order, who become nervous and cowardly if for one moment this order wavers, and helpless if they are torn away from their total incorporation in it . . . [I]t is in such an evolution that we are . . . caught up." Mayer, loc., p. 127.

36. The distinction between normative and comparative reference groups is influenced by Harold H. Kelley's, "Two Functions of Reference Groups," in Guy E. Swanson, Theodore M. Newcomb, and Eugene L. Hartley, eds., *Readings in Social Psychology*, rev. ed. (New York: Henry Holt and Company, 1952), pp. 410-14. See also Leon Festinger, "A Theory of Social Comparison Processes," *Human Relations*, VII (Spring 1954), 117-40; Ragnor Rommetveit, *Social Norms and Roles* (Minneapolis: University of Minnesota Press, 1954); and William A. Rushing, *The Psychiatric Professions: Power Conflict and Adaptation in a Psychiatric Hospital Staff* (Chapel Hill: The University of North Carolina Press, 1964), pp. 20-21, 144-45, 252-53.

37. Neal and Seeman, op. cit.

38. James B. McKee, *Introduction to Sociology* (New York: Holt, Rinehart, and Winston, Inc., 19xx), p. 341.

39. For example, see ibid., p. 346.

40. There is the possibility, of course, that the results reveal only how alienated farm workers really are. Because they are not aware of how powerless their situations make them, they are that much more alienated. Moreover, because they are accustomed to having little power they may not really know just how little power they do have. For a discussion of alienation from this perspective, see Israel, op. cit., pp. 80-86.

41. See note 17.

42. There are other parallels. For Marx, a major component in alienation was wage labor ("the wage is but a necessary consequence of labour's estrangement," *Economic and Philosophic Manuscripts of 1844*, op. cit., p. 75). Inasmuch as farmers receive guaranteed payments from the government, in a sense they receive wages for their labor. (There is a difference, of course, since Marx identified wage labor with private property [ibid.], and it is the farmer, not the government, who owns the land.) In still another sense, the relationship between labor and the product of labor, Marx's analysis of alienation is appropriate to the farmer's work conditions. Rather than being an end in itself, for many farmers labor is probably a "servant of the wage" (ibid.). If farming were an end in itself, why would farmers sell the products of their labor to the government, which does not always use them to feed hungry people, and why would they accept payment for products they do not even produce? Perhaps we are stretching Marx's formulation a little too far. Modern property relationships and wage relationships are more complicated than when Marx was writing, and it is not clear how his conception of private property and wage labor applies to certain contemporary situations, especially as they relate to alienation (powerlessness). Moreover, that aspect of alienation which Marx appears to have in mind in the current context appears to be closer to self-estrangement and estrangement from one's labor and the product of one's labor than to the powerlessness dimension. As noted, Marx meant several different things by alienation.

43. This is statistically significant at the .001 level, based on Chi-square, $2df$ (two-tail test).

44. This is statistically significant at the .001 level, based on Chi-square $2df$ (two-tail test).

45. The difference is statistically significant at the .05 level based on Chi-square test, $1df$, with powerlessness scores divided into two categories (0.2 and 3-6) (two-tail test).

Relative Deprivation, Normlessness, and Anomia: The Class Context

As we have noted, interpretations of the many differences between social classes frequently revolve around whether class differences are due to differences in the structure of one's class position or to the perception of one's position in the class structure.[1] The distinction is between structural and social-psychological approaches to social stratification. We have seen, of course, that perceived class position or deprivation appears to be a more important factor in determining powerlessness than class position itself. Different results may obtain for normlessness and anomia, however.

The issue involves still another question: Are there class differences in the relationships of relative deprivation to normlessness and anomia? Study results in Chapter 4 show that the relationship between relative deprivation and powerlessness is not affected by the class context since that relationship exists for both classes. A different situation may exist for normlessness and anomia, however; relationships may hold for farmers but not farm workers, or vice versa.

Social Class, Relative Deprivation, and Normlessness

Probably the most common sociological usage of alienation is normlessness or normative alienation. This usage is the focus of much of Emile Durkheim's work, and it is central in what may be Robert K. Merton's most influential work, "Social Structure and Anomie."[2] For these two theorists, as well as others, normlessness is linked to "anomie." However, because anomie and the related concept of anomia frequently do not refer to normlessness, let us distinguish between them.

As an attribute of society, *normlessness* is defined as the existence of little or no agreement as to what the dominant societal norms should be. Thus, when agreement is low we may speak of a *normless* culture or society. Viewed from the individual's perspective, however, normlessness refers to an orientation which accords primary legitimacy to one's own self-interests when those interests conflict with the interests of others. Thus, individual normlessness refers to an orientation away from the control of law, rule, and norms, and the tendency to use illegitimate means to further one's own interests and aspirations, that is, to the condition "in which calculations of personal advantage and fear of punishment are the [primary] regulating agencies."[3]

Several purported measures of normlessness have been developed. The best known is Srole's scale of anomia[4]; as we will note below, however, this scale does not appear to measure normlessness as such. Also, the Dean and McClosky-Shaar "normlessness' scales[5] appear to refer to unpredictability and meaningless-ness rather than to normlessness itself (e.g., "I often wonder what the meaning of life really is," "with everything so uncertain these days, it almost seems as though anything can happen," "with everything in such a state of disorder, it's hard for a person to know where he stands from one day to the next"); even when items refer more directly to normative matters they seem not to refer to a weak commitment to control by rules and laws so much as to problems encountered in trying to discover which rules and laws one should be committed to (e.g., "everything changes so quickly these days that I often have trouble deciding which are the right rules to follow").[6] In any case, pretests revealed that most items in the Dean and McClosky-Shaar scales are too abstract to have much meaning for many of the farm workers. More concrete items were needed. At the same time, since different cultural groups were included, we needed items that were not too specific with reference to particular norms of anglo-American (or Mexican-American) culture. Therefore, we attempted to develop questions comparing self-interest and personal advantage with order and the control of rules and laws that were not bound in content to anglo-American culture. We developed the following six yes-no questions:

1. In your opinion, is the honest life the best regardless of the hardships it may cause? (*Reverse scored.*)
2. Do you think a person is justified in doing almost anything if the reward is high enough?
3. In order to get ahead in the world today, some say you are almost forced to do some things that are not right. What do you think?
4. In your opinion, should a man obey the law no matter how much it interferes with his personal ambitions? (*Reverse scored.*)
5. Would you say that the main reason for obeying the law is the punishment that comes if one is caught?
6. Some people say that to be a success in this country it is usually necessary to be dishonest. Do you think this is true?

Total scores ranged from 0 to 6, with 6 representing the strongest normless attitude.[7]

At first glance, the items are clearly different from those used to measure powerlessness. Items for the latter refer to the individual's perceived ability to influence personal outcomes, whereas the normlessness items pertain to what people do or should do in reference to honesty and lawful behavior, particularly when such behavior may preclude personal advantage. That the two measures are largely independent is indicated by the low correlation between them; for farmers the product-moment correlation is .17 (Gamma = .10), whereas for farm workers it is .14 (Gamma = .17). Obviously, the two sets of items do not measure the same thing. It remains to be seen, however, whether they differ in terms of their relationship to social class and perceived relative deprivation.

Distributions of normlessness scores for both farmers and anglo-American farm workers resemble a J-curve, a recognized characteristic of much deviant behavior. The curve is somewhat steeper for farmers, however, indicating that normlessness is greater among workers. Average scores for the two groups are 0.62 and 1.16. Scores are higher for farm workers even when the effects of perceived deprivation are minimized. Farmers and workers are divided into "high" and "low" perceived deprivation categories, as in the previous chapter. Findings are given in the first three columns of Table 5-1.[8] In contrast to powerlessness, class status is associated with normlessness. Since the relationship holds for both levels of perceived deprivation, there is apparently something inherent in the structural differences between farmers and farm workers that contributes to normlessness.

At the same time, normlessness and powerlessness are both positively related to relative deprivation; for both the "high" deprivation category has the highest alienation score. Moreover, in both instances the relationship holds for farmers as well as farm workers. Hence, for neither is the relationship class specific. The significance of relative deprivation to normlessness is not limited to the lower class.

Social Class, Relative Deprivation, and Anomia

In a well-known paper in 1956, Leo Srole presented the concept of anomia, which he defined as "self-to-others alienation" or "interpersonal alienation."[9] He contended that the individual or psychological state of this type of alienation consists of several dimensions: the individual feels "that community leaders are detached from and indifferent to his needs"; he perceives the social order as "fickle" and unpredictable; he thinks his lot is getting worse; he feels a "sense of

Table 5-1
Average Normlessness and Anomia Scores by Class and Perceived Deprivation

	Normlessness Perceived Deprivation			Anomia Perceived Deprivation		
	Low[a]	High[a]	P[b]	Low[a]	High[a]	P[b]
Farmers	0.52	0.69	<.05	1.02	1.60	<.05
	(149)[c]	(66)		(148)	(67)	
Farm Workers	0.92	1.29	<.01	2.65	2.92	.07
(anglo-Americans)	(226)	(282)		(225)	(284)	
P[a]	.01	.01		.01	.01	

[a]Low is below 15 on the perceived deprivation scale (community); high is 15 and above.
[b]Probability based on both Chi-square and Student-t test (see note 8 for explanation) (two-tail test).
[c]Figures in parentheses are N.

meaninglessness of life itself"; and he feels that his personal relationships—"the very rock of social existence"—are no longer dependable. Srole proposed measuring these dimensions with five questionnaire items, which we have modified in light of pretest experience (see below). Unlike the original anomia questions, which are answerable in terms of agree-disagree, our questions are answered as either yes or no. Also, the original items are all scored positively (that is, an agree is scored as 1, a disagree as 0), whereas one of our items is reverse scored (that is, a "no" response is scored as 1)[10] to reduce the influence of response set tendencies, especially acquiescent ones, which might be stronger among farm workers. Furthermore, the five items were interspersed with three buffer items which we felt most respondents would be inclined to answer in the negative. The five anomia and three buffer items are given below with the percentage of "no's" for farmers (F) and farm workers (FW) given in parenthesis. Asterisked items are buffer items.[11]

1. *Do you think that most people really care what happens to the next fellow? (F = 29%; FW = 60%)
2. Some people say that a person does not really know whom he can count on anymore. Do you agree with them? (F = 65%; FW = 30%)
3. Do you think that the life of the average man (most people) is getting worse? (F = 79%; FW = 43%)
4. *Would you say that most people in the U.S. care what happens to farmers (farm workers)? (F = 58%; FW = 65%)
5. Do you think that nowadays a person has to live pretty much for today and let tomorrow take care of itself? (F = 74%; FW = 46%)
6. Do you think that it is fair to bring children into the world with the way things look for the future? *(Reverse scored)* (F = 15%; FW = 41%)
7. *Would you say that your life is an unhappy one now and that there is little hope of it getting any better? (F = 94%; FW = 86%)
8. Some people say that there is no use writing to public officials, such as senators, governors, and other government people, because often they are not really interested in the problems of most people. How do you feel about this; do you think it is true? (F = 79%; FW = 49%)

Our attempt to counter any tendencies toward acquiescence appears to have been moderately successful, particularly for farm workers. As can be seen, all three buffer items elicited a majority of negative responses among farm workers and two of the three did so for farmers; the exception among farmers is the first buffer item, which closely approximates the first anomia item in content but is its obverse in *form* (that is, a "no" to the first buffer item is roughly equivalent to a "yes" to the first anomia item). Note that the percentage of "no" answers is almost exactly opposite for the two questions. This suggests that respondents were responding to the content of the questions and not automatically complying with "yea" or "nay" tendencies.[12] We will have more to say about this below.

Scores for the five-item anomia scale vary between a theoretical maximum of

5 and a minimum of 0. Srole considers this score to be a general measure of one dimension of alienation. Sometimes the measure has been used synonymously with a measure of alienation in general.[13] In any case, the scale has been the basis of much research, and has been found to be correlated with socioeconomic status, race, religion, residence, political participation, racial prejudice, and other individual characteristics.[14]

Nevertheless, some question what the scale actually measures. Some agree with Srole and assume it measures a psychological effect of anomie (or normlessness as a societal state), that is, individuals from societies with little agreement on dominant norms should score high. Inspection of the five items suggests, however, that the common theme is pessimism, despair, hopelessness, fatalism: things are getting worse, the world is not safe for children, the future is unpredictable and bleak, and one can't depend on others. Whereas the powerlessness items pertain to what an individual thinks he can or cannot accomplish (primarily in reference to economic issues) and the normlessness items pertain to what persons do or should do in reference to honesty, rules, and law, anomia items refer to a general condition of social malaise. Also, in contrast to powerlessness, which measures the individual's perceived ability to influence outcomes largely within the context of his occupational role, anomia items concern more global aspects of one's situation.

We suggest that anomia items are related to the individual component of the situation which Durkheim called *fatalism*, involving "excessive regulation [in which] futures [are] pitilessly blocked and passions violently choked by oppressive discipline."[15] Fatalism thus results in a feeling of hopelessness or despair, and Durkheim felt it would be particularly high among groups who are severely constrained by the structure of their environments, such as slaves.[16] This interpretation of the scale as a generalized measure of despair or hopelessness is consistent with the interpretation given by others,[17] although such an interpretation is no less significant than that of alienation itself. Indeed, a generalized sense of hopelessness or despair may be considered to be a significant component of alienation.[18]

That the conditions of farm workers would be conducive to anomia or despair is certainly indicated from the analyses of journalists, which we reviewed in Chapter 2. Anomia may be typical of the poor in general; Thomas Gladwin states that poverty is "a climate of discouragement and despair," and Oscar Lewis characterizes the poor as having a "sense of resignation and fatalism based upon the realities of their difficult life situation."[19] If this is so, and if our interpretation of the anomia scale is valid, an unusually high anomia score would be expected among the poor, especially among farm workers whose situations are particularly constraining. These constraining features are not limited to occupational activity or to the pursuit of economic ends associated with occupation but also include the inability to affect political affairs, to enlist the aid of others, to find time to plan—or even think—of the future, and to free oneself from the day-to-day pursuit and toil of work. In short, anomia is the inability to effect changes in virtually any aspect of one's life situation. Consequently, we would expect farm workers to see little hope for the future, in contrast to farmers who have more freedom to influence aspects of their life situations beyond their occupational role, although they are also subject to occupational and bureaucratic constraints.

Inspection of the individual items in the anomia scale in conjunction with our previous descriptions of farm workers also leads us to expect a high score for this group. As we have seen, public officials and politicians have shown little interest in the problems of farm workers, the workers themselves have few social relationships on which they can depend in time of need,[20] and most were reared in poverty, all of which gives them little basis for expecting the lot of the average man to get better. And as will be shown in Chapter 7, their living conditions cause them to lead a "day-to-day" or "hand-to-mouth" existence rather than show concern for the future. The structure of the farm workers' situation is such that a high anomia score would be anticipated.

Findings are consistent with this expectation. Overall, the average anomia score for farmers is 1.24 (N = 234) in comparison to 2.83 (N = 539) for farm workers. Differences are not due to differences in perceived deprivation, since the disparity exists for the "high" and "low" perceived deprivation categories (see columns four and five of Table 5-1).[21] It thus seems that some aspect of the *structure* of class positions gives rise to different levels of anomia that are independent of how deprived an individual feels. In this respect, findings parallel those for normlessness but not powerlessness.[22]

However, findings for the relationship between perceived deprivation and anomia resemble those of both normlessness and powerlessness to deprivation. Farmers and farm workers in the high perceived deprivation category have a higher anomia score than those in the low perceived deprivation category. And the relationship for farm workers is close to the .05 level, which would indicate statistical significance. Overall, then, each of the three measures of alienation is associated with relative deprivation for both social classes. Our results suggest that some aspect of U.S. culture produces alienative attitudes (as we have measured them) when the individual feels that he is deprived relative to others.

This is not to say that class does not exert an effect independent of relative deprivation, a fact which is especially clear when Gammas are computed between class and low, medium, and high alienation scores and separately for high and low perceived deprivation categories.[23] That the effects of class are virtually independent of perceived deprivation is indicated by the fact that Gammas for class and normlessness are $-.28$ and $-.30$, respectively, for high and low perceived deprivation, and corresponding Gammas for anomia are $-.66$ and $-.68$ (a negative coefficient indicates that farm workers have the higher score). (Gammas for class and powerlessness are $+.04$ and $-.11$.) It is clear, therefore, that for normlessness and anomia the effect of class is independent of perceived deprivation. Although our data do not indicate what precise factor this class effect may stem from, it is clear that it does not originate from feelings of deprivation.

Despite the effect of class position, however, perceived relative deprivation exerts an effect on all three dimensions of alienation within each social class.[24] It is plausible to argue, therefore, that certain dynamics of alienation may be general with respect to social classes and, hence, stem from cultural conditions that are common to all classes in anglo-American society. We will explore this possibility in more detail in the next chapter. First, however, a few comments concerning the possible influence of acquiescence tendencies on our results are in order.

The Acquiescence Problem

A problem with many studies based on questionnaire and structured interview data is that some respondents may answer questions in the affirmative (or negative) regardless of question content. It is probably true, as many sociologists claim, that the tendency to acquiesce (to yeasay) is stronger at lower socioeconomic levels than at higher levels. The tendency may also be strong among certain minority groups. Anyone who has had much contact with southern blacks, especially those in the lower income level (but not limited to this level), are familiar with the phenomenon; these blacks may agree with almost anything a white person says.[25] In a recent investigation, Leslie Carr has unequivocally documented this tendency for low income southern blacks[26] by showing that respondents are apt to agree with the anomia items regardless of form. For example, 47% of the respondents in a sample agreed with all five anomia items and 35% of a comparable sample agreed with all five items when the items were stated in *obverse* form (for instance, "These days a person does not really know whom he can count on," versus the obverse form, "These days a person can know whom he can count on").[27] Overall, Carr estimates that approximately 50% of the responses in his samples were due to acquiescence. No doubt the figure is considerably less for other lower-class groups, although it may still be present to some degree.

If so, the phenomenon has important implications for many findings between socioeconomic status and anomia as well as other findings based on agree-disagree or yes-no questions, such as the questions we have used to measure normlessness and powerlessness. We have already briefly discussed the problem in connection with our efforts to counter possible acquiescence tendencies among farm workers, especially in response to the anomia items. We will now discuss it in more detail in connection with all three measures of alienation. We believe our results are not due to acquiescent tendencies for the following reasons:

First, interviewers observed a noticeable tendency among some farm workers, especially migrants, to be "disagreeable" or hostile in the interview situation.[28] Interviewers detected no tendency for farm workers to agree by giving routine "yes" answers or to give "dishonest" answers; they felt that in general most workers were frank and open. Neither did they detect any evidence of unusual deferential behavior.

In addition, as noted previously, we tried to guard against a stereotyped tendency to yeasay (or naysay) by changing the form of items (that is, by reverse scoring or stating items in the obverse form). In the case of the anomia scale, we also interspersed buffer items designed to elicit a predominantly negative answer. Of course, these measures do not prevent the stereotype response to yeasay (or naysay) if the tendency is strong enough; quite simply, to counter such a tendency respondents must be encouraged to examine each question carefully. Still, reverse scoring and the inclusion of buffer items do prevent or reduce the probability of artificially high scores due to acquiescence. But more compelling reasons indicate that our results are not due to this tendency.

First, note that only two "yes" responses to the six powerlessness items are scored as 1 (the other four are scored 0), in comparison to four of six and four of five for the normlessness and anomia items, respectively. Consequently, if acquiescent tendencies were especially strong among farm workers, a much lower score would be expected for powerlessness. To facilitate the comparisons, averages for the three measures for farmers and farm workers are presented together in Table 5-2. As can be seen, the score for powerlessness is higher than for both normlessness and anomia among farmers, and among farm workers it is higher than the score for normlessness and only slightly lower than the score for anomia. We feel also that the higher anomia scores relative to normlessness scores could not be due to acquiescent tendencies, since four anomia items and four normlessness items are positively scored.

There are other considerations. Given the scoring system used, and making the assumption that the acquiescent tendency is stronger among farm workers, a significantly *lower* powerlessness score would be expected for farm workers than for farmers. This, however, is not the case. Furthermore, a comparison of farmers and farm workers on responses to individual reverse scored items and

Table 5-2

Average Powerlessness, Normlessness, and Anomia Score for Farmers and Farm Workers

	Farmers	Farm Workers
Powerlessness	2.45	2.59
Normlessness	0.62	1.16
Anomia	1.24	2.83

nonreverse scored items in the normlessness scale reveals no significant difference; farm workers have a higher proportion of normlessness responses regardless of the form in which the questions are asked. And with regard to powerlessness items, for which the total scores show no significant difference between farmers and farm workers, farmers have a *higher* proportion of affirmative responses in five out of six instances (although only two of the items—one of which is reverse scored—show any substantial difference between the two groups). Moreover, we have noted that when buffer items were included in the anomia questions, farm workers did respond negatively to questions, sometimes in very high proportions, even when the buffer questions were followed by questions for which the response was overwhelmingly affirmative (see p. 80 above). Such results support our claim that responses are based on question content and are not merely or even primarily stereotyped acquiescent responses.

Even if we discount these observations, acquiescent tendencies cannot account for our results. Acquiescence does not explain why the powerlessness, normlessness, and anomia scales are associated with relative deprivation. Nor does it explain why powerlessness differs from normlessness and anomia in its relationship to social class. This is not to say, of course, that the problem of acquiescence does not exist or that there are no errors in the data because of it (and because of other factors, for that matter). It seems unlikely, however, that error stemming from this source could have produced the results we have obtained.

Conclusion

The findings of the last two chapters should make us cautious about generalizing about differences between social classes and alienation. First, these findings indicate that only two of three measures of alienation—normlessness and anomia—are significantly related to the distinction between farmers and farm workers. Still, these differences are substantial and reveal that the class structure is a significant factor in generating differences in alienative attitudes, as much theory and research have suggested. At the same time, however, the findings also reveal that class differences are not due to frustration associated with class deprivation, since class differences remain unchanged when the effects of perceived deprivation are reduced. Just what the influencing factor is our results do not say, but they do rule out status deprivation.

Second, however, the relationship between perceived deprivation and alienation exists within both classes, which, therefore, manifest a common pattern. Only in the case of anomia, for farm workers, does the relationship fail to reach statistical significance, and even here it is approached ($P = .07$).[29] Class similarities are much more apparent than class differences.

Although each of our measures of alienation is interpreted in terms of individual attitudes, each nevertheless reflects something about the individual's relationship to society: his ability to influence personal outcomes in society, to accept normative societal controls, and to be hopeful about his situation in society. A high score on each scale indicates estrangement from society and from one's position in that society. The less one gets from society and the less one perceives himself as getting, the more estranged from society one tends to be.

There is the further question, however, of whether this holds for persons of all cultural backgrounds. Differences in estrangement from society may not be associated with differences in the distribution of life chances and the perception of that distribution. Estrangement may, rather, result from various interpretations of differences in life chances and perception of those differences which may in turn depend on the cultural context. Although class is not the significant factor in the relationship between perceived deprivation and alienation, culture may be.

Notes

1. For an early approach, see Richard Centers, *The Psychology of Social Classes* (Princeton: Princeton University Press, 1949). For a recent study, see Roberta G. Simmons and Morris Rosenberg, "Functions of Children's Perceptions of the Stratification System," *American Sociological Review*, XXXVI (April 1971), 235-349.

2. Robert K. Merton, "Social Structure and Anomie," *American Sociological Review*, III (October 1938), 672-82. This paper has been reprinted a number of times. It is included in somewhat different form in Merton's *Social Theory and Social Structure*, rev. and enlr. ed. (New York: The Free Press, 1957), pp. 131-60. See also his chapter, "Continuities in the Theory of Social Structure and Anomie," in ibid., pp. 161-94.

3. Ibid. *Social Theory . . .* , p. 157. In this quote we have substituted the word "primary" for "only."

4. Leo Srole, "Social Integration and Certain Corollaries: An Exploratory Study," *American Sociological Review*, XXI (December 1956), 709-16.

5. Dwight G. Dean, "Alienation: Its Meaning and Measurement," *American Sociological Review*, XXVI (October 1961), 753-58.

6. For a scale of "illegitimate expediency," which is somewhat closer in manifest content to that desired here, see Wan Sang Han, "Discrepancy in Socioeconomic Level of Aspiration and Perception of Illegitimate Expediency," *American Journal of Sociology*, LXXIV (November 1968), 240-47.

7. As indicated, two items are reverse scored (a "no" response is scored as one). Scalogram analysis using the Goodenough technique produced a Rep of .88. Item analysis reveals that items discriminate well between high and low scoring respondents; with one item excluded, discriminatory power for the two samples ranges between 0.50 and 1.67 (the one exception was 0.38). In addition,

the score for each item is rather highly correlated with the total score in both samples; all Gammas are above 0.66.

8. Tests of significance reported in Table 5-1 are based on Chi-square as well as student-t (difference between means) tests. Whenever there is a difference in significance level, the more conservative result is reported. To help the reader visualize the differences more easily, however, results are reported for averages rather than proportions or frequencies.

9. See Srole, op. cit.

10. "No opinion" responses were classified as "yes" except for the reverse-scored items, which were treated as "no" responses. For all items the proportion of "no opinion" responses is small. For farmers the percentage for one item is 5% with the other four having 2% or less, and for farm workers three items have 4% or less with the other two having 8% and 10%.

11. Although the Rep for the five anomia items (based on the Goodenough technique) was low (.75), DP's were high (1.30, 1.51, 1.26, 1.13, and 1.25) as were Gammas between item score and total score (.66, .75, .57, .66, and .65).

12. It is possible, of course, that if these two questions were separated by several other questions different results would have been obtained. Respondents may be less apt to give contradictory responses when the question and its obverse form are not separated by other questions. In fact, one method of controlling for response set tendencies is to separate a question and its obverse form in the interview or questionnaire, and then disregard results for respondents who give contradictory answers (see Gerhard E. Lenski and John C. Leggett, "Caste, Class, and Deference in the Research Interview," *American Journal of Sociology*, LXV [March 1960], 463-67). Our approach to the problem is that rather than controlling for response set by omitting respondents after they have been interviewed, we have tried to reduce its occurrence.

13. Srole views the scale as a measure of "the individual's generalized, pervasive sense of 'self-to-others belongingness' at one extreme compared with 'self-to-others distance' and 'self-to-others alienation' at the other pole of the continuum." Srole, op. cit., p. 711.

14. For a review, see Charles M. Bonjean, Richard J. Hill, and S. Dale McLemore, *Sociological Measurement* (San Francisco: Chandler Publishing Company, 1967), pp. 33-37.

15. Emile Durkheim, *Suicide: A Sociological Study* (New York: The Free Press, 1961), p. 276.

16. Ibid.

17. See Dorothy L. Meier and Wendell Bell, "Anomie, Social Isolation and the Class Structure," *Sociometry*, XX (June 1957), 105-16; Edward L. McDill and Jeanne Clare Ridley, "Status, Anomia, Political Alienation, and Political Participation," *The American Journal of Sociology*, LXVIII (September 1962), 205-13; Russell Middleton, "Alienation, Race, and Education," *American Sociological Review*, XXVIII (December 1963), 973-77; and Gwynn Nettler, "A

Comment on 'Anomy,' " *American Sociological Review,* XXX (October 1965), 762-63.

18. The product-moment correlation between anomia and powerlessness is .27 (Gamma = .26) for farmers and .38 (Gamma = .37) for farm workers; corresponding coefficients for anomia and normlessness are .23 (Gamma = .27) for farmers and .24 (Gamma = .27) for farm workers. The correlations are low enough so that the overlap between anomia and the other two measures is not great. Hence, our assumption that the three measures are measuring different states would appear to be warranted.

19. Thomas Gladwin, *Poverty U.S.A.* (Boston: Little, Brown & Company, 1967), p. 119; and Oscar Lewis, *The Children of Sanchez* (New York: Random House, Inc., 1961), p. xxvi.

20. For example, in response to question about his fears for the future, a farm worker responded, "Not having enough to eat, enough [money] coming in, and having *nobody to go to for help.*"

21. Again, tests of significance are based on Chi-square and student-t.

22. Anomia and normlessness differ from powerlessness also in that neither is associated with age.

23. The classification of scores into low, medium, and high is as follows: 0, 1, and 2-6 for normlessness, 0, 1-2, and 3-5 for anomia, and 0-1, 2-3, and 4-6 for powerlessness.

24. Gammas for the relationship between perceived deprivation and the measures of alienation are reported in Chapter 6 in which cultural differences in the relationship are examined.

25. The author's experience in the past few years in comparison to his experience in the late forties and early fifties indicates to him that the pattern is less prevalent today, however.

26. Leslie G. Carr, "The Srole Items and Acquiescence," *American Sociological Review,* XXXVI (April 1971), 287-93.

27. The wording of the items in Carr's paper is the same as in Srole's original formulation, and hence differs slightly from the wording used in the present application.

28. See Appendix A. Our reference here is to anglo-Americans only. Virtually no hostility was detected among Mexican-Americans.

29. As a rule, the .05 level of statistical significance is the level at which a result is assumed not to be due to chance.

6

Culture, Relative Deprivation, and the Cultural Context

In the past three chapters we have examined the relationships between social class and perceived deprivation and those between each of these and powerlessness, normlessness, and anomia. In this chapter we follow a similar procedure except that culture replaces social class in the analysis. Therefore, cultural differences in perceived deprivation and the three measures of alienation will be investigated, but our primary concern is the question of cultural differences in the relationship between perceived deprivation and powerlessness, normlessness, and anomia. In the last two chapters we have found no class differences in these relationships, but there may be cultural differences. Before we investigate these issues, however, let us examine socioeconomic differences between the three cultural groups.

Socioeconomic Differences

Numerous studies of the American class structure have shown that ethnic-cultural minorities are not equally distributed in the class structure but are disproportionately concentrated at the lower end. We want to know, however, whether the effect of culture-ethnicity penetrates *into* the lower class. That is, do life chances within a lower class differ depending on cultural differences within this stratum? Data indicate that they do.

Education

Although all the study groups are deficient in education, pronounced differences exist between the three groups (see Table 6-1). Over one-fourth of non-English speakers have had no formal education as compared to 12% of bilinguals and 3% of anglo-Americans. Seventy percent of the first group have less than five years of schooling as compared to 41% and 12% for the other two groups, respectively.

Occupational Differences

Although occupational differences between ethnic groups were not systematically investigated, differences between anglo-Americans and Mexican-

Table 6-1
Relationship between Ethnicity and Education, in %

	None	1-4 Years	5-8 Years	More than 8 Years	N
Anglos	3	9	50	38	539
Bilinguals	12	29	49	10	297
Non-English Speakers	27	43	28	2	186

$$X^2 = 301.07 \ (p < .001, 6df)$$

Americans were apparent. First, Mexican-Americans tended to work in vegetable-growing areas whereas anglo-Americans were concentrated in fruit-growing areas. Interviewers observed, however, that even in mixed crop areas, anglo-Americans tended to work in orchards pruning trees and picking fruit, and Mexican-Americans worked exclusively at the more arduous "stoop labor" in the vegetable fields. (The interviewers could not recall a single case of a Mexican-American working in fruit orchards.)[1]

Income

Differences in occupation are also reflected in wages: work in the orchards generally brings higher pay than stoop labor does. Such income differences are somewhat evident for the three ethnic groups, although the difference between anglo-Americans and bilinguals is quite small; median annual family income is $3,431 for anglo-Americans, $3,229 for bilinguals, and $2,410 for non-English speakers.

These findings provide rather compelling evidence that cultural minority status is a unique disadvantage in the American class structure. Not only are cultural minorities disproportionately represented at the lower end of the class scale, but on the basis of our results, within the poverty class itself cultural minority status is associated with the greatest disadvantages. Our results, therefore, are consistent with the formulation in Chapter 3 that social and economic disadvantages are cumulative: the disadvantages of cultural minority status and discrimination are compounded by poorer jobs and lower income. Consequently, when we consider cultural differences in class perception and alienation, we must control for socioeconomic differences.

Culture and False Consciousness

Although the conception of false consciousness involves a number of elements in Marxian thought, the trait is essentially produced by structural conditions. One's perception of his position in the class structure, of his real interests, and so forth, is determined by his position in the class structure. Our analysis of false consciousness among farmers and farm workers provides at least some support for this position. Workers view themselves as lower in the community class structure than farmers do, and within both groups perceived deprivation is inversely related to income (see p. 46). However, cultural differences between the three groups of farm workers may be associated with differences in class perceptions. The less a group is assimilated into the dominant culture of a society, the less likely its members may be aware of their true position in the class structure of that society. Level of assimilation may influence the extent to which the class structure is visible to an individual, and hence influence the accuracy of one's perception of his class position. According to this reasoning, non-English speakers should be more falsely conscious of their position than bilinguals, and bilinguals should be more falsely conscious than anglo-Americans. Hence, non-English speakers should perceive themselves to be the least deprived, with bilinguals next, and anglo-Americans the most deprived.

In presenting the results of our analysis by cultural group we will report findings separately for residents and migrants, as well as for different income levels. Average scores for the perceived deprivation scale with the entire society as the frame of reference (see p. 45) are presented in Table 6-2. Because of the small number of families in three of the Mexican-American groups in the "over $6,000" income category, these cases are combined with the "$4,001-$6,000" category.

The data in Table 6-2 represent the perceived deprivation score by ethnic-cultural status for residence-income groups. Except for groups in the "over $6,000" category, there are three cultural comparisons each for residents and migrants for each income category. There are a total of nineteen comparisons, in thirteen of which the least assimilated group has the highest score on perceived deprivation. This, of course, is contrary to the hypothesis that lower cultural assimilation lowers the degree to which one perceives himself as deprived. Thus we can say that perceptions of bilinguals and non-English speakers are at least as realistic as those of anglo-Americans.

Comparisons between income categories for cultural-residence categories (e.g., compare anglo-American residents in the "over $6,000" category with anglo-American residents in the "$4,000-$6,000" category) support this conclusion. In ten of twelve comparisons for anglo-Americans the lower income category has the highest perceived deprivation score; for bilinguals the number is eight of nine; and for non-English speakers, five of six. Clearly, the tendency to perceive one's position in the class structure accurately does not vary with the extent to which one is assimilated into the dominant culture. Therefore, results indicate a structural rather than a cultural interpretation of class perception. The greater one's disadvantages, the more one is apt to view himself as disadvantaged.

At the same time, many workers do not perceive their positions to be as low

Table 6-2

Average Perceived Deprivation Based on Perceived Standing in the United States,[a] by Residence, Income, and Ethnicity for Farm Workers

		Anglo-Americans	Bilinguals	Non-English Speakers
Over $6,000	Residents	15.59 (33)[b]	16.53 (19)	c
	Migrants	14.31 (26)	c	c
$4,001-$6,000	Residents	16.36 (79)	17.07 (53)	18.91 (18)[d]
	Migrants	17.05 (45)	17.05 (15)[e]	17.71 (7)[f]
$2,001-$4,000	Residents	16.10 (92)	17.97 (99)	17.24 (28)
	Migrants	18.66 (99)	17.48 (34)	18.46 (32)
$2,000 and Below	Residents	18.11 (49)	17.86 (26)	21.47 (13)
	Migrants	18.59 (42)	18.05 (34)	21.19 (42)

[a]Perceived relative standing on income, education, housing, medical care, and good employment.
[b]Figures in parentheses are N.
[c]Negligible number: Combined with $4,001-$6,000 category.
[d]Includes four resident non-English speakers over $6,000.
[e]Includes five migrant bilinguals over $6,000.
[f]Includes two migrant non-English speakers over $6,000.

as they actually are. Certainly "almost everyone is better off" (the first alternative to the perceived deprivation items) than individuals in the lowest income level. Consequently, their perceived deprivation score should be the maximum, that is, a score of 25. But only the scores of non-English speakers approach this level (21.47 and 21.19), and then only 11% admit they are at the bottom for all five items. These perceptions are unrealistic. Therefore, the two patterns of class perceptions that were observed in Chapter 3 do not vary depending on the cultural context. However, we cannot judge whether the two patterns would obtain for other cultural groups and societies, although their existence for our three culturally distinct groups suggests that the characterization of the lower class as either conscious or falsely conscious of their class position is an oversimplification. To some degree lower-class persons are aware of their true positions and to some degree they are not. And the difference in awareness does not vary by culture. Hence, the perceptions of Mexican-Americans appear to be no more unrealistic (or realistic) than those of anglo-Americans. The hypothesis of a relationship between cultural integration and false consciousness is not tenable. The class context is a more important determinant of class awareness than cultural background.

Culture and Community Context

In Chapter 3 we reported that anglo-American farm workers were less apt to view themselves as deprived in comparison to other members of their community than when they were compared to the overall population (see pp. 50-51). We suggested that this was largely a function of community isolation. Because these workers rarely come in contact with persons whose standard of living is higher than their own, they are apt to view themselves as relatively better off than they really are. We now want to know whether there are cultural differences in this community effect. We would expect that both groups of Mexican-American farm workers, like their fellow anglo-American workers, would perceive themselves as less deprived when evaluating their life chances against other persons in their home community than against the entire population.

Results are consistent with this conclusion. A comparison of scores on the community relative deprivation scale (data not given) with those for the societal relative deprivation scale in Table 6-2 reveals that in all thirteen comparisons between residence-income categories among Mexican-Americans, the score is lower when community is used as the frame of reference. Again, factors which influence class perception do not differ among cultural groups. The community context appears to be a more important determinant of class perception than cultural background.

In summary, results are generally consistent with a neo-Marxian position that perception of class position is a product of that class position. Since our data also suggest that class perception is influenced by community position, findings consistently support the hypothesis that perception of class position is largely sociologically determined. Class perception is not associated with *cultural* differences, however, and the relationships between class perception, income, and community position do not vary with cultural background. Hence, class perception is largely a social rather than a cultural phenomenon.

The Relationship between Relative Deprivation and Alienation: The Cultural Context

Although perceived deprivation itself is not influenced by cultural background, its effect on powerlessness, normlessness or anomia may be. We believe that this is in fact the case because the meaning of relative deprivation varies between cultural groups. Cultural background may be an important factor influencing the salience of self-other comparisons, that is, how much significance one gives to how he compares with others.

The significance of "other direction" among anglo-Americans has been postulated by numerous writers for a number of years.[2] We do not contend, however, that the tendency to be aware of how one ranks in comparison to others is necessarily more prevalent in this society than in others. Instead, we believe that these social comparison processes[3] may have greater significance for members of this society than they do for members of other societies. The U.S. cultural ethos emphasizes that individual status is based on performance. Since the ethos also contends that opportunities are equal, level of achievement and status become an index of ability and performance; so if status is based on performance, then status must reflect a person's performance and ability.[4] Consequently, one's status—one's relative ranking on life changes—is particularly important. Although "life chances provide tangible evidence of individual worth,"[5] they do so only in terms of one's life chances relative to the life chances of others. Hence, one's comparison with other members of the community in class status is particularly important in an achievement-oriented society: the comparison has implications for self-worth.

In contrast to the above tendency, John Gillin states that among Latin American countries "each person is valued because of a unique inner quality or worth he possesses."[6] Unlike the North American who is valued and respected in relation to how he compares with other men, the Latin American is valued and respected because he "is special and unique."[7] Consequently, how one compares with others is obviously of less significance to Latin Americans than to anglo North Americans. Similarly, Cochran concludes that Latin American businessmen are more interested than anglo-American businessmen in "inner worth and justification by standards of personal feeling than they are in the opinion of peer groups."[8] It is doubtful if such an orientation could survive in an achievement-performance oriented society such as the United States.

Early socialization patterns may be involved. Heller contends that among Mexican-Americans, unlike anglo-Americans, parents' "love for their children is not conditional . . . on the child's level of performance as compared with his peers. . . ."[9] Consequently, the social perceptions of a Mexican-American may be less dependent on how he compares with his peers because he has not been socialized in such a way that one's relative achievements and position are emphasized. Indeed, Arthur J. Rubel, having studied Mexican-Americans in Texas, contends that early socialization practice is an important factor in the Mexican-American tendency to "attach qualities of anxiety and disaffection to their perception of persons" beyond their immediate family.[10] The experience of anxiety and disaffection toward nonfamily members may be an additional factor in the (postulated) Mexican-American tendency *not to pay much attention to how he compares with others.*

Note again that this does not imply that the process of social comparison occurs less frequently among Mexican-Americans than among anglo-Americans. We have seen that Mexican-Americans are able to assess their life chances relative to the life chances of other persons in the community as realistically (and unrealistically) as their anglo-American counterparts. The Mexican-American, to quote John Gillin, knows "that, from the point of view of social structure, he is *not* equal to everyone else, either in position [that is, life chances] or opportunity." The point, however, is that "as an individual he does *not* have to pay much *attention* to [this inequality]."[11] The anglo-American, however, attaches greater significance to self-other comparisons, and he does "pay attention to" how he compares with others. We suggest that this is true in any achievement-oriented society because differences in life chances are related to differences in performance and ability and, hence, perceptions of self-worth.

If this is so, one's perception of his position in the class structure should depend on one's culture. We would therefore expect that this perception would lead to different *consequences*, depending on the individual's cultural background. Inspection of Table 6-3 indicates that perception of position in the class structure does have different consequences for powerlessness. This table gives the relationship in percentages between perceived community deprivation—high and low (15 and below, and above 15)—and powerlessness—high, medium, and low (4-6, 2-3, 0-1). Examination of the Gammas shows a clear gradient depending on degree of cultural assimilation; the correlation is highest for anglo-Americans, lowest for non-English speakers, among whom it is actually negative. Control for income does not affect the result. If we divide respondents into groups of high and low income depending on whether they have more or less than a $4,000 annual income, coefficients for high and low income categories are .47 and .42 for anglo-Americans, .13 and .36 for bilinguals, and —.14 and .00 for non-English speakers. Hence, the significance of social comparisons for powerlessness differs with cultural background. The negative assessment of one's life chances relative to others leads to a negative assessment of one's ability to control his economic fate, depending on one's cultural background.

A comparison of the contextual effects of culture and class for relative deprivation and powerlessness can be made in Table 6-4 (column 2), in which Gammas are given for farmers along with the three groups of farm workers. In contrast to the rather striking gradient of Gammas by cultural group, Gammas for farmers and anglo-American farm workers are almost identical. Insofar as powerlessness is concerned, the significance of relative deprivation for alienation is more a cultural than a class phenomenon: it holds about equally well for the two classes of native Americans and less well for the two cultural minorities.

The same general conclusions can be made about normlessness (see Table 6-4, column 3). The Gammas for farmers and anglo-American workers are quite similar, and although neither of the Gammas for the two Mexican-American groups is statistically significant, the pattern is the same as for powerlessness: the positive effects of relative deprivation vary inversely with cultural assimilation. As for anomia, the lower coefficient for anglo-American farm workers relative to bilinguals varies from the pattern for powerlessness and normlessness. However, the relationship is statistically significant for farmers and approaches significance at the .05 level for anglo-American farm workers (p = .06), and the contextual effects of culture are obvious in the difference between bilinguals and non-English speakers. (As in the previous chapter, we distinguish between high, medium and low scores on both scales, corresponding to scores of 2-6, 1 and 0 for normlessness and 3-5, 1-2, and 0 for anomia.)

In summary, the striking features about Table 6-4 are the differences between

Table 6-3
Relationship between Perceived Deprivation and Powerlessness, in %, for Farm Workers

	Anglo-Americans: Perceived Deprivation			Bilinguals: Perceived Deprivation			Non-English Speakers: Perceived Deprivation		
	Low[a]	High[a]	N	Low[a]	High[a]	N	Low[a]	High[a]	N
Powerlessness									
High (4-6)	26	74	149	27	73	56	33	67	37
Medium (2-3)	45	55	215	37	63	149	30	70	95
Low (0-1)	64	36	144	44	56	85	24	76	33
Gamma		.46*			.22**			−.12	

[a]Low is below 15 on the perceived deprivation scale; high is 15 and above (community frame of reference).
*P < .001 (two-tail test).
**P = .06 (two-tail test).

Table 6-4

Gammas between Perceived Relative Deprivation (Community) and Each of the Three Dimensions of Alienation for Farmers and Farm Workers

	Powerlessness	Normlessness	Anomia	N[a]
Farmers	.44***	.32**	.26**	215
Farm Workers				
Anglo-Americans	.46***	.26**	.15	509
Bilinguals	.22	.08	.26*	290
Non-English Speakers	−.12	−.02	−.30	164

[a]N may deviate slightly for different measures of alienation.

*P ≤ .05 (two-tail test)

**P ≤ .01 (two-tail test)

***P ≤ .0001 (two-tail test)

different cultural groups of similar class status and the similarity between different classes of similar cultural backgrounds. Hence, the involvement of relative deprivation in the dynamics of powerlessness, normlessness, and anomia appears to be largely a matter of culture. Data thus support the hypothesis that the salience of social comparison processes (at least in reference to life chances) for alienation depends on the cultural context.

Since differences exist between cultural groups, a precise explanation for these differences is not immediately apparent. Groups with different cultural heritages and connections with wider cultures differ with respect to a large number of things. Consequently, the observation of a particular difference could conceivably be attributed to many single cultural elements or to configurations of elements. We suggest, however, that no single cultural difference accounts for our results; rather, the configuration of elements associated with achievement and ascriptive orientations is the determining factor. In an achievement-oriented society characterized by cultural assumptions that opportunities are equal and that status is the result of performance, one's ranking in the community class structure implies something about one's performance. To perceive one's rank as low is to recognize that one's performance and ability are inferior to that of other men. Therefore, those who perceive their performance as inferior to others are more apt to experience a sense of alienation than those who do not. That is, persons who view themselves as contributing little to or as receiving little from society are more apt to be alienated from it—to think they have less ability to influence their fate in society, to adopt attitudes that emphasize individual self-interest, and to feel hopeless and pessimistic about their situations in society.

It is clear that frustration deriving from relative deprivation per se cannot be the significant factor, since relative deprivation exists among Mexican-Americans as well as among anglo-Americans. But how perceived deprivation is interpreted is crucial, and this varies depending on culture.

Cultural Assimilation and Alienation

In addition to cultural differences in the above relationships, we want to know if cultural differences are associated with powerlessness, normlessness, and anomia when the influence of perceived deprivation is removed (or at least minimized). Consequently, we will compare the powerlessness, normlessness, and anomia scores of cultural groups separately for respondents who are high and low on perceived deprivation. First, however, let us consider the theoretical perspectives.

Two separate perspectives would lead us to expect cultural differences in alienation. The first focuses on the process by which ethnic minorities become assimilated into the dominant culture of a society, a process which in the United States is sometimes referred to as "Anglo-American conformity,"[12] since it refers to the adoption by immigrant minorities such as Italians, Greeks, Poles, Russians, Chinese, and Latin Americans of the language, beliefs, values, and attitudes of the dominant anglo culture.[13] When the differences between this dominant culture and the minority culture are great (or when there is prejudice and hostility of anglo-Americans toward the minority), the pace of assimilation may be particularly slow. Evidence suggests that this is especially the case among Mexican-Americans.[14] As applied to alienation, however, the assimilation hypothesis does not designate which of the three groups will be the most alienated, but does stipulate that the three groups will be ordered, with bilinguals in the middle since they occupy a middle point in level of assimilation.

Another perspective does suggest the direction of cultural differences. Eric Fromm states that "alienation differs from culture to culture, both in the specific spheres which are alienated, and in the thoroughness of the process."[15] According to Fromm and others, American culture is especially alienating, both in pervasiveness and completeness: "Alienation as we find it in modern society is almost total."[16] If one accepts this hypothesis, the degree of powerlessness, normlessness, and anomia should all be higher for anglo-Americans than for Mexican Americans.[17]

Analysis yields mixed results. For powerlessness there are no significant differences between cultural groups; averages are 2.59 (anglo-Americans), 2.38 (bilinguals), and 2.42 (non-English speakers). Averages for anomia show that bilinguals have a significantly lower score than the other two groups: 2.83 (anglo-Americans), 2.41 (bilinguals), and 2.85 (non-English speakers). Although this suggests that the "marginal status" of bilinguals may create conflict for this group and hence contribute to a higher level of anomia, one might argue that cultural conflict should have this effect for powerlessness as well. There is no apparent explanation for this disparity.[18]

Results for normlessness are even different. Overall, average normlessness scores are 1.16 for anglo-Americans, 1.59 for bilinguals, and 2.21 for non-English speakers. All differences are significant at the .001 level of statistical significance or beyond.[19] Further analysis indicates that the relationship remains unchanged even when the effects of income and perceived deprivation are controlled. Gammas are computed between cultural assimilation and the three levels of normlessness (low, medium, and high), separately for low and high income and perceived deprivation. Results are presented in Table 6-5. All Gammas are statistically significant, and three of the four are almost identical in magnitude. It would seem, then, that whereas the effects of relative deprivation depends on level of cultural assimilation, the effects of cultural assimilation does not depend on perceived deprivation (or income). We cannot say if such findings apply to persons higher in the class structure since middle-class groups from different cultural backgrounds are not represented in our samples. Besides, the question is academic because middle-class groups that parallel each of our three farm worker groups would be difficult to find, if they exist at all (e.g., there are few if any non-English speaking Mexican-Americans whose incomes compare with the incomes of our group of farmers). Nevertheless, in the absence of such comparisons, we do not know to what extent the cultural effect reflected in Table 6-5 is specific to the lower class.

Note that the direction of the relationship (anglo-Americans are lowest in normlessness, non-English speakers are highest) is contrary to the hypothesis that normlessness is higher among native Americans, as is suggested in Merton's formulation. Merton states that when the cultural emphasis of a society

shifts from the satisfactions deriving from competition itself to an almost exclusive concern with the outcome, the resultant stress makes for the breakdown of the regulatory structure. With this attenuation of institutional controls, there occurs an approximation to the situation erroneously held by the utilitarian philosophers to be typical of society, a situation in which calculations of personal advantage and fear of punishment are the only regulating agencies.[20]

The implication is that such a condition is more typical of American society than other societies, although it is more pervasive in the lower class than in the more advantaged strata.[21] Alvin W. Gouldner is more explicit; he claims that the attitude conveyed in the above quote is particularly characteristic of western and American society in which it is "a central component of the everyday culture of middle-class society."[22] Thus, according to Merton and Gouldner, we can say that normlessness should be higher among anglo-Americans than Mexican-Americans, although Merton argues that it would be higher for lower-class anglo-Americans than for those of the middle class, and Gouldner suggests that it might be higher for the middle class. Findings in the last chapter eliminate Gouldner's hypothesis for the subjects in the present study. And the findings in the present chapter provide no support for the hypothesis that a normless or utilitarian attitude is higher among native Americans in comparison to those whose native origin is an ascriptive society. Instead they suggest the hypothesis that normlessness is only one element of an estrangement syndrome; it increases as cultural estrangement or lack of assimilation in general increases.

Table 6-5

Relationship between Cultural Group and Normlessness, in %, for Level of Income and for Perceived Deprivation for Farm Workers

	Less Than $4,000 Annual Income					
	Low Perceived Deprivation[a]			High Perceived Deprivation[a]		
Normlessness	Anglo-Americans	Bilinguals	Non-English Speakers	Anglo-Americans	Bilinguals	Non-English Speakers
High (2-6)	23	53	71	40	53	65
Medium (1)	40	26	29	29	31	25
Low (0)	37	21	–	31	16	10
N	98	62	24	173	101	68
Gamma		-.55*			-.35*	

	More Than $4,000 Annual Income					
	Low Perceived Deprivation[a]			High Perceived Deprivation[a]		
Normlessness	Anglo-Americans	Bilinguals	Non-English Speakers	Anglo-Americans	Bilinguals	Non-English Speakers
High (2-6)	21	30	50	35	44	71
Medium (1)	32	36	50	31	40	14
Low (0)	47	33	–	34	16	14
N	106	33	10	80	50	14
Gamma		-.36*			-.33*	

aLow is 15 and below on the perceived deprivation scale (community); high is 15 and above.

*P ≤ .001 (two-tail test).

These results are consistent with some of those obtained by others. Jessor et al. report differences in "deviance-prone" scores between anglo- and Mexican-Americans in Colorado,[23] and Simpson reports that native Mexicans are significantly higher on a measure of normlessness than native North Americans.[24] Nevertheless, the theoretical interpretation of these results is not apparent. Jessor et al emphasize the structure of opportunity. In Chapter 9 we will investigate this issue by examining the relationship between perceived opportunity and normlessness.

In summary, we cannot say that cultural differences in alienation hold true for all measures of alienation. We can say, however, that there is no support for the hypothesis that the culture of the United States, in comparison to societies such as Mexico,[25] leads to feelings of powerlessness, normlessness, or anomia. Only in the case of normlessness are there systematic cultural differences, which are contrary to what the hypothesis predicts. The mixture of results does not permit us to make any overall generalization about differences in alienative attitudes between persons from ascriptive and achievement-oriented societies.

Conclusion

Results of this and the previous chapter provide interesting comparisons and contrasts in the effects of class and culture. With regard to the relationship of each to perceived deprivation and to the three measures of alienation, class is clearly the more important factor. Class is significantly associated with perceived deprivation, normlessness, and anomia, whereas cultural assimilation is associated only with normlessness.

As for the contextual effects of class and culture on the relationships between perceived deprivation and all three measures of alienation, quite different conclusions can be drawn. None of the three relationships is influenced by class differences; correlations are about as high or higher for the middle-class farmers as for the lower-class farm workers. This is not true for cultural differences, however. For powerlessness and normlessness, the correlation is higher among anglo-Americans than bilinguals, and for all three measures of alienation the (positive) correlation is higher for bilinguals than for non-English speakers.

We must thus distinguish between two approaches to the issues of cultural assimilation and alienation. One views alienation as an aspect of assimilation itself; in the case of normlessness it decreases as assimilation increases. The other views the sources or dynamics of alienation as different depending on the level of assimilation, that is, the factors that are associated with alienation and, presumably, contributing factors to it vary depending on cultural background. Despite the fact that cultural assimilation is not associated with perceived deprivation and two of three measures of alienation, it still influences the relationship between perceived deprivation and all three measures of alienation.

Thus, assimilation and perceived deprivation interact: the effects of perceived deprivation are not uniform but depend on the cultural context. (We assume here, of course, that perceived deprivation leads to alienation, not vice versa.) The dynamics of alienation are more closely associated with the assimilation process than is the level of alienation itself. In Part III we will examine the interaction between assimilation and another condition.

Notes

1. Not only does orchard work generally bring higher pay, it confers status as well, as reflected in the disparaging comments frequently volunteered by anglo-Americans about stoop labor and Mexican-Americans. Although the occupational differences reflect a familiar pattern—ethnic status and occupational status are related in the United States generally—its explanation in this particular case is not known. Since skills for all farm work can be acquired even by the illiterate, differences in status for various kinds of farm work are not due to differences in education. To what extent discriminatory hiring practices are reflected is not known. However, the foreman of a fruit ranch, when questioned about the absence of Mexican-Americans in his orchards, reported that Mexican-Americans never applied for work. Probably, a latent physical threat is involved, since on numerous occasions anglo-Americans volunteered hostile and prejudicial attitudes about Mexican-Americans. Thus, given these feelings, it is entirely possible that a Mexican-American who obtained orchard work would meet with physical violence. But regardless of the explanation, Mexican-Americans have the poorer jobs.

2. See David Riesman, *The Lonely Crowd* (New Haven: Yale University Press, 1950). A number of empirical assessments of Riesman's formulations have been made. See, for example, Richard A. Peterson, "Dimensions of Social Character: An Empirical Exploration of the Riesman Typology," *Sociometry*, XXVII (June 1964), 194-207. A number of studies are cited by Peterson, op. cit., p. 195, n. 6. For a general assessment and critique, see Seymour Martin Lipset and Leo Lowenthal, eds., *Culture and Social Character: The Work of David Riesman Reviewed* (New York: The Free Press, 1961). Our focus is considerably different from Riesman's, of course, since we are concerned with the salience of one's ranking in comparison to others and not the significance of the attitudes and opinions of others in modes of conformity. However, both could be generated by the same kinds of cultural and social conditions.

3. See Leon Festinger, "A Theory of Social Comparison Processes," *Human Relations*, VII (Spring 1954), 117-40.

4. The equation of status with ability is reflected in the question, "If you're so smart, why aren't you rich?" Although this may imply an emphasis on materialistic symbols in American society, it nevertheless reflects the assumption that people with ability will tend to acquire those symbols.

5. John P. Hewitt, *Social Stratification and Deviant Behavior* (New York: Random House, Inc., 1970), p. 48.

6. John Gillin, "Ethos Components in Modern Latin American Culture," in Dwight B. Heath and Richard N. Adams, eds., *Contemporary Cultures and Societies of Latin America* (New York: Random House, Inc., 1965), p. 507.

7. Ibid.

8. Thomas C. Cochran, *The Puerto Rican Businessman* (Philadelphia: University of Pennsylvania Press, 1959), p. 131.

9. Celia Heller, *Mexican-American Youth: Forgotten Youth at the Crossroads* (New York: Random House, Inc., 1968), pp. 36-37.

10. Arthur J. Rubel, "Perception of Social Relations: A Comparative Analysis," in John H. Burma, ed., *Mexican-Americans in the United States* (Cambridge: Schenkman Publishing Company, Inc., 1970), p. 105.

11. Gillin, op. cit., pp. 511, 512, 513; emphasis added.

12. Milton M. Gordon, *Assimilation in American Life: The Role of Race, Religion, and National Origins* (New York: Oxford University Press, Inc., 1964), pp. 88-114.

13. See Robert E. Park and Ernest W. Burgess, *Introduction to the Science of Sociology* (Chicago: The University of Chicago Press, 1921), p. 735; and Robert E. Park, "Assimilation, Social," in Edwin R.E. Seligman and Alvin Johnson, eds., *Encyclopedia of the Social Sciences* (New York: The Macmillan Company, 1931), II, 281.

14. Mexican-Americans may have stronger tendencies than other minorities to hold on to their native culture. See John H. Burma, ed., *Mexican-Americans in the United States* (Cambridge: Schenkman Publishing Co., 1970), p. 105. See also Clark S. Knowlton, "Petron-Peon Pattern among the Spanish Americans of New Mexico," *Social Forces*, XLI (October 1962), 12; and Ozzie G. Simmons, "The Mutual Images and Expectations of Anglo-Americans and Mexican-Americans," in Staten W. Webster, ed., *Knowing the Disadvantaged* (San Francisco: Chandler Publishing Company, 1966), pp. 134, 137-38.

15. Eric Fromm, *The Sane Society* (New York: Holt, Rinehart and Winston, Inc., 1955), p. 123.

16. Ibid., p. 114; see also pp. 111, 238.

17. A qualification may be in order with specific reference to Fromm, since Fromm's conception of alienation is not identical with the formulations of sociologists such as those referred to in this book. For a discussion, see Richard Schacht, *Alienation* (Garden City, N.Y.: Doubleday & Company, Inc., 1970). Nevertheless, the thesis that alienation is unusually high in the United States and similar societies is not limited to Fromm but is an assumption frequently made by others.

18. It would not appear to be due to a stronger tendency to acquiesce (to yeasay) among this group. (We recall that one item in the anomia scale is reverse scored.) Perhaps a stronger acquiescent tendency can be expected among non-English speakers and a weaker tendency among anglo-Americans; but there

is no difference between these two groups in anomia. Moreover, in Table 6-4 we see that there is no consistent tendency for lower income farm workers to score higher than higher income farm workers; the tendency to yeasay would probably be higher within the lower income category.

19. Probability is based on Chi-square analysis (median test, 2 if).

20. Robert K. Merton, *Social Theory and Social Structure*, rev. and enlr. ed. (New York: The Free Press, 1957), p. 157.

21. However, the thrust of Merton's theory is not so much that culture influences levels of normlessness but that culture affects the relationship between normlessness and another factor, i.e., blocked opportunity. This issue will be explored in Chapter 9.

22. Alvin Gouldner, *The Coming Crisis of Western Sociology* (New York: Basic Books, Inc., 1970), p. 61.

23. Richard Jessor, Theodore D. Graves, Robert C. Hanson, and Shirley L. Jessor, *Society, Personality, and Deviant Behavior: A Study of a Tri-Ethnic Community* (New York: Holt, Rinehart and Winston, Inc., 1968), p. 302. However, findings for a measure of "attitudes toward deviance" do not show Mexican-Americans to be significantly higher—ibid., p. 308.

24. Simpson also finds a similar relationship for a measure of powerlessness. Miles E. Simpson, "Social Mobility, Normlessness and Powerlessness in Two Cultural Contexts," *American Sociological Review*, XXXV (December 1970), 1002-13. However, let us not make too much of Simpson's findings in reference to our conceptions and measures of powerlessness and normlessness, since the manifest content of the items used in Simpson's study appear to be different from the content of our items.

25. We are assuming here, of course, that Mexican-Americans are controlled to a large degree by the Mexican culture, and that this is more true for non-English speakers than for bilinguals.

Part III: Opportunity and Alienation

7 Class, Culture, and Aspirations

In the next three chapters we will examine aspects of one of the most well-known theories in sociology, Robert K. Merton's "Social Structure and Anomia." The theory was first published in the *American Sociological Review* in 1938, and several additional statements have since appeared.[1] The theory basically is as follows:

In any society, members are encouraged to aspire to certain cultural goals and to pursue those goals in culturally prescribed ways. Both the goals pursued and the means used to pursue them are defined by cultural norms and values. Normlessness and deviant behavior occur when the goals and means are malintegrated, which can happen for several reasons. Individuals may emphasize the means more than the goals, in which case "rutalistic" attitudes and behavior result; the teacher who emphasizes methods of instruction and forgets the goals of student learning, the social worker who adheres strictly to welfare rules even though these may work against the interests or the needs of welfare recipients, or the nurse who wakes hospital patients to give them sleeping pills (because all patients of certain types are required to have sleeping pills)—all are examples of ritualistic behavior. In other instances, individuals may reject both goals and means, and withdraw from the cultural and social life surrounding them; this is called "retreatism" and is exemplified by psychotics, suicides, alcoholics, and drug addicts. Or individuals may retain cultural goals but reject the prescribed means by which these goals should be achieved; this is "innovation," and is often manifested by economic crime. Although Merton emphasizes economic and materialistic goals in this pattern, any goal identified with the individual's self-interest may be involved.

Merton gives "innovation" the most attention in his theory. He contends that this pattern is likely to occur in societies such as the United States wherein all persons are admonished to aspire to the same lofty goals, such as monetary success, and where the myth of equal opportunity exists but society denies to a large segment of the population the opportunities to achieve those same goals that it admonishes them to strive for. Differences in opportunity are generated by the social structure; hence, persons who are oriented toward goals which they do not have the means to achieve are apt to be found in the lower stratum of the class structure. Consequently, in this stratum, "there is strain toward the breakdown of norms, toward normlessness."[2]

Our brief review reveals that there are three major hypotheses in Merton's theory:

1. There is no difference between social classes in economic-occupational-materialistic goals and aspirations in the United States.
2. Regardless of differences in aspirations, lower-class persons perceive their opportunities to be more limited than members of the middle and upper strata.
3. Normlessness is higher in the lower class because perceived opportunity is lower in the lower class.[3]

An important issue emerges from the third hypothesis. Since the hypothesis states that class differences in normlessness are due to differences in perceived opportunity, it implies that the relationship between class and normlessness exists only if class differences in opportunity also exist. That is, the correlation between class and normlessness would disappear (or be significantly reduced in magnitude) if perceived opportunity were controlled. But what happens to perceived opportunity when the effects of class are controlled? Does the theory anticipate a relationship between perceived opportunity and normlessness *within* classes? In the next chapter we suggest that it does. Moreover, we will contend that this particular relationship is more a cultural phenomenon than a class phenomenon. Consequently, the relationship is expected to exist among middle-to upper-class farm workers as well as among lower-class farm workers, but not among Mexican-Americans who are not assimilated into the culture of the United States.

In the present chapter, our concern is with the first hypothesis and with whether there are cultural differences in goals and aspirations within the lower class. The other two hypotheses will be discussed in more detail in the next chapter, where we will investigate the class and cultural differences in the relationship postulated in these hypotheses. Then in Chapter 9, we will examine the relationship between perceived opportunity and powerlessness and anomia.

Social Class, Goals, and Aspirations

In any society members consider the pursuit of certain goals to be more important and worthy than others. Through the process of socialization individuals become acquainted with those goals and incorporate them in their individual life styles. In the United States, for example, it is usually assumed that occupational success is an important and worthy goal to strive for; indeed, the assessment and evaluation of an individual's worth is frequently made in terms of his occupational success. At the same time, it is also true that every member of every society is not expected to achieve the same level of success as other members; the caste system of India is a good example. In the United States, however, some sociologists say that goals and aspirations are generally the same for all groups, and that most American males regardless of class level are oriented to the same materialistic and occupational success goals. This follows from the cultural (and possibly sexually related) emphasis on achievement. Much of the controversy over Merton's theory revolves around this issue. In his original 1938 statement, Merton implies there is little if any difference between classes because of the "cultural axiom" that all persons, regardless of class background, "should strive for the same lofty goals since these are open to all."[4] According to this view, then, members of the lower class should be oriented just as much as members of the higher classes to the materialistic success goals which characterize many U.S. citizens. Others contend, however, that this is not the case, that lower-class persons have less lofty goals and aspirations; much evidence supports this latter position.[5]

There are good theoretical reasons for believing that each position is valid. Since members of the lower class are part of the broader society, they have been exposed since childhood to dominant middle-class goals and the belief that such goals are attainable to anyone willing to pay the price; to a degree some lower-class people have probably assimilated these goals and beliefs, or so Merton implies. However, the nature of the lower-class person's situation, as indicated by the findings for farm workers in Chapters 3 and 6, encourages adaptations that involve the acceptance of other types of goals and values which are more realistic given the constraints imposed by the structure of their situation. For example, lower-class people may be more concerned with economic security than with economic and materialistic success, as defined by dominant American standards.[6] Thus the goal orientations of lower-class persons such as farm workers may be determined by both the assimilation of middle-class culture *and* the realistic limitations imposed by the constraints under which they live.

Our results will be reported separately for farmers and farm workers and for different cultural groups among farm workers. Data are based on responses to: (1) structured questions concerning educational and occupational aspirations for children, and (2) open-ended questions dealing with hopes for and fears about the future.

Educational and Occupational Aspirations

Much of the data on class differences in goals and aspirations are based on responses to questions about the educational and occupational aspirations for one's children.[7] Similar questions were asked of farmers and farm workers. Parents who had school-age children living with them were asked how much education they wanted for their children. Although 868 workers (84%) and 210 farmers (89%) reported having school-age children, only 455 workers (44%) and 122 farmers (51%) reported children living with them at the time in this age range.[8] Among farmers, 91% wanted their children to have at least a college education, in comparison to 63% among all farm workers.

These results are consistent with those of other studies which have found that the aspirations are directly associated with class status. But, since 63% of all workers want a college education for their children (even 62% of those with incomes less than $4,000),[9] even though their aspirations are lower than those of farmers, the extent to which middle-class goals are assimilated by them would appear to be rather high. Such results probably reflect two patterns: the assimilation of middle-class values and hopes for children's success and the realistic adaptation to the structure of poverty.

Differences between cultural groups among farm workers are slight. Percentages wanting a college education for their children are: anglo-Americans, 64; bilinguals, 66; and non-English speakers, 57. Farm workers were also asked if they wanted their children to go into farm work. Since farm work is such a low-status occupation, a negative response would be assumed to reflect at least some upward aspiration for children and an affirmative response a lack of aspiration. The percentage having occupational aspirations for their children are: anglo-Americans, 82; bilinguals, 86; and non-English speakers, 90. None of the differences is statistically significant.

Goal Orientations

One difficulty with the educational and occupational aspiration questions is that they structure responses and limit the range of response alternatives; respondents are not free to express their concrete goals and *goal alternatives*.[10] It may be that although a respondent wishes his children to obtain a certain level of education, he may not consider it especially important that his children do so. Other concerns may be more important. In order to get a realistic picture of the range of concerns, respondents must be given greater freedom to express their views. Consequently, two open-ended questions were asked. The first was:

All of us want certain things out of life. When you think about what really matters in your life, what are your wishes and hopes for the future? In other words, if you imagined your future in the best possible light, what would your life look like then, if you are to be happy? Take your time answering; such things aren't easy to put into words.

We assume that the responses to this question are concrete expressions of major values and life goals.[11]

After responses to this question had been recorded, the following question was asked:

Now taking the other side of the picture, what are your fears and worries about the future? In other words, if you imagined your future in the worst possible light, what would life look like then? Again take your time in answering.

If we know a man's fears and worries we have clues about the goals toward which he is oriented, because they are opposite to the goal states he would like to achieve.

When respondents had difficulty responding to either question, it was repeated with the encouragement to "take your time." Probing was often necessary to get specific responses; for example, the answer, "a happy life," to the first question would be probed with the question, "What would it take to make your life happy?" until specific responses were given.

Class Differences

In all, 223 farmers (92%) and 986 workers (96%) gave responses to the first question; most respondents mentioned several things. Responses were coded into ten separate categories and percentages of each group who mentioned the category are given in Table 7-1. The percentages who mention the category as the first response are given separately because the first response may represent matters that are most salient. Responses are ordered according to the frequency with which they were mentioned.

Goals mentioned most frequently by both groups are economic advantages, good health, and children's success. There is no difference between farmers and workers in concern for children's success, and the farmers' greater concern for health probably reflects their older age (median age of 51 years versus 40 years for workers). Goals that have received most attention in the literature are economic; the discussion by Merton focuses on monetary goals. Our results show similarities as well as differences between farmers and workers in this area.

The two groups are similar in that economic goals are mentioned most often by both. Also, if home ownership and better housing are included, close to 100% of workers may have mentioned economic-monetary-materialistic goals (the exact percentage is not known because some workers who mentioned economic goals also mentioned home ownership or better housing). There are important differences between farmers and farm workers in type of economic and materialistic goals, however.

First, farmers, most of whom own their homes, do not mention home ownership at all and only a small percentage are concerned about improving their housing. Second, workers are far more concerned about achieving stable employment and obtaining some form of self-employment ("to have a piece of land [farm] of my own," "to have a little business of some kind"). Third, despite the similar proportions who wish for more money (which constitutes most of the "other" economic category), there is a difference in scale. Goals of workers include: "to make enough money to meet my living expenses," "to be able to buy all the whiskey I want," "to make some money to buy a housetrailer to live in," and "to get a $100 check every Saturday night." Farmers, however,

Table 7-1

Goal Orientations of Farmers and Farm Workers, in %, as Indicated by Responses to the First Question[a]

	Farmers		Farm Workers	
Economic:	41[b] (16)[c]		83 (52)	
Stable employment (e.g., "steady job")		4 (1)		43 (28)
Self-employment (e.g., "have my own farm")		2 (1)		12 (10)
Other (e.g., "more money")		35 (14)		28 (14)
Good Health	29 (22)		13 (8)	
Children's Success	20 (14)		19 (8)	
Secure Retirement	12 (5)		2 (1)	
Own Home	0 (0)		11 (6)	
Better Housing	3 (0)		10 (0)	
Peace	9 (5)		1 (1)	
Good Government	9 (4)		0 (0)	
Life Continue As Is	9 (9)		2 (1)	
Other and Unclassifiable	45 (26)		36 (23)	
Total responding	223		986	

[a]"All of us want certain things out of life. When you think about what really matters in your life, what are your wishes and hopes for the future? In other words, if you imagined your future in the best possible light, what would your life look like then, if you are to be happy?"

[b]Column totals to more than 100% because many respondents mentioned more than one goal.

[c]First response in parenthesis.

report such goals as: "to always get a good price for wheat," "to have sufficient income so I can travel six months out of the year," "to get my land paid off and out of debt to the bank," and "to make $150,000 this year."

Workers' hopes for self-employment, home ownership, and good housing are desires for things that farmers already have, and hence represent the assimilation of middle-class goals and apparently the wish to "get ahead" in the world. Other studies have revealed the importance attached to home ownership in achieving middle-class status in American society. Its importance for those who do not have it is clearly indicated in the results of Mizruchi's study of a small New York State community.[12] Respondents were asked to list, in order of importance, the things they believed to be "signs of success" in American society. The "class" distribution for those who mentioned home ownership (with class I being highest) is as follows:

Class (%)				
I	II	III	IV	V
8	16	32	31	41

Since actual home ownership is directly related to class status, the results suggest that symbols of middle-class status are assimilated by a substantial proportion of the lower class.[13] Even for persons as low in the class structure as farm workers, these are important values for a sizable proportion. In general, then, results provide some support for the hypothesis that goals of the lower class are not unlike the goals of the middle class.

At the same time, however, home ownership and other symbols of middle-class status, such as self-employment and good housing, are mentioned by only a third of the workers, and they constitute only 16% of the first responses. The most frequently mentioned goal is stable employment, being mentioned by 43% of all workers and constituting 28% of first responses. Workers appear to be less concerned with the "goal of monetary success,"[14] than they are with achieving economic stability. Examples are:

I just want a job all year round so money will keep coming in for living expenses.

Just to have a good living—a steady job. We [family] don't want nothing great, just so we have enough to eat, a place to live, a job.

Even the wish for more money is rather modest. In response to the question of how much farm workers thought they should make, the median hourly rate they think they should receive is $1.92, in comparison to the current median of $1.59.[15] Although the proportionate increase desired is substantial (21%), the level of living that could be achieved would be much too low to obtain the economic and material values that are associated with "monetary success" in the United States. The orientation reflected in these results, in contrast to these pertaining to self-employment and home ownership, is toward economic *survival* and *stability*. Thus, the hypothesis that lower-class persons are more apt to be oriented to "security" rather than "success"[16] is also strengthened. As with relative deprivation, two patterns are reflected in our data for farm workers. In contrast, farmers are concerned almost solely with economic enhancement and even greater monetary success.[17]

Other differences are revealed in desires for peace, secure retirement, and good government (e.g., one "that doesn't take away our freedoms"). Note that these desires are all temporally or spatially removed from the individual's current life situation; their effects are less immmediate, for example, than good employment, which helps explain why they are seldom mentioned by farm workers.

Although responses to the second question were fewer and less diverse (see Table 7-2) than those to the first, the same general trends and themes appear. Farmers and workers are both concerned most with economic matters, but different types. Workers worry about being unemployed and not having money for basic necessities such as food, rent, car payments, and doctor's bills; they're afraid of having "no place to live [because of no money for rent] and nothing to eat." Farmers, however, worry about "inflation getting way out of control," "going bankrupt and losing my farm," crop failures, decreases in price of farm goods, etc. Also, 45% of workers mention fears of physical survival: for example, "car burning up with my family in it," "have no place to live and nothing to eat," "car breakdown and we [family] have to live in the desert"; the corresponding figure for farmers is 23%, most of which concerned fear of poor health.

Such results are understandable in light of differences between farmers and farm workers in the structure of their situations. Given farm workers' income, unstable employment, and limited occupational skills, their concern with problems of employment and the basic necessities of day-to-day existence is to be expected. It is a realistic adaptation to their situations.

Perhaps members of the lower class do not plan for the future (a common assumption)[18] because matters of immediate physical and economic survival—a place to live, a dependable car, clothes and food for the family—are of such overriding importance to them.[19] Warren Haggstrom has stated, for example:

Table 7-2
Goal Orientations of Farmers and Farm Workers, in %, as Indicated by Responses to the Second Question[a]

	Farmers	Farm Workers
Economic:	43[b] (78)[c]	51 (38)
Unemployment	4 (4)	30 (22)
Money and Other	39 (24)	21 (16)
Physical		
(health, accidents, death, starvation)	23 (16)	45 (33)
Communism and Socialism	14 (10)	0 (0)
Government Oppression	17 (8)	0 (0)
War	16 (13)	8 (7)
Other and Unclassifiable	34 (25)	26 (22)
Total Responding	195	893

[a]"What are your fears and worries about the future? In other words, if you imagined your future in the worst possible light, what would life look like then?"
[b]Columns total to more than 100% because respondents mentioned more than one fear.
[c]First response in parentheses.

Caught in the present, the poor do not plan very much. They meet their troubles and take their pleasures on a moment-to-moment basis; their schemes are short-term. Their time perspective is foreshortened by their belief that it is futile to think of the future. Thus, when the poor use conventional words to refer to the future, those words tend to be empty of real meaning. They have little sense of the past and they go forward, but not forward to any preconceived place.[20]

Similarly, a witness to the President's Commission on Rural Poverty, A.J. McKnight of Louisiana, remarked that for the poor,

...there is no future; everything is today. They do not postpone satisfactions. When pleasure is available, they tend to take it immediately. They do not save, because for them there is no tomorrow.
• • •
The smug theorist of the middle-class would probably deplore this as showing a lack of traditional American virtues. Actually, it is the *logical* and natural reaction of a people living without hope, without a future.[21]

We would add, or make the qualification, that the reaction is a logical and natural response to the constraints of poverty by people who must constantly struggle to maintain basic physical and economic survival.[22] There is too little time to think of anything else.

This may partially explain why farmers are far more apt to be concerned about war and peace, and why workers, in contrast to farmers, hardly express a desire for good government or speak about problems of communism (and socialism) and government oppression at all (e.g., farmers mentioned "more government controls and loss of individual freedom," "socialistic or communistic government taking over"). Also, however, the farmers' have far more to lose economically from external factors such as war and changes in the existing government than do workers. Farmers have more vested interests in maintaining the status quo (the existing system undisturbed by war or changes in form of government) than workers who do not fare nearly as well under it anyway.

Cultural Differences

There are three cultural differences expressed by groups of farm workers on the first question (see Table 7-3). Both groups of Mexican-Americans expressed the wish for their children's success more than anglo-Americans, which probably reflects the value placed on children in Mexican culture, although this may at first seem to be a direct contradiction of what we said earlier about the American success ethic. Wish for self-employment is directly related to extent of assimilation into the broader culture; anglo-Americans appear to have assimilated the American value of self-employment more than Mexican-Americans, and bilinguals more than non-English speakers. The wish for steady and permanent

Table 7-3
Cultural Differences in Goal Orientations, in %

	First Question[a]		
	Self-employment	Children's Welfare and Success	Secure Employment
Anglos (N = 526)	16[b](13)[c]	10 (5)	29 (19)
Bilinguals (N = 289)	11 (10)	36 (14)	54 (35)
Non-English Speakers (N = 171)	1 (1)	23 (12)	65 (49)

	Second Question[a]	
	Physical Survival	Unemployment
Anglos (N = 448)	49 (39)	19 (13)
Bilinguals (N = 272)	42 (29)	33 (25)
Non-English Speakers (N = 153)	41 (25)	59 (46)

[a]See Tables 7-1 and 7-2.
[b]Total response.
[c]First response in parentheses.

employment under someone else, however, is inversely related to cultural assimilation. Analysis of responses to the second question gives much the same result for unemployment (although anglo-Americans were slightly more concerned about health, death, etc.). Concern for economic security appears to be more pervasive among Mexican-Americans than among anglo-Americans and is particularly extensive among the non-English speakers. Results suggest, therefore, that cultural assimilation is inversely related to goal orientation for the lower class which represents a realistic adaptation to the structure of lower-class existence. Unfortunately, however, responses cannot be cross-classified by income and culture groups because of the particular coding operations used.[23] But considering that there is so little difference between anglo-Americans and bilinguals in income (see p. 90), results are probably due to cultural factors rather than class factors. Apparently, cultural differences within the lower class contribute to significant differences in the types of goal orientation adopted.

Conclusion and Theoretical Implications

The question of whether lower-class persons have assimilated middle-class goals is not simple; we cannot give a categorical answer to it. As we have seen, some workers *are* concerned with such goals, as is indicated by those who wish to be self-employed, to own their homes, and perhaps those who want better housing as well. Examples are:

I just hope I don't have to work like this all my life. We would like to have a little motel, sports goods store, or restaurant. . . .

I'm in hope maybe to get me a home and settle down and it would be farm work [farming] cause that's all I know how to do.

However, for many workers economic security, survival, and stability are foremost.

Such findings indicate the presence of two patterns of goal orientations in the lower class, thus putting the controversy concerning the goals of lower-class persons in a different light. The hypothesis that goals and values are different receives support as does the hypothesis that dominant cultural values are assimilated by members of the lower class. Both hypotheses appear to be correct.[24]

This finding, along with those for relative deprivation and for alienation, indicate that describing the lower class in terms of any one pattern is an oversimplification, even if that pattern is more characteristic of the lower class than the middle and upper classes. Contradictory patterns may exist in the lower class, as they apparently do in society generally.[25] We saw in Chapters 3 and 6 that although farm workers feel more deprived than more advantaged persons, they do not feel as deprived as they actually are; in Chapters 4 and 5 we found that they may be more alienated than farmers in some respects but not in all; and in this chapter we have observed different patterns of goals and aspirations. Disagreements over the characteristics of the lower class may exist because different observers have focused on one particular pattern rather than others.[26]

The findings for goal orientations have further significance for the "poverty subculture" concept. Although they do not reveal that the orientations of farm workers are predominantly middle-class, they also do not indicate that they are shaped primarily by lower-class subcultural norms and values. Farm workers' orientations appear to be shaped more by structural than by cultural aspects of poverty. (Indeed, to the extent that they *are* shaped by cultural elements and orientations, it would appear that such elements and orientations are lodged in a culture of much greater scope than one which is unique to poverty.)

Other observers have made similar conclusions concerning the situational versus subcultural conceptions of the lower class.[27] Liebow, for example, on the basis of his study of lower-class urban blacks, states that the values of lower-class persons, in comparison to those of the higher classes, seem to be vague images reflected by forced or adaptive behavior rather than real values with a positive determining influence on behavior or choice.[28]

Let us also note responses of farmers and farm workers to two questions: "Would you say that a man's occupation is probably the most important thing in his life"? and "Would you say that money is the only real reason for a man to work?" The first question measures the pervasiveness of occupation in one's life—or the extent to which one's life is structured by occupational activity; the second measures the extent to which occupation is viewed only in terms of its economic security and survival function.[29]

To the first question, 39% of farmers and 60% of farm workers answered in the affirmative. Such results are consistent with our belief that the life situations of farm workers are more apt to revolve around the pursuit of work; just having an occupation (a job) is of central importance, and almost everything else depends on that. Since economic security and survival are so basic and of such overriding importance, life becomes to a great extent structured around the pursuit of job activity.[30]

At the same time, however, occupational pursuit in the lower class is probably tied to a limited range of interests, e.g., economic security, whereas among the middle and upper classes it may be a means to a wider range of values, e.g., prestige, luxury, self-fulfillment.[31] It is not that occupation is not unimportant to farmers, but only that occupation may be more apt to be divorced from the pursuit of economic security. *That* problem resolved, occupation is viewed as a means to other ends. Thus, in response to the second question, "Would you say that money is the only real reason for a man to work?" 7% of farmers answered in the affirmative, in comparison with 39% among farm workers. This difference probably reflects an economic fact: to survive you must first have money. Hence, farm workers are more apt to view occupational pursuit only in terms of economic survival and security. Workers' higher proportion of affirmative responses to both questions probably reflects their realistic adaptation to the structure of lower-class existence.[32]

Finally, results of this chapter may be viewed in terms of two general, but in many respects contradictory, theoretical frameworks of social structure: (1) Marxist or neo-marxist theory and (2) functionalist theory. According to the former, the class structure generates feelings, such as relative deprivation and alienation, which, when combined with other factors such as interaction and social organization among workers, lead to worker rebellion and the eventual change of the class structure. The functionalist perspective emphasizes forces which contribute to the stability and continuity of the social structure; the social (class) structure is viewed as generating sentiments and attitudes which serve to reinforce the existing structural arrangements.[33] Findings in this chapter would appear, on balance, to be more consistent with the functionalist perspective. We have noted previously that the nature of the lower-class status and the principle of cumulative disadvantage make it difficult for an individual to modify his status. They constitute structural factors that, to a great extent, make class status self-perpetuating (see pp. 43-44). Others contend that attitudes, motivation, and behavior (the inability to defer gratification, lack of discipline, and so forth) also contribute to lower-class status. We suggest, however, that the structure of lower-class status generates types of behavior that make it difficult for an individual to modify his status, regardless of his attitudes and motivations. Because of the nature of their structural positions, most poor persons are oriented to a "day-to-day" and "hand-to-mouth" existence. Their primary difficulties revolve around problems generated by the structure of their class position—finding a new job every few days, paying bills, and "making ends meet." For most farm workers, goals emphasized in the wider culture, such as monetary success, are simply beyond their reach so they are not oriented toward their achievement. Farm workers are too busy with the problems of existence to be concerned with the lofty goals that a large proportion of the affluent population strives for and often takes for granted.[34] This probably makes upward movement in the class structure still less probable, and hence helps to perpetuate current class status.

Also, because of the pressing nature of the worker's economic and physical problems, most farm workers are probably unable to sustain militant efforts, such as strikes, union campaigns, work slowdowns, and even violence and sabotage that could, either by virtue of purpose or consequence, lead to a redistribution of economic rewards between farmers and workers and hence result in the modification of the class structure. In this connection we might note a finding of a study of blacks in the United States.[35] It was found that 14% of "lower-class" blacks, 31% of "middle-class" blacks, and 45% of "upper-class" blacks held militant orientations ("middle" and "upper" correspond to relative distinctions among blacks, not to their positions in American class structure overall) opposite to that which would be expected from a Marxian viewpoint. Our interpretation is that deprivation in the lower class may not lead to militant attitudes and activity because deprivation for this stratum is so severe and basic that it forces one to attend almost exclusively to the day-to-day problems of deprivation. Other concerns become secondary by necessity. The development of militant orientations requires the expenditure of at least some time and energy after the basic economic essentials of life have been provided for. But eking out a living from day to day is so debilitating that most farm workers have little time or energy left for orientations and actions that are not designed to bring immediate changes to their economic situations. Even when time is available (e.g., because work is not available) we suggest that farm workers (and perhaps most of the poor) are too concerned with finding work and with sheer economic survival to care about actions and programs that may lead to a modification of their economic and social situations in the distant future.

Notes

1. Robert K. Merton, *Social Theory and Social Structure*, rev. and enlr. ed. (New York: The Free Press, 1957), pp. 131-94. The original statement appeared in "Social Structure and Anomie," *American Sociological Review*, III (October 1938), 672-82. See also Robert K. Merton, "Anomia, Anomie, and Social

Interaction: Contexts of Deviant Behavior," in Marshall B. Clinard, ed., *Anomie and Deviant Behavior: A Discussion and Critique* (New York: The Free Press, 1964), pp. 243-82.

2. Ibid. (*Social Theory . . .*), p. 162.

3. In presenting these hypotheses we do not imply that no other conditions are mentioned in Merton's formulation or that the relationships in these hypotheses are not influenced by them. See ibid., p. 175. We should also note that these hypotheses represent our own construction of Merton's statement. For each hypothesis questions may exist as to whether it is an accurate rendering of Merton's formulation. Our primary concern, however, is not with whether we have stated these hypotheses precisely as Merton did, but whether they are valid. All are plausible hypotheses and, although they are based on our interpretation of Merton's work, they are no less plausible even if our interpretation of Merton's work is subject to debate.

4. Ibid., p. 137.

5. See Richard Centers and Hadley Cantril, "Income Satisfaction and Income Aspiration," *Journal of Abnormal and Social Psychology*, XLI (January 1946), 64-69; Genevieve Knupfer, "Portrait of the Underdog," and Herbert H. Hyman, "The Value Systems of Different Classes: A Social Psychological Contribution to the Analysis of Stratification," both in Reinhard Bendix and Seymour M. Lipset, eds., *Class, Status, and Power: A Reader in Social Stratification* (New York: The Free Press, 1953), pp. 255-63, 426-42; Ephraim H. Mizruchi, "Aspiration and Poverty: A Neglected Aspect of Merton's Anomie," *Sociological Quarterly*, VIII (Autumn 1967), 439-46; and Audrey Wendling and Delbert S. Elliott, "Class and Race Differentials in Parental Aspirations and Expectations," *Pacific Sociological Review*, II (Fall, 1968), 126-36. See also Seymour M. Lipset and Reinhard Bendix, *Social Mobility in Industrial Society* (Berkeley: University of California Press, 1959), pp. 286-87; and Talcott Parsons, "A Revised Analytical Approach to the Theory of Social Stratification," in Bendix and Lipset, *Class, Status and Power*, op. cit., p. 125.

6. Hyman (ibid.), pp. 491-93; see also Susan Keller and Marisa Zavallonni, "Ambition and Social Class: A Respecification," *Social Forces*, XLIII (October 1964), 58-70.

7. See Centers and Cantril, op. cit.; Hyman, op. cit.; Wendling and Elliott, op. cit.; William S. Bennett, Jr. and Noel P. Gist, "Class and Family Influences on Student Aspirations," *Social Forces*, XLIII (December 1964) 167-73.

8. School-age children were defined as children between 6 and 16. Only 454 workers reported children currently living with them in this age range. The precise validity of this figure may be questioned because in some states workers have been accused of allowing or coercing their children to work in the fields (Karl Koos, *They Follow the Sun* [Jacksonville: Bureau of Maternal and Child Health, Florida State Board of Health, 1957]) and may have concealed the fact that children were living with them. Although we detected no evidence of

children at work and have no other data that would question the validity of the responses given, workers may well have concealed the presence of children to interviewers. However, given the cramped living quarters of most workers, this is unlikely.

9. There is the question of how much fantasy enters these responses, and the extent to which workers are actually *committed* to the idea of a college education for their children. The issue is difficult to assess and is not unrelated to the perennial question of whether there is any necessary relationship between verbal statements and overt behavior. (For a general statement, see Melvin L. DeFleur and Frank R. Westie, "Verbal Attitudes and Overt Acts," *American Sociological Review*, XXIII [December 1958], 667-73; and for a review of the evidence see Lyle G. Warner and Melvin L. DeFleur, "Attitudes as an Interactional Concept: Social Constraint and Social Distance as Intervening Variables between Attitudes and Actions," *American Sociological Review*, XXXIV [April 1969], 153-69. In specific reference to the lower class, Haggstrom has stated the problem as follows: "the poor frequently verbalize middle-class values without practicing them. Their verbalizations are useful in protecting their self-conceptions and in dealing with the affluent rather than in any pronounced relationship to non-verbal behavior. This does not imply deliberate falsification; a poor person may have the necessary sincerity, intention, and skill to embark on a course of action but there is so much unconscious uncertainty about achieving psychological returns through success that the action may never be seriously attempted." Warren C. Haggstrom, "The Power of the Poor," in Frank Reissman, Jerome Cohen, and Arthur Pearl, eds., *Mental Health of the Poor* (New York: The Free Press, 1964), p. 216. Indeed, study interviewers felt that for many workers the term "college" was a vague concept and did not imply the same specific commitment that the term did for farmers. Consequently, endorsement of college education by many workers, in contrast to farmers, may represent little more than verbal allegiance to middle-class standards. But this does not mean that lower-class persons who endorse such goals do not *want* them; one can want something and still recognize realistic constraints which prevent him from achieving it. Indeed, as we shall see in Chapters 8 and 9, differences in aspirations within farm workers are associated with perceived opportunity.

10. Merton, *Social Theory . . .*, op. cit., p. 157; and Hyman Rodman, "The Lower-Class Value Stretch," in Louis A. Ferman, Joyce L. Kornbluh, and Alan Haber, eds., *Poverty in America* (Ann Arbor: University of Michigan Press, 1965), pp. 270-84.

11. This question and the next are taken from Hadley Cantril, "A Study of Aspirations," *Scientific American*, CCVIII (January 1963), 41-45.

12. Ephriam Mizruchi, *Success and Opportunity: Class Values and Anomie in American Life* (London: The Free Press, Collier-MacMillan Limited, 1964), 72.

13. Vidich and Benson state, for example, that for a major segment of the

"middle-class" in "Springdale," home ownership has top priority in expenditure of income, and home improvement also ranks high in the scale of values. Arthur J. Vidich and Joseph Benson, *Small Town in Mass Society: Class, Power, and Religion in a Rural Community* (Garden City, N.Y.: Doubleday & Company, Inc., 1958), p. 58. Also, Lipset and Bendix comment: "A man who can buy his own house will feel that he has moved up in the world even if he has not changed his occupational position." Op. cit., p. 109.

14. This is the goal emphasized in Merton's original analysis. See his *Social Theory . . .* , op. cit., pp. 136-37.

15. This figure is for the three cultural groups combined in contrast to the figure for anglo-Americans (see p. 52).

16. Hyman, op. cit., pp. 492-93; and Keller and Zavallonni, op. cit.

17. Such an orientation would appear to be consistent with cultural values in the United States, that is, one should continue to work hard and improve himself. This is not to say, however, that such an orientation leads to the ultimate satisfaction of life, and it is in this sense that many have described American culture as essentially alienating. See, for example, Eric Fromm, *The Sane Society* (New York: Holt, Rinehart and Winston, 1955), esp. pp. 134-36. This orientation which Fromm describes as the "receptive orientation" (p. 136), was characterized by Durkheim as the "disease of the infinity" and was considered to be major determinant of suicide. See Emile Durkheim, *Suicide, A Study in Sociology* (New York: The Free Press, 1951). Mizruchi (op. cit.) argues that this is a major dynamic of alienation (anomia) in the middle class; we will have more to say about this in the next two chapters.

18. See Elizabeth Herzog, "Some Assumptions about the Poor," *Social Service Review*, XXXVII (December 1963) 391-400; and Lawrence L. LeShan, "Time Orientation and Social Class," *Journal of Abnormal and Social Psychology*, XLVII (June 1952), 589-92.

19. An alternative interpretation of the tendency for lower-class persons to "live for today" is that they have weak "impulse control" and are unable to "defer gratification," which some claim is due to class differences in child training and socialization. See, for example, Allison Davis, "Social Class and Color Differences in Child-Rearing," *American Sociological Review*, XI (December 1946), 698-710.

20. Haggstrom, op. cit., pp. 206-7.

21. Report by the President's National Advisory Commission on Rural Poverty, *The People Left Behind* (Washington, D.C.: U.S. Government Printing Office, 1967, p. 8 (emphasis added).

22. In a similar vein, Keller and Zavallonni suggest "that before lower-class individuals seriously pursue prestige or power goals in the society at large, they must first concentrate on getting and holding jobs . . . " (op. cit., p. 66).

23. The problem stemmed from an oversight by the author in issuing instructions to coders. (By the time the omission was discovered, the author had

moved and the original interview data were lost in process.) There were other differences between anglos and Mexican-Americans, but these involved only a few members of either group. For example, several Mexican-Americans mentioned the wish for more babies and a happy family life, but no anglos wanted more babies and less than 1% mentioned the wish for a happy family life. On the basis of interviews with 65 Mexican-Americans from four southwestern states, Ulibarri concluded: "The most obvious and intense concern of the total group was in the area of earning a living. Usually, the greater part of the interview was related to the problems of earning a living and the difficulties encountered in providing adequately for their families." Horacio Ulibarri, "Social and Attitudinal Characteristics of Spanish-Speaking Migrant and Ex-Migrant Workers in the Southwest," in John H. Burma, ed., *Mexican-Americans in the United States: A Reader* (New York: Harper & Row, 1970), p. 32.

24. On balance, of course, results are somewhat more consistent with the hypothesis of a class difference. Hypotheses which emphasize universalistic goal orientations are refuted by the evidence inasmuch as there *is* a class difference in goals and aspirations. At the same time, however, the fact that the values and goals of a substantial proportion of lower-class farm workers resemble those of farmers cannot be ignored.

25. See Michael Mann, "The Social Cohesion of Liberal Democracy," *American Sociological Review*, XXXV (June 1970), 423-39.

26. The problem is apparently not confined to students of modern society; it may apply equally to students of simple societies. The presence of contradictory patterns in such societies was noted years ago by Bronislaw Malinowski, although his caveat has often been ignored by many of his sociological descendents. See his *Crime and Custom in Savage Society* (Paterson, N.J.: Littlefield, Adams and Company, 1962 (originally published by Routledge & Kegan Paul Ltd., London, 1925). The problem is illustrated by anthropological studies of preliterate societies in which different observers come away with different and sometimes conflicting conclusions. Studies of the Hopi are an example. David F. Aberle states that, "Hopi society is often described as peaceful, harmonious, and operating with a minimum of physician coercion, yet child rearing is said to be repressive and adult life constrained, and the Hopi are often characterized as anxious, mistrustful, and full of suppressed hostility." He continues, however, by saying that the explanation is not that one or the other pattern exists and that the truth does not just lie "somewhere in between," but that both patterns exist. See David F. Aberle, "The Psychological Analysis of a Hopi Life History," *Comparative Psychology Monographs*, XXI (1951), 1. If this is true for societies such as the Hopi, it is even more likely to occur in a complex society such as the United States. If farm workers are representative, contradictory patterns exist within the entire lower class in the United States. S.M. Miller, "The American Lower Classes: A Typological Approach," in Frank Reissman, Jerome Cohen, and Arthur Cohen, eds., *Mental Health of the Poor* (New York: The Free Press, 1964), p. 151.

27. Miller, op. cit., p. 151. See also Thomas Gladwin, *Poverty U.S.A.* (Boston: Little, Brown & Company, 1968), esp. p. 73; Peter H. Rossi and Zahava A. Blum, "Class, Status, and Poverty," in Daniel P. Moynihan, ed., *On Understanding Poverty: Perspectives from the Social Sciences,* (New York: Basic Books, Inc., 1968), I, 36-63; and Leonard Reissman and Michael N. Halstead, "The Subject is Class," *Sociology and Social Research,* LIV (April 1970), 293-305.

28. Elliott Liebow, *Tally's Corner: A Study of Negro Streetcorner Men* (Boston: Little, Brown & Company, 1967), p. 211, n. 3.

29. These two questions were in a series of ten questions concerned with commitment to work, occupation, and job and which were designed to form a scale of "occupational primacy." Several were adapted from other studies of "occupational primacy," i.e., Joseph A. Kahl, "Some Measurements of Achievement Orientation," *American Journal of Sociology,* LXX (May 1955), 670-71; and idem, *The Measurement of Modernism: A Study of Values in Brazil and Mexico* (Austin: The University of Texas Press, 1968), p. 19. The other eight questions are:

3. When looking for a job, do you think a person should find a job in a place located near his parents, even if it means turning down a good job in another place? [Reverse scored.]
4. Do you think the best way to judge a man is by the job he has?
5. Would you say that the most important qualities of a real man are determination, great ambition and hard work?
6. Some say that Americans place too much importance on occupational success. Do you think so? [Reverse scored.]
7. Do you think a man should always try to get farther ahead in the world than his parents, regardless of how hard he has to work?
8. Do you think the job should come first, even if it means giving up time for recreation?
9. Do you think you would turn down a much better paying job than you now have if it meant being away from your family a lot more? [Reverse scored.]
10. Do you think a man ought to continue to try to get ahead and to make more money no matter how well off he is or how much money he has, even if he has to work real hard to do so?

The total scale (theoretical maximum score is 10, the minimum is 0) produced no meaningful results. For example, average scores are 4.21 for farmers, and 4.70, 5.23, and 4.22 for anglo-American, bilingual, and non-English speaking farm workers, respectively. Moreover, although several individual items are significantly related to class (occupation), income, or ethnic status, no meaningful overall pattern can be discerned.

30. Keller and Zavallonni (op. cit., p. 65) state: "For those who cannot take security for granted it may not only loom as important but it may overshadow all other claims and ambition. However, this striving for security in the lower class is striving to attain something one does not have and is thus different in

nature from the similar striving among middle-class individuals. Economic security (not wealth) is taken for granted in the middle-class where everyone has a job, goes to work, can afford a car, a vacation, and adequate housing. In the lower class this much cannot be taken for granted—unemployment, being laid off from work, plant shutdowns, etc. are familiar and dreaded experiences. The drive for security is thus in a very real sense comparable to the middle-class drive for respectability—it is something to be achieved and carefully guarded."

31. Kahl and Hamblin suggest that successful men take their success more for granted and hence "turn their attention to the 'higher things of life,' " Joseph A. Kahl and Robert L. Hamblin, "Socioeconomic Status and Ideological Attitudes: A Nonlinear Pattern" (unpublished manuscript, 1961, cited in Kahl, "Some Measurements . . . " op. cit., pp. 671-72). Miller distinguishes between the "insecure" lower-class (prolonged unemployment, irregular employment, and low income) in contrast to the "secure" lower class. S.M. Miller, "The American Lower Classes: A Typological Approach," in Reissman, Cohen, and Pearl, op. cit., pp. 139-54. To the extent that this is a valid distinction, farm workers would belong to the "insecure" category. Findings, therefore, may be true for only one segment of the lower class.

32. It is doubtful that results are due to the farm workers' greater tendency to acquiesce. First, if acquiescence were the explanation, it would influence the total scale score as well as responses to individual items. We have seen, however, that total scale scores are not necessarily higher among farm workers (non-English speakers have almost the identical scale score as farmers—see note 29, above). Moreover, inspection of patterns of responses to individual items reveals no consistent tendency for "yes" responses to be higher for farm workers or to be inversely related to ethnic status or income level of farm workers. For example, on two questions, non-English speakers and farmers give exactly the same proportion of affirmative responses, both of which are significantly higher than those given by anglo-Americans and bilinguals. One question was, "Do you think you would turn down a much better paying job than the one you now have if it meant being away from your family a lot more?" Percentages of affirmative responses were 69% for farmers and non-English speaking farm workers, and 53% and 43% for anglo-Americans and bilinguals. Obviously, such a pattern could not result from the greater tendency among farm workers to "yeasay."

33. Specific reference here is to the functionalist framework of Radcliffe-Brown, which although not a theory of social stratification per se, is a general theory of social structure and, hence, includes stratification. See A.R. Radcliffe-Brown, *Structure and Function in Primitive Society* (New York: The Free Press, 1952), esp. pp. 1-14.

34. Robert Coles' comments about rural Mississippi Negroes are relevant here. In discussing the case of Ruth, who is the wife of a sharecropper, mother of several children, cook, and maid in an affluent white landowner's home, Coles

states: "Life is hard and even brutal for Ruth, and to survive has cost her a lot. But . . . in the words of contemporary psychoanalysis, her mind has learned to be 'adaptive'—and so has her overworked, tired body. . . . [She] goes back and forth between two worlds; everyday she does. . . . She doesn't get 'overinvolved,' though. When she and they [landowner's family] part company she knows how to go back to her own life and live it. If she has 'fantasies' about her life over there in The House, she controls them, buries them, or more likely, lets them quietly come and quickly go. (Oh, every once in awhile I ask myself why God did things the way He did and made me me and her [landowner's wife] her; but pretty soon *there's the next thing I have to tend to.*')" Robert Coles, "Whose Strength, Whose Weakness?" *The American Scholar*, XXXVII (Autumn 1968), 613-14; emphasis added. For "Ruth" and her family to survive, she must do many things—cook for her family, care for her own children, wash her own family's clothes, etc., as well as cook, babysit, and wash for the landowner's family. The obvious implication: there is little time left to aspire to the middle-class "goals of monetary success."

35. Gary T. Marx, *Protest and Prejudice* (New York: Harper & Row, 1967).

8   Class, Culture and Opportunity: Contexts of Normlessness

In this chapter we will investigate the second and third hypotheses which were presented in the previous chapter. The second stipulates a relationship between class and perceived opportunity regardless of level of aspiration. As an adjunct, we want to know whether there are cultural differences among farm workers in this particular relationship.

The third hypothesis is concerned with the relationship of social class and perceived opportunity to normlessness. This is the crucial hypothesis in our theory since Merton's primary concern is with explaining deviance and normative estrangement in the lower class, traits which he contends are due to class differences in denied or blocked opportunity. In our formulation, perceived opportunity is an intervening variable in the relationship between class and normlessness. Thus, the theory anticipates no particular relationship between class and normlessness if there are no class differences in perceived opportunity. Consequently, if there is a (negative) correlation between social class and normlessness, we would expect the correlation to decrease in magnitude when perceived opportunity is statistically controlled. But, since most studies of the relationship between social class and deviance and attitudinal measures of normative estrangement have generally failed to include measures of perceived opportunity, the separate effects of class and perceived opportunity have heretofore not been examined.

In addition, cultural differences may influence the relationships proposed in the third hypothesis. Since we did not study middle-class groups of Mexican-Americans we will be unable to investigate cultural differences in the relationship between social class and normlessness. However, we can investigate cultural differences in the relationship between perceived opportunity and normlessness among lower-class farm workers. This will permit us to compare the influence of the class and cultural contexts on the relationship between perceived opportunity and normlessness, and thus to assess "opportunity theory" as primarily a "class theory" or a "cultural theory." If we find no difference between classes in the relationship between perceived opportunity and normlessness but do find significant differences between the cultural groups in this relationship, we will be able to say that the influence of perceived opportunity on normlessness should be viewed from a cultural perspective rather than a class perspective.

In addition to these issues, we will also investigate the relationship between cultural assimilation and normlessness, which we presented in Chapter 6. However, we will now control for perceived opportunity. If our hypothesis that

127

normlessness is one element in an assimilation syndrome is valid, normlessness should be inversely related to cultural assimilation even when perceived opportunity is statistically controlled.

Social Class, Culture, and Opportunity

Theoretically, opportunity to realize one's aspirations can be just as limited for persons whose aspirations are low as for persons whose aspirations are high. According to our hypothesis, in any population even if there is a smaller proportion of lower-class persons than middle- and upper-class persons who have middle- to upper-class aspirations, there should be a larger proportion of the lower class who perceive their opportunities to be blocked.[1] In our study, however, such perception would presumably be most probable among farm workers who have assimilated middle-class goals. We have seen that the assimilation of middle-class goals does penetrate to the workers' level. That some workers perceive their opportunities as limited is exemplified in the remarks of a farm worker in response to the question about his hopes for the future:

I'd like to have a lot of money, a good job, a nice home, a place to live. That would make a man happy. There's no way to get that.

Moreover, perception of denied opportunity is not limited to isolated cases. After respondents were asked about their educational aspirations for their children, they were asked how good they thought the chances were that their children would receive the amount of education desired; possible responses were "very good," "fairly good," and "not good at all" (classified as "poor"). Results are reported in Table 8-1. Regardless of aspiration, farm workers perceive that their opportunities are more limited than do farmers. Thus, data support our second hypothesis, that is, the existence of class differences in perceived opportunity.[2]

But, let us note that no relationship exists between culture and perceived opportunity (see Table 8-1). Results are thus consistent with findings for culture and perceived deprivation in Chapter 6; culture has no apparent influence on either perceived deprivation or perceived opportunity. Both are largely a matter of position in the class structure, not ethnic-cultural group affiliation.

Opportunity, Normlessness, and the Class Context

Although Merton's primary concern is with normlessness in the lower class, the relationship between perceived opportunity and normlessness is crucial in his theory[3] because class differences in normlessness stem from class differences in

Table 8-1

Relationship of Class and Culture to Perceived Opportunity, in %, by Level of Aspiration

	College[a]				Less than College[a]			
	Very Good	Fairly Good	Poor	N	Very Good	Fairly Good	Poor	N
Farmers	59	39	2	110	75	25	–	12
Farm Workers								
Anglo-Americans	18	54	28	120	31	55	13[b]	67
Mexican-Americans	20	54	25[b]	157	30	54	16	99

[a]For college category, X^2 = 51.13 between farmers and anglo-American farm workers ($p <$ 001; 2 df); for less than college, X^2 = 8.23 ($p < .01$; 1 df–nine farm workers in "poor" category combined with "fairly good").

[b]Row does not add to 100% because of rounding.

opportunity. Those who perceive their opportunities as unequal ("blocked") are more apt to be normatively alienated than those who do not. This is so because of the discrepancy between the value which American culture places on equal opportunity in principle and the fact that opportunities are unequal in practice. This formulation has become a popular but much criticized theory of deviate behavior. Several attempts have been made to extend and integrate it with other theories,[4] and a number of research studies have been construed as bearing upon it.[5] In addition, the formulation "rings true" for many; intuitively, it is a plausible explanation for much deviant behavior in the United States.

Among the criticisms which have been made of this theory, we will mention four. One is that the theory oversimplifies a very complex phenomenon—the relationship between the class structure and deviant behavior.[6] The criticism is valid, but then the same criticism can be made of virtually any theory about society and social behavior (or anything else for that matter). Any generalization about reality is an oversimplification of reality. To say that unequal opportunity is a significant factor in class differences in deviant behavior and normative estrangement is not to say that there are no other factors involved or even that this is the only factor in the influence of social class; also, this does not deny that the processes of deviance and their consequences are important. The theory, however, does not address itself to these other issues but is concerned with class differences in normative estrangement and postulates that unequal opportunity is a significant factor in these differences.

A second criticism maintains that Merton's distinction between culture and social structure is largely artificial, and cannot be usefully maintained in the analysis of data. This criticism seems to derive from Merton's claim that culture "defines, regulates and controls" behavior while, at the same time, he uses culture "to describe modal tendencies in the behavior" of persons in society,[7] such as most Americans aspiring to the same materialistic success goals. Merton does claim that Americans believe that materialistic success goals are (and should be) universalistic (open to all); and he may imply that the behavior pattern that is consistent with this principle constitutes evidence for widespread belief in this principle. The reasoning is circular of course and is the source of the criticism. But it is not the pursuit of cultural goals that Merton wishes to explain. He wants to explain deviant behavior in the American lower class and the cultural emphasis on universalistic goals is one element of the explanation.[8] In this writer's opinion the place of culture in Merton's formulation should be viewed as follows. First, the emphasis on the principles of universalistic goals and equal opportunity are the primary cultural variables. These are taken as given for the United States; no effort is made to account for them. Under these cultural conditions a relationship between perceived blocked opportunity and normative alienation is expected; when belief in these principles is not widespread in a society such a relationship is not anticipated. In such a formulation the distinction between class structure and culture is certainly not artificial; each variable is clearly distinguished from the other. Individuals with different cultural backgrounds may be equal in terms of actual and perceived opportunity.

Third, some criticize Merton's theory because it is limited to explaining lower-class deviance and normlessness and ignores the higher strata.[9] As will become clear below, we do not agree with this criticism. (Even if true it is a *limitation* of the theory more than a criticism of the logical or empirical adequacy of the theory for explaining lower-class deviance-normlessness.) However, the theory does emphasize lower-class behavior and attitudes, and this may create a problem because the cultural context in which the theory is held to be valid may not receive its proper attention.

Finally, the theory has been criticized because there is little direct evidence to support it. Some critics claim it is invalid because the goals and aspirations of lower-class groups are lower than those of middle- and upper-class groups.[10] In addition, studies which show that crime and delinquency vary inversely with class status[11] do not constitute direct support for the theory because social classes differ with respect to a number of factors, many of which could theoretically account for the class differences in crime and delinquency. Also, even though opportunities are fewer in the lower than in the middle and upper strata, individuals in the lower stratum who are deviants may not have the most limited opportunities although the theory implies that they do. Moreover, as noted in Chapter 5, most attitudinal measures that have been developed[12] appear not to measure the precise attitude that Merton's formulation implies. And, conclusions about the significance of class differences in opportunity have been based on the assumption that the goals of different classes are similar;[13] however, considering the fact that aspirations and goals may be different for different classes, the validity of this assumption may be questioned.[14]

On balance, then, there is little evidence to provide direct support for the class-opportunity hypothesis of deviance and normative estrangement. At the same time, however, there is very little evidence that clearly contradicts the hypothesis either, and some studies do provide at least some tenuous support for it.[15] Quite simply, too few data bear on the relationship between class and deviance-normlessness as this relationship is mediated by perceived opportunity.

A test for the relationship between social class and normlessness requires measures of both social class and perceived opportunity. If denied opportunity is the significant factor in the class influence, then the correlation between class and normlessness should disappear or be considerably reduced when perceived opportunity is controlled. To test this possibility Gamma coefficients have been computed between class (farmers and farm workers) and normlessness for different levels of perceived opportunity.

As noted above, after respondents had been asked about the educational aspirations for their children (see pp. 109-10), they were asked how good they thought the chances were that their children would be able to get the amount of education desired; response alternatives were "very good," "fairly good," and "not good at all" (classified as "poor"). Because so few farmers gave "poor" responses, the second and third groups of responses were combined. Hence, the correlation between class and normlessness was derived for only two levels of perceived opportunity. As in the previous analysis (see p. 95), normlessness scores were divided into low, medium, and high (0, 1, and 2-6).

For all respondents who responded to the perceived educational opportunity questions, the Gamma between class and normlessness is −.39 (a negative Gamma indicates that normlessness is higher among farm workers). We found that there is little difference in the Gammas between class and normlessness for persons in the two perceived opportunity categories. Gammas are −.38 for those in the "very good" category (N = 117) and −.32 for those in the "fairly good" category (N = 186). Thus, the relationship between class and normlessness cannot be due to perceived opportunity; indeed, on the basis of these results, we can say that perceived opportunity appears not to contribute to the social class-normlessness relationship at all. (Nor is the relationship between class and normlessness influenced by aspirations, since Gammas are −.38 and −.40, respectively, for those who want a college education for their children [N = 227] and those who do not [N = 79].)

Consequently, to the extent that Merton's theory explains the high rate of normlessness in the lower class, our results provide little support; the relationship between social class and normlessness is independent of perceived opportunity. However, statements indicate that the theory is concerned with the sources of normative alienation and deviance in the United States *in general*, not just in the lower class.[16] In any case, there is nothing in the logic of the hypothesis that precludes a relationship between perceived opportunity and normlessness for all levels of the class structure. Indeed, this is the crucial hypothesis, with the proposed relationship between social class and normlessness being a corollary. The most significant factor should be the contradiction between the principle of equal opportunity and the fact of unequal opportunity. If this is so, the relationship between perceived denied opportunity and normlessness in the middle and upper classes will be no different from the relationship in the lower class. The source and dynamics of normative estrangement, as they are related to denied opportunity, may be cultural phenomena that transcend class boundaries.

According to Merton, aspiration may be an important factor in the relationship between denied opportunity and normlessness.[17] Consequently, the relationship may exist for lower-class persons who have middle-class aspirations but not for lower-class persons who have less lofty aspirations. We will refer to those who want a college education for their children as *aspirants* and to those who want less than a college education as *nonaspirants*. Evidence in Table 8-2 indicates that the relationship does hold for the aspiring workers but not for the nonaspiring workers: the Gamma for farm worker aspirants is −.28, that for nonaspirants −.07.

Note that virtually the same result is obtained for aspiring farmers, for whom

Table 8-2
Relationship between Perceived Opportunity and Normlessness, by Class and Level of Aspiration (College or Less Than College Education), in %

| | Farmers: Aspirants Perceived Opportunity | | | | Farm Workers: Aspirants Perceived Opportunity | | | |
	Very Good	Fairly Good	Poor	N	Very Good	Fairly Good	Poor	N
Normlessness								
High (2-6)	27	64	9	11	11	56	33	44
Medium (1)	59	41	−	39	18	50	32	38
Low (0)	66	32	2	59	25	59	16	36
Gamma		−.32*				−.28*		

| | Farmer: Nonaspirants Perceived Opportunity | | | | Farm Workers: Nonaspirants Perceived Opportunity | | | |
	Very Good	Fairly Good	Poor	N	Very Good	Fairly Good	Poor	N
Normlessness								
High (2-6)	100	−	−	1	27	58	15	26
Medium (1)	100	−	−	6	40	45	15	20
Low (0)	40	60	−	5	29	62	10	21[a]
Gamma		+1.00				−.07		

*Significant at the .001 level of significance or beyond (one-tail test).
[a]Adds to more than 100% because of rounding.

Gamma is $-.32$. For nonaspiring farmers the Gamma is in the opposite (positive) direction, but the number of cases (twelve cases for nine cells) makes this result meaningless. Nevertheless, the fact that a negative relationship exists for aspirants of both classes indicates that the influence of perceived denied opportunity on normlessness transcends class boundaries in the United States and is not specific to the lower class. The most significant factor may be American culture rather than the class structure.[18]

Opportunity, Normlessness, and the Cultural Context

The significance of cultural differences has not received much attention in discussions of Merton's theory. Implicit throughout Merton's own statements, however, is a cross-cultural perspective. Indeed, the importance Merton attaches to American cultural ideology requires that the postulated relationship between opportunity and normative estrangement be viewed within a particular cultural context. It would not appear to be blocked opportunity per se that leads to normative estrangement, but blocked opportunity in a cultural setting wherein achievement criteria rather than ascriptive criteria are emphasized. Merton states:

there is something peculiar about the emphasis on success in *an open-class society*. Aspirations for place, recognition, wealth, and socially prized accomplishments are culturally held to be appropriate for all, whatever their origins or present conditions. To a degree not true of other types of society, people are expected to reach out for worldly success. The emphasis may be assimilated in varying degree by those occupying different positions in the social structure. Nevertheless, the accent on success is more widespread than in a society where *ascribed* status dominates. ... American society comes as close as any in history to arguing that going up in the world is an absolute value. And here we come to an untidy paradox we would do better to acknowledge rather than explain away. Precisely because the opportunity-structure is comparatively open, substantial numbers of men in each social stratum aspire to worldly success. ... Yet we know that in this same society that proclaims the right, and even the duty of lofty aspirations for all, men do not have equal access to the opportunity structure. Social origins do variously facilitate or hamper access to the forms of success represented by wealth or recognition or substantial power. Confronted with this contradiction in experience, appreciable numbers of people become estranged from a society that promises them in principle what they are denied in reality.[19]

In short, blocked opportunities to realize one's aspirations are most apt to lead to normative estrangement in societies which emphasize universalistic goal orientations and achieved rather than ascribed status, and wherein the ideology of equal opportunity is institutionalized in cultural mythology more than in actual fact. Only then does blocked opportunity lead to a contradiction in experience.

This particular hypothesis does not deal with cultural differences in the level of normative estrangement itself but stipulates that the relationship between perceived opportunity and normative estrangement varies depending on the relative cultural emphasis given to achieved status and equal opportunity. The two hypotheses do not emerge merely from different theoretical formulations; they require different methods of procedure. If one wants to explore cultural differences in normlessness, the appropriate procedure is to examine the relationship between cultural differences and normlessness and, when possible, to control for other relevant variables; this we will do in the next section. Let us note, however, that we must control for culture when we assess cultural differences in the relationship between perceived opportunity and normlessness. We will do this by examining the relationship for different cultural groups.[20]

Although Merton does not explicitly address himself to cultural differences within the United States, his rationale for differences *between* societies may be extended to cultural groups *within* society. Both study groups of Mexican-Americans originate from a society wherein the cultural ideology concerning equal opportunity differs from that of the United States; certainly such an ideology is not imbedded in the cultural tradition of Mexico, or of Latin America generally, to the extent that it is in the United States. We would also expect variations between the two Mexican-American groups because of the language difference. Bilinguals are more assimilated and therefore more apt to be influenced than non-English speakers by the ideology of achieved status and the mythology of equal opportunity.

The above quote from Merton makes it clear that his theory is specific to achievement-oriented societies which emphasize an open-class system ideology and it postulates that when people of such a society are denied opportunity they suffer a contradiction in experience and thus become normatively estranged from society. This suggests that blocked opportunity per se is less important than how blocked opportunity is *interpreted*, and that such interpretation will differ depending upon one's cultural background. That is, the (perceived) opportunity structure and culture may interact in their effects on normlessness. Specifically, in our study, the negative correlation between perceived opportunity and normlessness should be highest for anglo-Americans and lowest for non-English speakers, with bilinguals in between.

In presenting this hypothesis, we do not claim that individuals are necessarily conscious or aware of the contradiction in experience. Indeed, there may be no cultural differences in the proportion who give verbal allegiance to the principle of achieved status. We say only that there are differences in cultural ideology between the United States and Mexico which determines how members of the three groups respond to perceived blocked opportunity.

John Gillin draws the following contrasts between the cultures of the United States and those of Latin America, including Mexico: In the United States the culture stresses that each individual "has the right to 'an equal chance' or opportunity with other persons" and does not encourage the individual to accept his place in the social order.[21] Indeed, he is expected to improve his position in the class structure. In Latin America, however, although the individual "may rise in the social scale . . . , [he] recognizes and accepts . . . his position in society. *He has no right to expect more.*"[22] Ascribed status is a dominant cultural principle. This is not to say that members of different cultures differ in terms of their *perception* of barriers to the achievement of desired goals and aspirations; as we have seen, there appear to be no differences in this perception. But, the individual's *interpretation* of existing barriers will differ depending on his cultural background. In ascriptive societies blocked opportunities are interpreted as part of the natural order whereas in achievement-oriented societies they are not.

If the above is valid, we would not expect Latin Americans to react to blocked perceived opportunity for their children in the same way that U.S. residents might. For them, blocked opportunity does not constitute a contradiction between personal experience and cultural ideology. As we have seen, however, blocked opportunity is important to American natives because opportunities in this country are supposed to be equal; therefore, one has a right to expect that opportunities will be equal. To perceive them as otherwise constitutes a contradiction between personal experience and cultural ideology, and any such contradiction may form the basis for attitudes of normative estrangement.

These reasons may be extended to the three cultural groups. Although the groups do not differ in educational aspirations and perceived opportunity (such differences appear to be more a function of class than culture), they may differ in their reactions to perceived blocked opportunity.

Our results are consistent with this hypothesis. Unlike our comparison between farmers and farm workers wherein results were based only on perceived educational opportunity, we have compared farm workers for perceived educational and occupational opportunity. Results based on perceived educational opportunity are presented in Table 8-3. This table shows no significant relationship for any group among the nonaspiring, and among the aspiring the only significant relationship is that for anglo-Americans. Results are somewhat different for occupational opportunity, although they are consistent with the hypothesis of cultural differences in the effect of perceived denied opportunity. After respondents had been asked whether they wanted their children to become farm workers[23] they were asked what they thought the chances were that their children would end up in farm work (with alternative responses being "definitely yes," "probably yes," "definitely no," and "probably no"); affirmative responses were classified as "poor" perceived opportunity and negative responses as "good" perceived opportunity, as listed in Table 8-4. Note that all Gammas are statistically significant and moderately high in magnitude, but only for anglo-Americans and bilinguals are they negative.

Table 8-3

Gammas between Perceived Educational Opportunity and Normlessness,[a] by Culture and Level of Aspiration (College or Less than College Education), for Farm Workers

	College	N	Less Than College	N
Anglo-Americans	−.28*	118	−.07	67
Bilinguals	−.05	97	.01	51
Non-English Speakers	+.07	61	+.11	48

[a]For three categories of opportunity (good, fair, and poor) and three levels of normlessness (0, 1, 2-6).
*Significant at the .001 level (one-tail X^2 test).

It would seem, therefore, that the relationship between perceived opportunity and normlessness does vary by cultural status; results consistently reveal statistically significant negative relationships for anglo-Americans and no such relationships for non-English speakers, with both relationships for bilinguals being negative, of which one is statistically significant. Consequently, the findings support the hypothesis that the cultural interpretation given to perceived opportunity is crucial in normlessness and not perceived opportunity per se.

The relationship may require even further specification. It may exist only for persons whose aspirations are linked to middle-class goals. Because of the way the occupational aspiration and perceived opportunity questions are phrased, the meaning of responses to the perceived occupational opportunity question is not clear for the nonaspiring (that is, for those who want their children to enter farm work).[24] However, none of the Gammas between perceived opportunity and normlessness for the three groups of respondents who want less than a college education for their children is negative and statistically significant (see Table 8-3).[25]

To conclude, then, our results reveal that culture and perceived opportunity interact, and are thus consistent with our derivations from Merton's theory. Cultural interpretation appears to be an important contingency in the operation of perceived opportunity, and it is our hypothesis that differences in interpretation derive from cultural differences in the relative emphasis given to the principles of achieved status and ascribed status.

The Contextual Effects of Opportunity

We want to explore one final issue in this chapter: the influence of perceived opportunity on the relationships between culture and normlessness. In Chapter 6

Table 8-4

Relationship between Perceived Occupational Opportunity and Normlessness, in %, by Cultural Group, for Farm Workers Who Want Something Other Than Farm Work for Their Children

	Anglo-Americans: Perceived Opportunity			Bilinguals: Perceived Opportunity			Non-English Speakers: Perceived Opportunity		
	Good	Poor	N	Good	Poor	N	Good	Poor	N
Normlessness									
High (2-6)	82	18	55	87	13	23	57	43	7
Medium (1)	90	10	51	72	28	46	68	32	28
Low (0)	67	45	45	41	59	59	81	19	62
Gamma		−.28*			−.57*			+.36[a]	

*Significant at the .001 level of significance or beyond (one-tail test).

[a]Contrary to predicted direction.

we observed that the inverse correlation between cultural assimilation or commitment remains unchanged even when perceived deprivation is statistically controlled. Results are different when perceived opportunity is controlled. Table 8-5 reveals that the realtionship is closer when perceived occupational opportunity is good (−.51) than when it is poor (−.11). Findings for perceived educational opportunity are similar; the magnitude of Gamma consistently decreases from good to poor perceived opportunity. In both cases, then, the relationship between culture and normlessness is closest when the opportunity structure is perceived as being open.[26]

Results indicate, then, that the process of normative estrangement, insofar as it is inversely associated with cultural assimilation, is not a matter of cultural assimilation per se since the extent to which the two variables are related depends on perceived opportunity. Cultural commitment involves a corresponding decrease in normlessness only when the (perceived) constraints of poor educational and occupational opportunities are eliminated or reduced. This means, therefore, that cultural assimilation and the perceived opportunity structure interact; the effects of cultural assimilation are not uniform but depend on conditions of the opportunity structure. In order for differences in cultural assimilation to exert an effect on normative estrangement, the opportunity structure must be open (at least as reflected in people's perceptions) or the constraints of the class structure would presumably be strong enough to override the effects of cultural commitment. Just as culture influences the effects of opportunity, so does the opportunity structure (or the perception thereof) influence the effects of culture. Consequently, there are two types of interactive effects between culture and opportunity.

Conclusion

The principle of equal opportunity is one of the major aspects (perhaps it is the central aspect) of the democratic ideology of the United States. It has also been

Table 8-5
Gammas between Cultural Assimilation and Normlessness,[a] by Perceived Opportunity, for Farm Workers

| | Perceived Occupational Opportunity | | Perceived Educational Opportunity | | |
	Good	Poor	Very Good	Fairly Poor	Poor
	−.51*	−.11	−.51*	−.40*	−.25*
N	271	105	106	240	96

[a]For three levels of normlessness (0, 1, 2-6).
*Significant at the .01 level or beyond (two-tail test).

cited as a principle that exposes important contradictions in the social structure and the hypocrisy that is often said to characterize American society. The problem is particularly acute, of course, for persons at the bottom of the class structure, as much literature attests. Rossi and Blum state: "The common thread running through [the literature on poverty] is the psychologically punishing situation of those on the bottom of a stratification system in a society that stresses achievement for all and universalism as a mode of selection for occupational placement."[27] Rossi and Blum caution, however, that "there is no reason to restrict this process only to those on the very bottom of the stratification hierarchy."[28] Since our findings reveal that the relationship between perceived opportunity and normlessness exists in both classes and does not diminish in strength in the higher classes, our results are consistent with this general perspective. Factors (in this case, perceived opportunity) that influence persons in the lower class also have an effect on individuals in the higher classes. Even though perceived opportunity is itself closely related to the class structure, its effects on normlessness are fairly constant regardless of the individual's location in the class structure. Thus, perceived blocked opportunity has the same meaning to individual persons at different places in the class structure. If this is so, the effect of perceived opportunity on normlessness cannot originate solely from the class structure itself but must originate from some other source. We propose that the source is the broader culture of society, specifically, the cultural emphasis that status should be achieved and the dicta that are implied in that emphasis—that the same goals are available to all and opportunities are equal for all.

Therefore, the cultural assimilation process may be viewed from two perspectives. One is that most members of the society in which the cultural minority lives possess certain attributes. Hence, Mexican-Americans become more like anglo-Americans in normative estrangement as they are assimilated. Second, however, assimilation may be viewed in more dynamic terms—the relationship between different attributes, here, that between perceived opportunity and normative estrangement. Therefore, although greater assimilation may lead to a reduction in level of normative estrangement, it increases the probability that certain factors will cause such estrangement.

Questions about class and cultural differences in normlessness must be distinguished from questions about class and cultural differences in the dynamics of normlessness—that is, the factors that are correlated with normlessness and are theoretical causes of it. *The dynamics may be similar for different classes even though both the level of normlessness and perceived opportunity may differ between classes.* But they may be different for different cultural groups who occupy similar positions in the class structure. The cultural ideology may pervade the class structure to such an extent that certain dynamic processes (in this instance, the effect of perceived opportunity on normlessness) are similar throughout the class structure for persons who are assimilated into that ideology.

Finally, results agree in part with both Merton's theory and some of the criticisms of his theory. Support is found for the criticism that the theory does not adequately explain class differences in deviance and normative estrangement. Indeed, according to our findings, perceived opportunity apparently has little if anything to do with class differences in estrangement. However, results do reveal that perceived denied opportunity is a significant factor in normlessness, and this is consistent with the theory. Moreover, we can say that the significance of perceived opportunity is based on cultural factors and not class factors. Thus, although results support the hypothesis of a relationship between perceived opportunity and normlessness, they reveal that the hypothesis should be viewed from a cultural rather than a social class perspective. As a "cultural hypothesis" it has validity, but as a "class hypothesis" it apparently does not.

Notes

1. Robert K. Merton, *Social Theory and Social Structure*, rev. and enlr. ed. (New York: The Free Press, 1957), p. 174. This may not be a correct statement of Merton's formulation, since he states that the theory is only concerned with class differences in *absolute* frequencies (p. 174). The *percentage* of lower-class persons who experience limited opportunity might be less than the percentage for the middle and upper strata, but the absolute number of persons who experience limited opportunity may be greater in the lower stratum (because the total number of lower-stratum persons may be much greater than the totals in other strata). We believe that Merton is only partially correct. If we are concerned with the *effects* of normlessness and deviant behavior (or other types of attitudes and behavior) on society, the absolute number of persons in different strata is the most significant factor. It is in this context that Merton states that absolute frequencies are more important than proportions (p. 175, n. 28). However, to the extent that we are concerned with the class-linked *sources* of normlessness and deviant behavior—and this seems to be the most central concern of the theory—then proportion is the most significant datum. Others have commented on the ambiguity that a focus on absolute frequencies imposes on the theory. See Ephraim H. Mizruchi, *Success and Opportunity: Class Values and Anomie* (New York: The Free Press, 1964), p. 134; and Judith Blake and Kingsley Davis, "Norms, Values and Sanctions," in Robert E.L. Faris, ed., *Handbook of Modern Sociology* (Chicago: Rand McNally, 1964), p. 474.

2. There is some similarity, of course, between perceived opportunity and our measure of relative deprivation. Relative deprivation, however, refers to the respondent's comparison of his performance or achievement with that of others in the community. Perceived opportunity, however, refers to how the individual perceives his opportunity to achieve something that he would like to achieve. For farmers there is a significant relationship between high and low scorers on

relative deprivation and perceived opportunity for their children to achieve college educations (X^2 = 8.64; $p < .02$; 2 df). However, for none of the three groups of farm workers is the relationship statistically significant.

3. A qualification may be in order here. Although this is the crucial hypothesis as we have reconstructed Merton's theory, let us remember that Merton's specific objective is to explain class variations in deviant *behavior*. Our focus, of course, is on attitudes rather than behavior; the degree to which normlessness and deviant behavior are associated (if at all) is unknown. Nevertheless, a concern with normlessness attitudes is not irrelevant to Merton's theory, as we have noted.

4. See Robert Dubin, "Deviant Behavior and Social Structure: Continuities in Social Theory," *American Sociological Review* XXIV (April 1959), 147-64; Richard A. Cloward, "Illegitimate Means, Anomie, and Deviant Behavior," *American Sociological Review*, XXIV (April 1959), 164-76; and Albert K. Cohen, "The Sociology of the Deviant Act: Anomie Theory and Beyond," *American Sociological Review*, XXX (February 1965), 5-14.

5. See Marshall B. Clinard, *Anomie and Deviant Behavior: A Discussion and Critique* (New York: The Free Press, 1964), pp. 243-82.

6. See Edwin M. Lemert, "Social Structure, Social Control, and Deviation," in Clinard, op. cit., pp. 57-97, esp. p. 73.

7. Ibid., pp. 59-60.

8. Another criticism Lemert makes is that Merton's paradigm is inadequate for explaining a variety of types of deviant behavior, such as alcoholism, suicide, and drug addiction (ibid., pp. 71-73, 74). I generally agree with this, but our concern is with the hypothesis which stipulates a relationship between perceived blocked opportunity and alienation. Merton does not claim that alcoholism, suicide, and drug addiction stem from blocked opportunity; they are "retreatist" reactions. See Merton, op. cit., p. 153.

9. Travis Hirschi, *Causes of Delinquency*, Berkeley: University of California Press, 1969, 7-8.

10. See Herbert H. Hyman, "The Value Systems of Different Classes: A Social Psychological Contribution to the Analysis of Stratification," in Reinhard Bendix and Seymour M. Lipset, eds., *Class, Status, and Power: A Reader in Social Stratification* (New York: The Free Press, 1953), pp. 426-42.

11. For a review of the evidence, see Robert K. Merton and Robert A. Nisbet, eds., *Contemporary Social Problems*, 2nd ed. (New York: Harcourt Brace Jovanovich, 1966), pp. 95, 157-59.

12. The most frequently used attitudinal measure is the Srole scale. See the discussion on pp. 77-78.

13. See Dorothy L. Meier and Wendell Bell, "Anomia and Differential Access to the Achievement of Life Goals," *American Sociological Review*, XXIV (April 1959), 190-202.

14. In addition to the previous chapter, see the following: Richard Centers

and Hadley Cantril, "Income Satisfaction and Income Aspiration," *Journal of Abnormal and Social Psychology*, XLI (January 1946), 64-69; Genevieve Knupfer, "Portrait of the Underdog," in Reinhard Bendix and Seymour M. Lipset, eds., *Class, Status, and Power: A Reader in Social Stratification* (New York: The Free Press, 1953), pp. 255-63; Hyman, op. cit.; Audren Wendling and Delberg S. Elliott, "Class and Race Differentials in Parental Aspirations and Expectations," *Pacific Sociological Review*, XI (Fall 1968), 123-36. See also Seymour M. Lipset and Reinhard Bendix, *Social Mobility in Industrial Society* (Berkeley: University of California Press, 1959), pp. 286-87; and Talcott Parsons, "A Revised Analytical Approach to the Theory of Social Stratification," in Reinhard Bendix and Seymour M. Lipset, eds., *Class, Status, and Power: A Reader in Social Stratification* (New York: The Free Press, 1953).

15. In his study, Delbert S. Elliott concludes that "Delinquents [from the lower and middle classes] quite uniformly perceive lower opportunity to achieve success goals than do non-delinquents." "Delinquency and Perceived Opportunity," *Sociological Inquiry*, XII (Spring 1962), 227. The data reported by James F. Short, Jr. on delinquency and perceived opportunity are consistent with Merton's hypothesis, though his data on aspirations are not; see "Gang Delinquency and Anomie," in Clinard, op. cit., pp. 105-15.

16. Merton, op. cit., pp. 134-39.

17. Ibid., p. 175.

18. Gammas computed for the relationship between aspirations and normlessness yield coefficients of $-.64$ for farmers and $-.18$ for farm workers. This suggests that both aspirations and perceived opportunity may be related to normlessness, but the influence of aspirations is much less in the lower class. However, when these coefficients are compared with cultural differences in the relationship between aspiration and normlessness (see note 20), no meaningful statement can be made about such a relationship.

19. Robert K. Merton, "Anomie, Anomia, and Social Interaction: Contexts of Deviant Behavior," in Marshall Clinard, ed., *Anomia and Deviant Behavior: A Discussion in Critique* (New York: The Free Press, 1964), pp. 217-18; emphasis added.

20. In some instances it appears that Merton is largely concerned with the first issue; see p. 99. The general thrust of Merton's argument, however, focuses on the issue of *sources* of normlessness in American society, especially in the lower class, and the question of cultural variation in the perceived opportunity-normlessness relationship, rather than the degree of normlessness in the United States in comparison to other societies. But in any case, it is necessary to keep the two questions separate for methodological reasons no less than the fact that they stem from different theoretical questions.

21. John Gillin, "Ethos Components in Modern Latin American Culture," in Dwight B. Heath and Richard N. Adams, eds., *Contemporary Cultures and Societies of Latin America* (New York: Random House, Inc., 1965), p. 507.

22. Ibid., pp. 512-13; emphasis added.

23. See p. 110.

24. Those who want their children to enter farm work could mean two different things when they say they believe their children will not end up in farm work: either their children may do better than farm work or they may do worse (e.g., become drifters, hoboes, skidrow bums, or beggars, etc.). The same problem is not encountered with the educational questions, since the perceived educational opportunity question asks respondents about the chances their children have of getting the amount of education desired. Therefore, poor perceived opportunity always indicates the expectation of a lower amount than is desired.

25. We have noted (note 13) that the Gammas between aspirations and normlessness for farmers and anglo-American farm workers are $-.64$ and $-.18$. For bilingual farm workers, Gamma is $+.12$ and for non-English speakers it is $-.46$. Only for farmers and non-English speakers is the relationship significant. Given these results we cannot say anything about the similarity and differences between classes and cultural groups in the relationship between aspirations and normlessness. Moreover, for none of the farm worker groups is there a significant relationship between occupational aspirants—nonaspirants and normlessness. Gammas for anglo-Americans, bilinguals, and non-English speakers are $-.04$, $+.11$, and $-.09$.

26. No systematic differences are observed between aspirants and nonaspirants. Gammas between cultural assimilation and normlessness are $-.37$ and $-.43$ for educational aspirants (N = 276) and $-.45$ and $-.34$ for nonaspirants (N = 51).

27. Peter H. Rossi and Zahava D. Blum, "Class, Status, and Poverty," in Daniel P. Moynihan, ed., *On Understanding Poverty: Perspectives From the Social Sciences* (New York: Basic Books, Inc., 1969), I, 49.

28. Ibid.

Opportunity Theory, Powerlessness, and Anomia

Although denied opportunity is usually viewed in reference to normlessness, it may be related to powerlessness and anomia as well. If this is so, then we have a basis for extending Merton's theory; but, if results are different for powerlessness and anomia then the theory is more specific and applies only to normlessness.

Our analysis in this chapter will follow much the same procedure as it did in the previous chapter. The relationship of perceived opportunity to powerlessness and anomia will be examined separately by class and culture. If the hypothesis is to be extended, we would expect the correlations between perceived opportunity and powerlessness and anomia to hold for farmers and farm workers, and among farm workers the correlations should be highest for anglo-Americans and lowest for the non-English speakers. To facilitate the comparisons, correlations for normlessness will be presented along with those for powerlessness and anomia. Class comparisons will be made between farmers and anglo-American farm workers whereas cultural comparisons will be made between the three groups of farm workers.

Opportunity and Anomia

Social Class

We noted in Chapter 5 that although anomia is sometimes confused with what we have called normlessness, the theoretical rationale for the connection between anomia and Merton's formulation of opportunity theory is not clear. In fact, most of the studies which purport to show an empirical association between opportunity and anomia have actually shown a relationship between socioeconomic status and anomia. Although the latter two are associated, we have seen that normlessness is higher among lower-class farm workers even when perceived opportunity and aspirations are controlled. It does not follow, therefore, that because anomia and socioeconomic status are related the association must be due to class differences in opportunity. Most researchers have assumed that the relationship between socioeconomic status and anomia is due to more limited opportunity in the lower class. This is based on the further assumption that the goals and aspirations of different classes are essentially the same.[1] If we consider that goals vary to some degree by social class, the validity of such an assumption is in doubt. One study does suggest, however, that a relationship may exist between anomia and perceived opportunity. As measures of perceived opportunity, Mizruchi asked respondents how good they thought their chances were of getting ahead ("excellent" vs. "limited") and whether a person with ambition could get as far today as he could in the past (responses were classified as "relatively open" and "relatively closed"). He reports that the relationship between these measures of perceived opportunity and anomia may be closer in the "higher" classes (I, II, and III) than in the "lower" classes (IV and V).[2]

Our data are not exactly comparable to Mizruchi's. The socioeconomic difference between farmers and farm workers is much greater than that between Mizruchi's "high" and "low" classes. Also, Mizruchi's findings are for men and women combined, whereas ours are only for men. In addition, we do not use exactly the same measures of perceived opportunity as Mizruchi, and we distinguish between aspirants and nonaspirants (those who want a college education for their children and those who do not), which Mizruchi does not do. Despite these differences, our results are not totally inconsistent with his. We find that perceived opportunity is inversely related to anomia for both classes in our study. However, the Gamma for aspiring farm workers (−.41) is somewhat higher than that for aspiring farmers (−.29) (see the first part of Table 9-1; our analysis is based on the distinction between low, medium, and high anomia, corresponding to scores of 0, 1-2, and 3-5 on the anomia scale). Both are significant beyond the .01 level of statistical significance. Because of the small number of nonaspiring farmers, meaningful class comparisons cannot be made concerning differences between aspirants and nonaspirants in the relationship between perceived opportunity and anomia. Among farm workers, however, the Gamma for the nonaspiring is only about half as high as for the aspiring, although it is still significant at the .01 level with the conservative two-tail test (see the middle part of Table 9-1).[3] Thus, the difference between aspirants and nonaspirants in the relationship between perceived opportunity and anomia is not as clear-cut as the difference in the relationship between perceived opportunity and normlessness.[4]

Cultural Differences

The correlation between perceived occupational opportunity and anomia is negative for all three cultural groups of farm workers, but is highest for anglo-Americans and lowest for non-English speakers (see the bottom part of Table 9-1). Results for perceived educational opportunity reveal that the coefficient is higher for anglo-Americans than for the other two groups among both the aspiring and nonaspiring. For the latter, however, there is no difference in the coefficient between bilinguals and Mexican-Americans. With this excep-

Table 9-1

Gamma Coefficients between Perceived Opportunity and Each of Three Dimensions of Alienation, by Cultural Group

	Normlessness	Anomia	Powerlessness	N[a]
Perceived Educational Opportunity				
Aspirants				
Farmers	−.32*	−.29*	−.14*	109
Farm Workers				
Anglo-Americans	−.28*	−.41*	−.35*	118
Bilinguals	−.05	−.07	−.05	97
Non-English speakers	+.07	−.08	−.33*	61
Nonaspirants (Farm Workers Only)				
Anglo-Americans	−.03	−.21*	−.46*	67
Bilinguals	.01	−.14	−.17	51
Non-English speakers	+.11	+.15	−.30*	48
Perceived Occupational Opportunity				
(Farm Workers Only)				
Anglo-Americans	−.27*	−.65*	−.72*	151
Bilinguals	−.63*	−.34*	−.41*	128
Non-English speakers	+.34	−.21*	+.03	97

[a]N may vary slightly for different dimensions of alienation due to variation in nonrespondents.

*Significant at the .01 level or beyond.

tion, our results are consistent with those for normlessness, with the magnitude of the negative correlation increasing as cultural assimilation increases. Unlike normlessness, however, this pattern also occurs for the nonaspiring, although all Gammas are low in magnitude. The cultural hypothesis of a correlation between perceived denied opportunity and alienation appears to be just as valid for anomia as for normlessness, and for anomia it may not be limited to those whose aspirations are linked to middle-class goals.[5]

Opportunity and Powerlessness

Although Merton's theory does not consider powerlessness, some advocates of the theory have moved from a focus on normative estrangement and deviance to powerlessness.[6] Moreover, there has been a tendency among some groups, particularly blacks and university students, to associate lack of power with blocked opportunities. The demand for more power among those groups (and others) is sometimes justified as necessary in order to achieve the goals that are being denied them, although the goals in each case may vary.

Social Class

Table 9-1 shows that for aspiring farmers and farm workers results are similar to the findings for normlessness because perceived opportunity and powerlessness are significantly related for both groups. If we distinguish between high, medium, and low powerlessness scores (0-1, 2-3, and 4-6), the Gammas are −.14 for farmers and −.35 for farm workers. Although both are significant at the .01 level or beyond, the coefficient is quite low for farmers. (This, however, is due to the particular placement of the cutting points on the powerlessness scale; if we distinguish between only two categories, 0-2 and 3-6, Gammas are −.35 for farmers and −.41 for farm workers.) Unlike the relationship for normlessness, however, the relationship for powerlessness is slightly stronger for the non-aspiring farm workers (Gamma = −.46). Therefore, perceived opportunity is associated with powerlessness as well as normlessness, but the association is not limited to farm workers whose aspirations are linked to middle-class goals.

Cultural Differences

For occupational opportunity there are statistically significant negative correlations between perceived opportunity and powerlessness for anglo-American and bilingual farm workers; the magnitude of the correlation is directly related to degree of cultural assimilation (see the bottom part of Table 9-1). Results for perceived educational opportunity are similar in that the correlation is highest for anglo-Americans, but only slightly higher than for non-English speakers, and much higher for both of these groups than for bilinguals. The same pattern exists for aspirants and nonaspirants. Therefore, except for occupational opportunity, there is no clear cultural gradient in the magnitude of Gamma for powerlessness. However, our finding that the correlation is higher for anglo-Americans than the other two groups is consistent with the cultural hypothesis.[7]

In general, results support the hypothesis that degree of cultural assimilation—assimilation to a culture in which achieved status is dominent—influences the extent to which perceived opportunity is associated with alienation. Of course, the gradient in the coefficients is not precisely the same in all cases—that is, the negative coefficient is not always highest for anglo-Americans, next highest for bilinguals, and lowest for non-English speakers. But, as we can see in Table 9-1, this pattern does exist in five of nine instances (though the correlations are extremely low for normlessness among nonaspirants). In addition, in three of the four instances wherein results deviate from the expected pattern (anomia and powerlessness for educational aspirants and powerlessness for nonaspirants), anglo-Americans have the highest coefficient, and in the fourth case non-English speakers have the lowest (negative) coefficient (+.34 for occupational opportunity and normlessness).

On balance, then, our results provide rather substantial support for the hypothesis that cultural assimilation does influence the relationship between perceived opportunity and alienation, and that the influence follows a gradient pattern with the effects of culture increasing as assimilation increases. Clearly, the contextual effect of culture is stronger than the contextual effect of class.

The Cultural Context of Opportunity and
Alienation: Further Considerations

In the case of normlessness results are what a priori theory leads us to expect. Perceived opportunity is more apt to lead to normative estrangement among individuals from achievement-oriented societies in which equal opportunity is assumed to be the birthright of everyone but does not in fact exist for everyone. The effects, however, appear to be general and are not limited to normlessness.

It is difficult to reconcile our results with interpretations that emphasize class differences in the effect of opportunity. True, these results do show that there are class differences in perceived opportunity and for normlessness and anomia. But in the *relationships* between opportunity and measures of alienation, the similarities are far more striking than any differences; this is not consistent with the theories of some that the significance of blocked opportunity varies depending on social class. We have noted, for example, that Mizruchi argues that although anomia is higher in the lower than in the middle class, the relationship between perceived blocked opportunity and anomia is stronger in the middle class.[8] He contends that the significance of aspirations and opportunity differ between the two classes as follows: In the middle class, anomia is a product of unlimited aspirations whereas in the lower class it is the product of blocked opportunity to achieve more modest aspirations.[9] Our findings presented in Chapter 7 support Mizruchi's hypothesis about middle-class goals and aspirations; the goals and aspirations of some farmers appear to be quite unlimited, and, once they reach a particular level, an even higher goal is sought. According to Mizruchi, this lack of restraint is an important factor in middle-class anomia, and he seems to believe that it is at least as significant in generating anomia in the middle class as is the presence of blocked opportunity within the lower class.[10]

Unfortunately, since we have no measure of the degree of goal restraint, the bearing of our results on this hypothesis is problematical. Although an orientation toward constantly rising aspirations is apparent among some farmers on the basis of their open-ended responses, we cannot differentiate between farmers in terms of *aspiration restraint.* Our measure of aspirations (educational level) is probably inadequate for this; it does not represent an orientation to unlimited aspirations, especially for middle-class persons. Instead, it is a measure of an orientation to a culturally approved goal that is nearly universal in the middle-class and that the majority of the lower class accept. From this perspective, perceived blocked opportunity among middle-class farmers may have much the same meaning for farmers that it has for farm workers; for both, there is a denial of opportunity to achieve something that most people would like to achieve.

Although our emphasis on cultural similarity or integration between social classes differs from Mizruchi's focus on class differentiation, it is possible that both hypotheses are correct. Unlimited aspiration as well as perceived blocked opportunity may be a factor in middle-class alienation but we have no data which bear on the former.[11] Our data refer to the relationship between perceived blocked opportunity and alienation and indicate class similarity rather than class difference; hence, they suggest a cultural rather than a class interpretation. Given that the relationships are similar for farmers and farm workers but different between cultural groups, our findings indicate that farmers and farm workers are integrated in the same overall cultural pattern. We suggest that this occurs because the interpretation of blocked opportunity varies depending on cultural background rather than social class, and the differences between the cultural groups of farm workers in this respect are wider than the differences between anglo-American farmers and farm workers.

Our hypothesis, of course, is that the specific cultural emphasis on achievement and equal opportunity, along with the perception of unequal opportunity (or at least the perception that opportunity is not good), contributes to alienative attitudes.[12] To perceive one's opportunities as blocked generates a contradiction between personal experience, on the one hand, and cultural definition and prescription, on the other, leading to disaffection with and estrangement from society. The contradiction holds for the middle and lower classes alike. Moreover, such disaffection and estrangement appear not to be limited to the normative sector, but also affect one's perceived ability to exert control over his economic fate in society and a general sense of optimism-pessimism about society and one's position in it. Although this interpretation is consistent with Merton's theory, it is also an extension of that theory since it incorporates findings for powerlessness and anomia. The contradiction between personal experience and cultural ideology concerning education-occupational opportunity contributes to alienation generally, not just to normlessness. We suggest that this more general formulation may be a specific instance of a still more general formulation.

A More General Formulation

Our findings may have implications beyond their specific reference to cultural achievement and ascriptive orientations, and educational and occupational opportunity. At a more general level, they indicate that a condition leading to alienative attitudes may be one in which (1) there is a conflict between the desire to achieve culturally valued objectives (such as, but not limited to, higher education and middle-class occupations for children) and the actual opportunities to reach them, and (2) there exists a cultural myth that claims opportunities are equal and hence, in effect, denies the existence of the conflict. That is, cultural mythology contradicts the underlying social reality and the contradiction is reflected in personal experience. This does not deny the validity of Merton's formulation, but it does put it in a more general perspective and views alienation as stemming from contradictions inherent in the social and cultural orders.

The formulation need not be limited to normative estrangement, but is more general in scope, as our results suggest. Furthermore, it need not be limited to contradictions between cultural mythology and the underlying social reality in reference to economic, materialistic, or occupational ends. An alienating condition may exist to the extent that one is unable to achieve culturally approved goals because of the social constraints that influence one when the cultural ideology denies that those constraints exist. It suggests, therefore, that alienation among groups from ascriptive societies stems from the cultural myths of that society which contradict aspects of its social and political structure.

We are not presenting merely another cultural conflict hypothesis. Conflicts in beliefs, religions, languages, etc., in themselves do not constitute grounds for alienation, according to this formulation. The conflict must be a contradiction between the *socially imposed constraints to realize culturally valued ends and a cultural ideology which denies that those constraints exist.* Or, we can say that a condition of alienation exists when the constraints of the social structure are inconsistent with the cultural ideology of the society and prevent the individual from making the ideology a reality in his personal experience.

According to this formulation, individuals who are most alienated from society should come disproportionately from two different categories: (1) those who are denied access to the means for culturally approved ends (and perceive this), and (2) those who, because of their particular location in the social structure, their education and experience, or their native endowment, have unusually keen perception of the cultural ideology and social structure of their society and the relationship between them.[13]

This suggests, then, that all cultures are alienating to some degree; probably no society exists in which there are no contradictions between what the cultural ideology says an individual can or should do and the existence of institutionalized constraints which prevent him from doing so. Naturally, the specific conditions that tend to generate alienative attitudes will vary from society to society. But the level of alienation in any society should vary with the number and severity of the constraints on achieving culturally valued objectives along with a cultural belief system which denies that those constraints exist.

On balance, our results do not agree with the claim that American society has a particularly alienating culture, since anglo-Americans do not have significantly higher powerlessness, normlessness, or anomia scores than Mexican-Americans.[14] Of course, our results are based on investigation of a specific occupation, and findings for members of other occupations might be different. At the same time, our data do reveal that the dynamics of normlessness, powerlessness, and anomia are consistent with the descriptions of persons who have written about the significance or (perceived) denied opportunity in the United States. It seems clear that Merton's assertion that, "appreciable numbers of people become estranged from a society that promises them in principle what they are denied in reality,"[15] is not limited to normative estrangement.

A Concluding Note

We noted in Chapter 1 that the concept of alienation means different things to different people. Given this diversity of meanings it is problematical if a general conception of alienation could be arrived at. Richard Schacht contends that it cannot, at least insofar as the concept has been used by sociologists, and he questions whether there is any relationship between the various states referred to as alienation or even if they are all part of the same general phenomenon.[16] Our findings that the correlations between our three measures are not particularly great lends support to Schacht's argument.[17]

Despite this, however, we suggest that the three measures of alienation do represent one's relationship to or estrangement from society: (1) perceived ability to influence one's fate in society, (2) estrangement from the normative system of society, and (3) optimism and confidence about one's place in society. Moreover, even if they are not homogeneous with each other, that is, highly related among themselves, their relationships to *other variables* are quite similar. Depending on the *cultural conditions*, all are influenced by one's perceived position in the class structure (perceived deprivation) and perceived barriers to one's aspirations. Therefore, the three states reflected in our measures of alienation are *causally* homogeneous with respect to certain social and cultural conditions—specifically, perception of class position and opportunity depending on the cultural emphasis given to achieved status.[18] In this sense, then, all three measures of alienation appear to be aspects of the same general social and cultural process and, hence, are aspects of the same general phenomenon.

Notes

1. Dorothy L. Meier and Wendell Bell, "Anomia and Differential Access to the Achievement of Life Goals," *American Sociological Review*, XXIV (April 1959), 190-202.

2. Ephraim H. Mizruchi, *Success and Opportunity: Class Values and Anomie in American Life* (London: The Free Press; Collier-Macmillan, Ltd., 1964), pp. 97-98. Although Mizruchi reports the relationship may be stronger for the middle class, it is not clear that this is true; our analysis of the data reported in his study produces Gamma coefficients (Q's) of $-.69$ and $-.52$ for the "middle" class and $-.38$ and $-.71$ for the "low" class (the computations here are ours, not Mizruchi's). In addition, in one set of computations we have taken the liberty of using a different cut-off point on the anomia scale than that used by Mizruchi. In the analysis based on how respondents felt about their chances of getting ahead (ibid., Table VI, p. 97), Mizruchi distinguishes between respondents who scored less than 1 and 1 or more on the scale; the Q's for this table are $-.69$ and $-.38$, the highest coefficient being for the middle class. In the analysis based on the other question, however, Mizruchi uses three cut-off points (0, 1-2, and 3-5) (ibid., Table VII, p. 99). We reconstructed Mizruchi's Table VII using the same cut-off points as those used in his Table VI, and found Q's of $-.52$ and $-.71$, with the highest coefficient being for the *lower* class. On the basis of these results, no class difference in the relationship would appear to be indicated.

3. Two-tailed tests are computed for anomia and powerlessness since, unlike normlessness, there is no a priori reason for predicting a relationship between them and perceived opportunity. In our view, only the attitude measured by our normlessness scale is within the purview of Merton's statements on social structure and anomie.

4. The relationship between class and anomia (see p. 82) is not a function of class differences in aspirations or perceived opportunity, since the Gamma is virtually the same for different levels of aspiration and perceived opportunity. For aspirants ($N = 228$) and nonaspirants ($N = 79$), respectively, Gammas are $-.61$ and $-.67$, whereas for those who perceived their children's educational opportunity as "good," Gamma between class and anomia is $-.72$ ($N = 116$) in comparison to a Gamma of $-.74$ ($N = 189$) for persons who perceive opportunity as "fairly good" and "poor."

5. Anomia is also similar to normlessness in that there is no tendency for aspirations and anomia to be inversely related. For farmers, anomia scores for aspirants and nonaspirants are 1.13 ($N = 110$) and 1.33 ($N = 12$), neither of which is statistically significant. For all farm workers, the averages for occupational aspirants and nonaspirants are 2.72 ($N = 388$) and 2.55 ($N = 51$) and for educational aspirants and nonaspirants they are 2.65 ($N = 279$) and 2.81 ($N = 166$). Within cultural groups, none of the differences are statistically significant, and in two of three instances occupational aspirants have a higher score than occupational nonaspirants; for educational aspirations the nonaspirants have the higher score in two of three instances. Hence, no significant relationship or even a suggested pattern exists between aspirations and anomia.

6. See Daniel P. Moynihan's comments in *Maximum Feasible Misunder-*

standing: Community Action in the War on Poverty (New York: The Free Press, 1969), esp. pp. 107-9.

7. As with normlessness and anomia, aspirations do not affect powerlessness. For farmers, average scores for aspirants and nonaspirants are 2.41 (N = 109) and 1.92 (N = 12), which is statistically significant, but with aspirants having the *higher* score. Among farm workers the averages are 2.44 and 2.39 for occupational aspirants (N = 388) and nonaspirants (N = 51), and 2.42 for both educational aspirants (N = 277) and nonaspirants (N = 166). For two of three farm worker groups, occupational aspirants have the highest score, whereas in only one group do educational aspirants have the highest score. Thus, there is no tendency for lower aspirations to be associated with powerlessness in any class or cultural group.

8. Mizruchi, op. cit., pp. 97-98. We have noted, however, that Mizruchi does not distinguish between people depending on their level of aspiration.

9. Ibid., pp. 97-100, 117, 126-37.

10. Ibid., esp. pp. 97 and 127.

11. It is possible that the questions Mizruchi asked of his respondents more nearly measure unlimited aspirations ("boundlessness") than do ours. (We might recall, however, that in our re-examination of Mizruchi's findings in note 2, we found little basis for a class difference.) In any case, our results indicate that the relationship between perceived opportunity and dimensions of anomia is just as close for lower-class anglo-American farm workers as for the middle-class farmers.

12. Mizruchi also emphasizes achievement cultural orientation in his interpretation (op. cit., pp. 61-90, 97). However, he attributes this orientation primarily to the middle class, whereas in our emphasis we do not limit its influence to the middle class.

13. This formulation suggests that Dadaists, who fight against cultural ideology being used to rationalize (or act as a "protective shield" for) an unjust social and political structure, would be particularly alienated. Since there is no society without cultural myths, Dadaists are prone to be alienated from *any* society. One expression of alienation, of course, is to remove oneself physically from the society. This process of disengagement is dramatically revealed in Richard Huelsenbeck's statement of why he, a Dadaist, left the United States for Switzerland after spending 34 years in New York. But, alas, do not all societies have the same kind of problem to some degree? Huelsenbeck states: "Being unable to solve [my conflict] entirely, I try to solve it by changing scenes. But it is a mistake. I know it. . . ." He believes, nevertheless, that the change may have "curative qualities," since he is able to see his problem more clearly: "America is a tragic land, and the Americans are a tragic people. Their grandiose try to found a free society has failed, and now they are in an unsolvable conflict." Being the true Dadaist that he is, he doesn't "claim to be in a much better situation [in Switzerland]." Despite the American failure to build a free society, he wonders

"whether liberty really existed anywhere, and that the American attempt to bring it about (although it has failed) has been one of the most sincere attempts." Richard Huelsenbeck, "Reflection on Leaving America for Good," *The American Scholar*, XXXIX (Winter 1969-70), pp. 80-85, quotes at p. 85. Hence, a major reason for alienation in American society may be that a "free society" (i.e., equal opportunity to pursue universalistic goals) is such an important cultural value which, despite the cultural mythology to the contrary notwithstanding, has never really been achieved. Hence, individuals in a society who accept the central cultural values of society but who also view cultural myths *as* cultural myths are among those who would be expected to be most alienated. Dadaists would be in this group, since their explicit focus is in analyzing cultural ideology and exposing it as myth when it is contrary to their conception of what a just social and political order should be. This is not to say that a Dadaist is alienated by the same processes as a farm worker. We suggest, however, that the major difference is the Dadaist's explicit recognition of a contradiction between cultural ideology and the reality of social structure in a general or abstract rather than a personal sense (that is, his own life situation).

14. It is possible that there are more inherent contradictions in the American culture and social structure than in most other societies, yet its citizens may not be any more alienated than citizens of other societies. This could occur because the conditions which tend to generate alienation among people are counter-balanced by other conditions. For example, although blocked opportunity may contribute to a high degree of alienation in the United States, this trend may be counterbalanced by trends stemming from other factors. Two such factors are the presence of false consciousness and the presence of a high level of perceived opportunity (relative to other societies): only 26% of anglo-American farm workers considered their children's opportunity to achieve a college education to be poor, and only 28% of those who wanted their children not to become workers thought they definitely or probably would end up in farm work. Simmons and Rosenberg have commented on the presence of false class consciousness and optimism about upward mobility as mechanisms which possibly dampen class conflict. See Roberta G. Simmons and Morris Rosenberg, "Functions of Children's Perceptions of the Stratification System," *American Sociological Review*, XXXVI (April 1971), 235-349. Such mechanisms may also lower the level of alienation. The conditions producing alienation no less than alienation itself are complex, and any general statement on the relationship between alienation and its presumed causes oversimplifies a process containing social, cultural, and social-psychological elements.

15. Robert K. Merton, "Anomia, Anomie, and Social Interaction: Contexts of Deviant Behavior," in Marshall B. Clinard, ed., *Anomie and Deviant Behavior: Discussion and Critique* (New York: The Free Press, 1965), p. 218.

16. Richard Schacht, *Alienation* (Garden City, N.Y.: Doubleday & Company, Inc., 1970), pp. 155-96.

17. See pp. 78, 81 (n. 18).

18. We assume here that, causally, perceived deprivation and perceived blocked opportunity lead to normlessness, powerlessness, and anomia (under specified cultural conditions, of course) and not the other way around. The conception of causal homogeneity focuses on the relationships between each of several factors (that are usually assumed to be aspects of the same thing), considered to be the dependent variables, and some other variables (or a series of variables) considered to be the independent variables. It is possible for factors to be rather highly correlated with each other but only weakly or not at all correlated with some third factor, and a series of factors that are not or only weakly correlated with each other may all be correlated with a third factor. Hence, questions about factors as aspects of the same general phenomenon and questions about those same factors as aspects of the same social and cultural causal process must be kept separate. For a discussion of the concept of causal homogeneity, see Jack P. Gibbs, "Needed: Analytical Typologies in Criminology," *Southwestern Social Science Quarterly*, XL (March 1960), 321-29; and William A. Rushing, "Organizational Size and Administration: The Problems of Causal Homogeneity and a Heterogeneous Category," *Pacific Sociological Review*, IX (Fall 1966), 100-108.

Part IV: Overview and Implications

 **Class Stability and Change**

Although our primary focus has been on the class and cultural contexts of alienation, our results also have implications for the dynamics of class stability and change. This is especially true with reference to findings on the structure of the farm workers' position and class differences in relative deprivation, goals, aspirations, and powerlessness. In this chapter we will outline what we consider these implications to be, reserving for the next chapter conclusions and implications as they relate to the class and cultural contexts of alienation.

Class Position and the Structure of Poverty

We have considered the structure of poverty in terms of objective socioeconomic external attributes which distinguish between a poor and a nonpoor population. We found in Chapter 3 that the different attributes are themselves interrelated, that a person deprived in one respect tends to be deprived in other respects. Poverty thus does not consist of any one factor, such as low income, but involves several interrelated factors. The external attributes thus form a pattern, which we suggest can be summarized in terms of the principle of cumulative disadvantage. The principle applies to differences between classes (farmers and farm workers) and to some extent to differences within the lower class (that is, cultural differences among farm workers). We suggest that this principle has far-reaching implications for understanding the class structure.

It is within the structure of the pattern of cumulative disadvantage that much behavior typical of the lower class, which disturbs and puzzles the middle class, might best be understood. Perplexing questions are frequently asked about poverty groups:

Why . . . are they so little interested in improving their lives? How can they resign themselves to acceptance of minimal welfare payments and then adopt the "dole" as a permanent way of life? Why aren't they more eager to leave their hopeless environment . . . for areas of greater opportunity? What, in short, explains their lack of ambition, their "episodic" view of life, and their inability to arouse themselves to sustained efforts? Admittedly, their past has been bleak and hopeless, but why should this prevent them from responding to the opportunities of the present?[1]

Richard Ball and others attribute much of the behavior of poverty groups which lead to these types of questions to an "analgesic subculture," which is the institutionalization of (that is, the development of norms, beliefs, and values around) "frustration-instigated" (or "nongoal-oriented irrational") behavior, rather than "motivation-instigated" (or "goal oriented rational") behavior. Ball emphasizes the emergence of norms and values (e.g., the encouragement of dependence on one's family among the South Appalachian poor) which are not only responses to life conditions, but which lead to behavior that reinforces those life conditions (e.g., the inability of a South Appalachian to break away from his family of orientation and take advantage of an available opportunity).[2] Coser has also noted that certain aspects of lower-class values and life styles—specifically, the prevalence and social acceptance of matrifocality, serial marriage, and high divorce rates—negatively affect children's achievement motivation and access to the occupational opportunity structure.[3]

Without necessarily disagreeing with these formulations, we will formulate the problem somewhat differently. The characteristics of any social position impose situational constraints on individual behavior but we suggest that the situation of the poor is particularly constraining. For example, a person with a low income and little education has few behavior alternatives open to him, at least in the occupational sphere. Furthermore, class background or social inheritance will determine to an important degree the extent to which one is exposed to the broader culture (e.g., the "nonanalgesic" culture), which in turn will influence the behavior alternatives that one perceives. And, of course, the more dependent one is on a low-paying job such as farm work, the fewer the occupational alternatives. That farm workers are severely restrained by the external characteristics of their position is clearly indicated in the results of this study. Even assuming that a farm worker is ambitious and is "motivation" or "goal-oriented" rather than "frustration" or "nongoal-oriented," *the structure of his situation* may provide him with too few degrees of freedom to take advantage of the opportunities that may be available. This would be true regardless of subcultural norms.

These considerations indicate that the nature of the class structure, especially the structure of poverty, contains a built-in dynamic of class stability. Although extreme differences in life chances may be necessary conditions for class conflict and demands (violent and otherwise) for structural change, the same conditions that generate those demands may produce forces of stability as well. Thus, contradictory forces are generated in the lower class. Given the structure of lower-class existence—low income, poor education, limited occupational and technical skills, little or no political power, community isolation, etc.—there is little that many lower-class persons can do as individuals to improve their station in life. Because of the principle of cumulative disadvantage, vertical movement in the class structure is not probable.

Class and Relative Deprivation

Contradictory patterns originating in the class structure are also reflected in findings for relative deprivation. Although farm workers are much more deprived than farmers, and some farm workers are more deprived than others, there is the further question of whether perceived deprivation parallels the degree of objective deprivation. Our results indicate two trends. On the one hand, farm workers feel deprived of basic life chances to a greater extent than farmers, and within farm workers perceived deprivation is inversely related to objective deprivation as measured by income level. On the other hand, considering the low structural position of farm workers, few feel as deprived as would be expected; most imagine a large proportion of the population to be at least as badly off as they. Hence, both realistic perceptions and false consciousness exist.

These trends parallel expectations based on contradictory theoretical frameworks of social class—structure-function theory and Marxist theory. If it is true that perceived deprivation is a necessary though not sufficient condition for militant actions, our results suggest that false perceptions may be a major reason why militancy among farm workers has been so weak. A lack of militancy, of course, helps to maintain and preserve the class structure in its present state, a consequence which some functional theorists emphasize. Interviewers were struck by the farm workers' apparent acceptance of and resignation to their situation; there were few indications of bitterness, resentfulness, or hostility. This is not to say there was no discontent, but it arose from the problems of a "day-to-day" or "hand-to-mouth" existence. Furthermore, farm workers appeared not to be preoccupied with *changing* this form of existence; most appeared not even to have thought about it at all. Such tendencies help to preserve the class structure in its present state.

But, because perceived deprivation is higher among farm workers than among farmers and increases as socioeconomic status decreases among workers, the psychological foundation of militancy may be present among farm workers, at least incipiently. And interviewers did report a feeling of hostility among a minority of farm workers, although this appeared to be limited mostly to the anglo-Americans.

There are other aspects of perceived deprivation. Although there are theoretical reasons for expecting community isolation to influence perceived deprivation, one may wonder whether this influences the perceptions of people whose life chances are extremely low; nonsocial factors might be expected to override any influence that social factors might otherwise exert. However, community position does influence perceived deprivation. Farm workers in comparison to farmers are isolated and largely segregated from the rest of the community, physically and socially; the residential patterns of most workers, residents as well as migrants, keep workers separated from the community so that they have little social contact with other members of the community, formally or informally. Results suggest that such exclusion from the community lowers the workers' reference points for comparing their life chances with others; farm workers perceive their life chances as higher when their "home communities" are used as the frame of reference for comparison than when the entire society is used, whereas the opposite is the case for farmers.

These results indicate that, even among a lower-class group such as farm workers, deprivation is largely a matter of the social comparison process. Patterns observed for anglo-Americans were also observed for bilinguals and non-English speakers. Therefore, how deprived a farm worker feels depends on the actual objective extent of his deprivation and the points of comparison he uses when assessing his life chances, but not on his cultural background.

If isolation and segregation from the community function to lower one's reference points of comparison, integration in the community may raise one's reference points. It is probably true that militancy among deprived groups is associated not so much with deprivation in any absolute sense as it is with how well these groups fare vis-à-vis others with whom they compare themselves. The promotion of greater integration of poverty groups with more affluent groups in the community may, therefore, lead to greater community tension. Such tension is the price communities may have to pay before inequities in life chances are eliminated, or at least substantially reduced.

Goals, Aspirations, and Opportunity

As with perceived deprivation, two trends are indicated in the goal orientations and aspirations of farm workers. The dominant pattern in goal orientations is economic security, for most workers are oriented to the pursuit of stable employment and enough money "to make ends meet." Fewer workers are oriented to a middle-class pattern and the pursuit of such goals as self-employment and home ownership. The constraints of day-to-day life do not permit the pursuit—or perhaps even the thought—of such goals for many farm workers. Hence, it is doubtful that the goal orientations of the lower class are essentially the same as those of the middle-class. At the same time, however, such goals do penetrate to the lower class, indicating that the hypothesis of class similarity in goals receives some support. Furthermore, Merton's statement of the hypothesis emphasizes the similarity of middle and lower classes *in the United States*. It may be that for societies which do not emphasize the universalistic acceptance of cultural success goals or the myth of equal opportunity, class differences in success goals are much wider.

The analysis of class differences in aspirations shows much the same thing as other studies; lower-class farm workers have lower aspirations than farmers (e.g., fewer wish for a college education for their children). At the same time, when the low structural position of farm workers is considered, their aspirations are actually rather high (for example, 62% want a college education for their children).

These trends suggest two consequences. The economic security orientation and lower aspirations of lower-class people help to preserve the class structure unchanged; farm workers must invest too much of their time and energy in the problems of day-to-day living for many of them to be concerned very much with the achievement of middle-class goals and meaningful economic enhancement. Furthermore, they have little time to develop organized efforts to modify the distribution of life chances in the rural population. However, because some do want to achieve middle-class goals and have aspirations that are higher than might be expected on the basis of their low structural position, dormant strains and potential tensions also exist in the class structure. The fact that the proportion who perceive their opportunities to be poor is greater among farm workers than among farmers reflects such strain and tension quite clearly. Hence, the theoretical positions of "conflict sociology" and structure-function sociology which postulate conflicting tendencies in the class structure are both supported. It is not that one might be right and the other wrong; patterns emphasized by each are present.[4] Moreover, there appear to be no cultural differences in these patterns since the same results are obtained for all three cultural groups among farm workers. This, of course, is consistent with the findings for perceived deprivation. For both class perception and perception of opportunity, class is a more significant factor than culture.

Class and Powerlessness

Given the highly structured position of farm workers—their low education, limited occupational skills, almost nonexistent political power, and dependence on farm work—there is relatively little that they can do to improve their economic situation. Nevertheless, they do not feel any more powerless to influence their economic fates than do farmers. Although this may to some degree reflect differences in level of economic aspirations, the fact remains that farmers are better organized and have considerably greater power. Of course, the consequent societal integration may give one a sense of less rather than greater individual power. The issue is complicated, and different types of social involvement (participation) may have different results,[5] but the fact that farmers as a group are more integrated than farm workers suggests that societal integration and powerlessness are inversely related.

We can speculate further. If a feeling of powerlessness produces occupationally based economic-political voluntary associations, the presence of such associations may create a social-psychological dynamic which insures their continued growth; thus, feelings of powerlessness lead to associational growth which in turn leads to greater feelings of individual powerlessness, and so on in a vicious circle. As a result, the organization of the poor, such as farm workers, may actually increase feelings of individual powerlessness among such groups. In any case, our findings question the hypothesis that power associated with position in the system of production is directly related to perceived personal power. It suggests further that apparent class differences in perceived power may not be due to differences in position power but to differences in income, perceived deprivation, or other variables.

Implications for Public Policy

If our analysis is valid, it is of more than passing academic interest for it will influence the success of programs designed to alleviate poverty. Indeed, it may help explain why poverty assistance programs frequently fail. To alleviate one element (e.g., income) of the overall pattern of poverty, and then only slightly (as with welfare payments), does not modify the basic structure, that is, the constraining and cumulative character of the poverty pattern. To provide income supplements to the poor individual does not change the constraints that keep him in low-income jobs. Nor does the provision of opportunities for education and occupational training eliminate the basic economic necessity for him to continue working at low-paying jobs in order to make minimum provision for his family, thus restraining him from taking advantage of such opportunities as are available. One major difficulty is that most assistance programs have been piece-meal, that is, they have focused on only one element of a broader problem: a person who is disadvantaged in one respect tends to be disadvantaged in others, and unless all or nearly all of his problems are attended to, none may be alleviated. All are severe, and left unresolved any one may dominate the individual's life style. Hence, the overall problem must be the focus of attack.

It is probably true that an affluent society like the United States could, if it wished, eliminate the problems of hunger, malnutrition, and minimum income. Restrictions on agricultural production could be lifted so that those in need might benefit, and a negative income tax or guaranteed annual income could provide an income floor beneath those persons who, because of their educational and occupational skill limitations, are unable to earn anything but poverty wages. Such programs are not without their problems, of course. An increase in agricultural production might lead to overproduction such that food prices would be severely depressed and hence contribute to a depression among farmers. And a negative income tax or guaranteed annual income has important political and cultural restraints and consequences; there are basic American values which emphasize that income should be earned. But even if we disregard these problems, solutions to the hunger and income problem would only solve *part* of the poverty problem. They do not solve the problem of deficient education and limited occupational skills. Nor do they necessarily influence the quality of social experience, values, and education of poverty children. This is not an argument against such programs. But *structurally*, poverty involves several less conspicuous dimensions—educational, occupational, and social—as well as the more obvious income and hunger problems. To be successful, programs designed to alleviate the problem of poverty must be multidimensional in focus.

At the same time, one may well wonder whether such programs could be successful for many of the farm workers included in this study. Of course, providing enough food and income is a basic and continuous problem for many members of this class; minimum provision of such necessities would at least make their lives more humane. But what can be done to improve the educational, occupational, and social aspects of the lives of persons of whom most have less than a fifth-grade education? The question has no easy answer, and merely to assert, as we have done, that the problem is multidimensional does not indicate specific strategies to alleviate the problem. Several issues are raised, however.

It may well be that the most that can be done for impoverished adults is to assure them minimum income and medical care and enough food for subsistence. Efforts to reduce the problem should focus on the children of the poor. Of course, simply to assert that special efforts should be directed to the educational and occupational training of these children amounts to little more than a current cliché. Furthermore, it does not deal with the question of how family and neighborhood influences are to be counteracted in such programs. Nevertheless, the fact that poverty tends to be part of one's social inheritance involving a series of disadvantages that cannot be quickly changed indicates that the problem of poverty must be attacked at the juncture of generations—that is, before the disadvantage of being born in low-income families is combined with poor education, a lack of occupational skills, limited social experiences, and other contraints. To concentrate on the income and food subsistence dimensions of poverty families to the exclusion of all else may do little to eliminate social inheritance in poverty. One need only consider that one generation of welfare families tends to produce the next generation of welfare families to understand this.[6]

One should take note of another factor before calling the situation hopeless. This generation of poverty children will live in a society much different from the one their parents entered and live in today. Although no one can say exactly what this society will be like, it will probably be technologically more complex with an even greater premium placed on the acquisition of technical knowledge and technical occupational skills. Thus, the children of farm workers may be able to fare even *less* well than their parents; relative to most other occupational groups, they may be much worse off than their parents. In addition, children of farm workers may not accept their plight in life as passively as their parents have. The violent actions of the urban black ghetto inhabitants, many of whom are young males, may be but a prelude to the coming reactions of the poor generally. One need not ponder the consequences of this very long to realize that society cannot afford to postpone actions that are designed to modify the structure of poverty and, certainly, to eliminate poverty as a social inheritance.

Even assuming that programs which focus on the future adult generation are valid, there are specific problems in connection with farm workers. Many farm workers are migrants or residents who work in different communities in their home states. Consequently, the problem is not only how to develop programs that orient individuals in the direction of educational and occupational upgrading, but also how to apply such directions consistently, from day to day, to the same individuals. Cultural and language barriers further hamper the applications of such programs.

Thus, as we have noted, the success of policy programs to alleviate poverty will be influenced by the nature of poverty itself. Specifically, they will be influenced by the fact that class structure and poverty contain powerful self-perpetuating mechanisms. The class structure with its extreme inequities in life chances contains both forces which preserve the class structure in its present state and the seeds of structural change (if, of course, we accept the dictum that inequities in the distribution of life chances breed discontent and class conflict which lead, in turn, to changes in that distribution). Forces of stability are important factors which help determine the eventual outcome of policy programs.

Findings for powerlessness are especially interesting in light of the frequently proposed recommendation that steps must be taken to give poor persons more power to control their fate. Without questioning how this can be accomplished, we would caution against too much emphasis on this particular issue.

Although powerlessness does appear to be negatively related to economic outcomes (that is, income) within each of the two classes, there is no difference between classes. Since the two classes differ widely with respect to economic outcomes, results suggest that other factors associated with the two structural positions are more important than income differences. These factors probably include processes of a bureaucratic society, social comparison processes, and the level of economic goals and aspirations. If this is true, an emphasis on feelings of powerlessness among the poor may be misplaced because it may not lead to a modification of the objective situation of the poor since powerlessness is not systematically related to that situation.

Objective collective power appears to be the most significant phenomenon. Such power makes a difference in terms of objective political reality (which may not be related to a feeling that one has power, as results from farmers suggest) and the economic outcomes that are influenced by the political process. Although farmers are no less powerlessness than farm workers, collectively they are much more integrated in the political process, and they have thereby been able to influence their economic outcomes. Hence, collective power, rather than the individual's perception of having power, is the significant factor. This power is associated with class differences, and it is more apt to influence economic outcomes.

From the foregoing discussion we can see that our efforts might be better directed if they were focused on developing collective rather than individual subjective power among poverty groups such as farm workers. Unionization among farm workers would be an example. This is not to say that this process may give the individual farm workers a sense of power, but it may allow farm workers collectively to influence the political process and hence their economic outcomes.

Even assuming the validity of the above, all of the consequences of collective power among lower-class groups are not necessarily desirable. For example, the use of power by farm workers (e.g., conducting strikes during harvest season) can seriously disrupt the food production process for the nation. An increase in food prices can result. Moreover, although an increase in collective power may modify the objective situation and the economic outcomes of these groups, perceived deprivation is largely a relative matter and may not be reflected in subjective awareness. Greater economic outcomes may not lead to a greater sense of satisfaction with the outcomes received. And it may not give the individual a greater sense of power, which may only lead to efforts to strengthen collective power, and so on.

These consequences will no doubt generate societal tensions. But this may be the necessary price to avoid the disruptions of violence that can surely be expected if changes in collective power and, hence, the economic outcomes among groups such as farmers are not forthcoming. Farmers are a case in point: they continue to generate tensions in society by lobbying for farm bills which part of the population opposes, by threatening "withholding actions" (and sometimes following through), and by being recipients of federally sponsored farm programs which are supported by tax dollars and which many taxpayers therefore oppose. Be this as it may, farmers do not usually use violence to achieve their economic ends. Thus, although collective power may not raise the level of "satisfaction" of individuals or even their sense of power, it may channel the way dissatisfaction and feelings of powerlessness are expressed.[7]

Conclusion

The inequitable distribution of life chances has frequently been cited as a condition that leads to social change, since it generates class tensions and conflict in society. Less frequently noted, however, is that the same structure of inequality may contain forces which tend to preserve the class structure in its present state.[8] Because lower-class status involves deprivation of a number of kinds, it is extremely difficult for a lower-class individual to modify his status even when assistance is provided. Unfortunately, the philosophy of many advocates of the poor is that all the poor need is a little assistance to "shore them up" until they can get on their feet. Indeed, much of the New Deal Program was oriented to this philosophy. To the extent that these programs were directed to individuals who possessed occupational and educational skills—which they generally were[9]—they were successful. They did help people who were out of work find work again. But such people were out of work not because they did not have skills to offer, but because the economy did not have jobs for them. The poor of today, if farm workers are an example, are not to be confused with this class. They do not have occupational skills and their educational levels are too low to allow them to qualify for anything except the most unskilled jobs. Such persons do not require "shoring up" but a restructuring of their lives which only occupational skills and education can provide, given the current economic and social system in which they live. But, because the acquisition of occupational and educational skills is a complex process, and is itself interrelated with other social, economic, and cultural components, even systematic and concentrated efforts to raise the occupational and educational skill levels of the poor cannot be expected to have quick results in the lives of most poor persons. Such policies will be constrained by the conservative (preserving) tendencies inherent in the class structure.

The problem, of course, is distributional—the distribution of life chances. True, a general increase in economic growth may raise the overall standard of living, so that fewer people live in conditions of poverty. But this may not affect the distributional problem, which relates to a relative conception of poverty. From this perspective, before the poor can be eliminated or their numbers even significantly reduced, those people higher in the class structure must be willing to give up some of *their* advantages. Given our findings that farmers view themselves as lower in the class structure than they actually are and as being even less satisfied with their income than are farm workers, one cannot be optimistic that the distribution of life chances is going to be more equitable in the future. Just as there are constraining forces emanating from the lower class, there are constraining forces to be found in the higher levels of the class structure. A redistribution of life chances will require that persons in the higher levels of the class structure be willing to give up some of their advantages so that the disadvantages of those at the bottom of the class structure will be less.

Notes

1. Richard A. Ball, "A Poverty Case: The Analgesic Subculture of the Southern Appalachians," *American Sociological Review*, XXXIII (December 1968), 885-95, quotes at p. 890.

2. Ibid.

3. Lewis A. Coser, "Unanticipated Conservative Consequences of Liberal Theorizing," *Social Problems*, XVI (Winter 1969), 263-72. A study by the Duncans provides strong evidence for Coser's thesis. See Beverly Duncan and Otis Dudley Duncan, "Family Stability and Occupational Success," *Social Problems*, XVI (Winter 1969), 273-85. See also Melvin Kohn, "Social Class and Parent-Child Relationships: An Interpretation," *American Journal of Sociology*, LXVIII (January 1963), 471-80. Differences between family patterns in the lower class (particularly among blacks) and the rest of society, and the potential negative consequences of this for the lower class and blacks, raised considerable public controversy when stated by President Johnson in his 1965 address at

Howard University. The President's address was based on the now famous "Moynihan Report." For an analysis of the events leading up to this report, its acceptance by the President, and reactions to it, see Lee Rainwater and William L. Yancey, *The Moynihan Report and the Politics of Controversy* (Cambridge, Mass.: The M.I.T. Press, 1967).

4. This is not to say that there are no important (and perhaps irreconcilable) differences between the various types of theories. See Ralph Dahrendorf, *Class and Class Conflict in Industrial Society* (Palo Alto: Stanford University Press, 1959). In raising this issue, we do not equate it with issues of political "conservatism" or "liberalism" (or "radicalism"). To point to the presence of patterns that function to preserve the class structure does not commit one to a politically conservative position any more than recognizing that there are disruptive forces commits one to endorsing political policies and programs which aim to change the class structure. Although it may be that social scientists who emphasize one pattern rather than another tend to be politically more "conservative" (or "liberal" or "radical") than those who emphasize the other, this need not be true. Also, the fact that politicians of one persuasion accept and endorse one point of view over another does not in any way commit the theorist to the political point of view being advocated.

5. There are two themes on social participation and powerlessness. One argues that organizations are the source of power in modern society and that persons who are unaffiliated with organizations are powerlessness. The other argues that even as a member of organizations the individual is powerlessness to do much about the policy and operations of the organizations, and he feels powerlessness as a result. See William Kornhauser, *The Politics of Mass Society* (New York: The Free Press, 1959), pp. 93, 110. See also Scott Greer and Peter Orleans, "The Mass Society and the Parapolitical Structure," *American Sociological Review*, XXVII (October 1962), 635. It is entirely possible that different types of organizations produce different results, a significant factor in this difference perhaps being the types of propaganda generated by organizations that are relevant to the issue of power.

6. On the basis of his assessment of the existing evidence, Kriesberg concludes: "Without question, families now dependent upon public assistance come disproportionally from families which had also been dependent upon assistance." Louis Kriesberg, *Mothers in Poverty: Patterns of Poverty and Broken Families* (Chicago: Aldine Publishing Company, 1970), pp. 173-77, quotes at p. 175. See also M. Elaine Burgess and Daniel O. Price, *An American Dependency Challenge* (Chicago: American Public Welfare Association, 1963); Greenleigh Associates, *Public Welfare: Poverty—Prevention or Perpetuation* (New York: Greenleigh Associates, 1964); and Norman S. Weissberg, "On Generational Welfare Dependency: A Critical Review," *Social Problems*, XVIII (Fall 1970), 257-74. This does not mean, however, that *all* welfare cases are recruited from welfare families or that all welfare families produce only

individuals who subsequently end up on welfare. No data have been collected that reflect exactly what proportion of individuals from nonwelfare origins are themselves recipients. See Kriesberg, op. cit., p. 175.

7. The findings of Ransford are relevant here. He finds that only among persons characterized as lower class is there a relationship between his measure of powerlessness and a tendency to use violence in the interest of racial justice. See H. Edward Ransford, "Isolation, Powerlessness, and Violence: A Study of Attitudes and Participation in the Watts Riot," *American Journal of Sociology*, LXXIII (March 1968), 581-91, esp. 589-90.

8. A similar analysis of inequality between nations as well as within nations is presented by Ronald G. Parris in "Inequality and Control in a Colonial Bureaucracy—Barbados: 1955-62," *Journal of Black Studies* (forthcoming) and his forthcoming dissertation, "Race, Inequality and Development in Barbados: 1627-1971" (Yale University).

9. See Thomas Gladwin, *Poverty U.S.A.* (Boston: Little, Brown & Company, 1967).

11 Alienation: Class and Cultural Dynamics

Our primary objective in this book has been to examine the class and cultural influences on alienation with regards to (1) the effects of class and culture on alienation itself and (2) the contextual effect of class and culture on the relationship of perceived deprivation and opportunity to alienation. In reviewing our findings and implications, we will discuss the former effects first.

Class, Culture, and Alienation

As expected, normlessness and anomia are inversely related to social class; our results are thus consistent with findings of other studies. At the same time, the relationships are apparently independent of the influence of perceived deprivation and perceived denied opportunity, and this is *not* consistent with much thinking about the influence of social class on anomia and normlessness. Although our findings do not reveal what aspect of lower-class life contributes to a higher level of anomia and normlessness, they do reveal that the factors involved are *not* high perceived deprivation and low perceived opportunity. Results are thus consistent with perspectives that contend that deviant behavior in the lower class is due to tradition, values, and subculture rather than feelings of deprivation and denied opportunity.[1] We of course have no measures of tradition, values, and subculture, and our measures of anomia and normlessness are, at best, only moderately good indicators of deviant behavior. Still results are at least not inconsistent with these perspectives. However, they are clearly inconsistent with perspectives that stress perceived deprivation and denied opportunity as crucial factors in *class* differences in deviant behavior and attitudes.

As for culture, only in the case of normlessness is there a systematic relationship. Even here, however, the effects of culture are modified by perceived opportunity. The negative relationship between cultural assimilation and normlessness is strongest when the effects of perceived opportunity are minimized. Thus, the effects of culture on normlessness are apt to be most apparent when the opportunity structure is perceived as open. Perceived opportunity and culture interact.

To account for this result we suggest a general cultural commitment or assimilation hypothesis. Normlessness is one expression of general cultural involvement, commitment, or assimilation. However, before a decrease in normlessness is associated with this general process, the individual must perceive the opportunity structure to be open. Perceived constraints on opportunity tend to counteract the effect of cultural assimilation or commitment in society.[2]

The findings for normlessness plus the finding of no relationship between culture and either anomia or powerlessness negate the view that alienation is especially high in American society. Class differences are clearly more apparent than cultural differences. This conclusion is consistent with the findings of other studies which have compared Mexican residents with United States residents and Mexican-Americans with anglo-Americans.[3]

In addition, the cultural difference in normlessness is consistent with the finding of another study; Simpson also reports that normlessness is higher among Mexican residents than North American residents.[4] It is not clear, however, that Simpson's measure of normlessness measures the same thing that our measure does. However, we can say generally that normlessness would seem to be higher among persons influenced by the Mexican culture than among those influenced by U.S. culture. Overall, then, results provide little support for the view that the culture of the United States has a particularly alienating effect on individuals.

Given our mixed results, it is difficult to know what if any significance should be attributed to cultural differences in level of alienation. It seems fair to say that class differences are probably more important than cultural differences. But, the cultural *context* is more important than the class context for the relationship between alienation and other variables, i.e., relative deprivation and perceived opportunity.

Relative Deprivation, Opportunity, and Alienation: Class or Cultural Dynamics?

We have seen that classes differ in perceived deprivation, aspiration, perceived opportunity, and in two of three dimensions of alienation. Although these findings are consistent with what theory and much research would lead us to expect, we have noted that they do not support some common assumptions about the effects of social class—that class and alienation are inversely related because class is inversely related to perceived deprivation and to denied opportunity. Class differences in normlessness and anomia remain after we control for both these variables. More significant, the relationships of perceived deprivation and opportunity to the three measures of alienation exist within both anglo-American class groups.

Our major hypothesis is that the dynamics of relative deprivation and opportunity derive from cultural rather than class factors, even though the levels of relative deprivation and opportunity are class determined to a large degree. At the same time, findings reveal that cultural differences are not related to relative deprivation and perceived opportunity, and only for normlessness is there a difference in alienation. Yet results rather consistently show that the magnitude of the correlations between relative deprivation and perceived opportunity, on the one hand, and measures of alienation, on the other, systematically increase with the level of cultural assimilation. Such results reveal that culture and the perceived social structure interact. Thus, perceived deprivation and blocked opportunity per se do not give rise to alienation, but the way perceived deprivation and opportunity are interpreted does. This, in turn, depends on cultural background. We suggest that our results for both perceived deprivation and opportunity are due to a different emphasis in Mexican and North American cultures on achieved and ascribed status.

Only in a society wherein the culture stresses that opportunities are (or should be) equal and wherein the same lofty goals are considered to be attainable by anyone regardless of class background—only in such a society does the denial of opportunity generate alienative attitudes. To be denied something that the culture both encourages one to strive for and insists is available to all, regardless of evidence to the contrary, is a condition that tends to generate alienation. This condition is not limited to the lower class, that is, farm workers, but also exists among the more advantaged farmers. Consequently, although results are consistent with critics of Merton's theory, that is, class differences in deviance and normative estrangement are not due to perceived denied opportunity, results are consistent with the emphasis Merton's theory places on denied opportunity in American society. The significance of this factor is cultural rather than class-related and hence may have a more general effect than Merton postulates, since it holds for powerlessness and anomia as well as normlessness.

Our interpretation of the effect of relative deprivation is somewhat different, although it is also derived from the differences in achievement and ascriptive orientations. Because in achievement-oriented societies, performance is equated with status, perceived class status (or relative deprivation as we have measured it) is important to a person's conception of his self-worth. Low status implies that one's performance is inferior to the performance of others. Thus, when one perceives himself as contributing little to and receiving little from society, one tends to become alienated from society. Generally, then, poor performers in an achievement-oriented society tend to be alienated from that society.

This is not to say that the perception of one's opportunities as blocked and one's performance as poor are the only factors contributing to alienation in an achievement-oriented society. As we have seen, class differences remain even when these two factors are controlled. Our hypothesis concerns only cultural differences in the relationship between these two factors and alienation.

The issue of cultural differences in alienation can now be seen in a different perspective. The most significant cultural phenomenon is not the level of alienation itself, but the dynamics of alienation. Although the assimilation of cultural minorities in the dominant culture of the United States may have little or no influence in raising the level of alienation (and on the basis of our results for normlessness, it may lower it), this phenomenon does help guarantee that certain factors will be associated with alienation. These factors may change with level of assimilation even if the level of alienation itself does not change.

We do not know, of course, whether the same results would be obtained for cultural minorities other than Mexican-Americans. According to our hypothesis, however, similar results would obtain only for minorities whose cultural heritage emphasizes ascribed status. Our hypothesis further contends that similar results would be obtained for comparisons between societies which differ in their emphasis on achievement and ascriptive orientations.

Our findings, of course, may measure specific differences between North American and Mexican cultures rather than general differences between achievement and ascriptive cultures. Only by completing additional comparative research on culturally distinct groups and societies which differ in achievement and ascriptive orientations can we ascertain if the patterns observed here are manifestations of general patterns associated with achievement and ascriptive cultures or if they are specific to the groups we have studied.

Social Class, the Lower Class, and the Differentiation-Integration of the Poor in Society

In concluding, we raise the question of whether the poverty or lower-class stratum could not be viewed in terms of its integration in society as well as its differentiation. It is true that the poor are different from the nonpoor in many respects. Farmers and farm workers differ as regards the structure of their life situations, perceived deprivation, goals and aspirations, perceived opportunity, and alienation. Since a high degree of alienation connotes a low degree of integration, the fact that farm workers are higher in normlessness and anomia indicates that they are less integrated into society than farmers. But in terms of the relationship between alienation and other factors (perceived deprivation and opportunity) farm workers are integrated, depending on their overall level of cultural assimilation.

This is not to say that social class is of no significance in these patterns. Indeed, as we have seen, relative deprivation and perceived opportunity are closely associated with the class structure and are largely determined by it. But in the responses individuals make to these factors, cultural differences are of greater significance than class differences. The broader culture shapes the individual's response to these factors and, hence, produces similarities rather than differences between persons in different positions in the class structure. In this sense, then, the poor and nonpoor are integrated in the broader culture of American society.

Conclusion

Like other investigations that are based on individuals from a particular geographical area, the general applicability of our results is problematical. Since the respondents are not probability samples of farmers and farm workers in the United States, generalizations for even these respective populations in the United States as a whole may be questioned. Furthermore, since samples are from rural populations, the extent to which our results apply to the more general lower-class and middle-class populations is problematical.

However, the income and other socioeconomic characteristics of most farmers clearly place this group in the middle- to upper-class level for the United States as a whole, and the characteristics of farm workers are definitely those of persons at the lower end of the class structure. Indeed, characteristics of farm workers—low income, low education, unstable unemployment, community isolation, poor housing—are frequently used to define lower-class status. Also, many of the differences between farmers and farm workers in social-psychological matters—perceived deprivation, goal orientations, aspirations, normlessness, and anomia—are consistent with existing fragmentary evidence and considerable theoretical speculation about differences between the middle and lower classes in the United States. Given also the widespread influence of the mass media and modern transportation, which permit affluent farmers to remove barriers which would otherwise keep them physically isolated from urban America, our results would not appear to be unique to class differences in the state of Washington or to peculiarities of the rural class structure. Consequently, our findings appear to have significant implications for class differences and poverty groups in general.

In addition, since the three groups of farm workers differ with respect to national origin and language, as well as other characteristics that would be expected to be associated with cultural assimilation, they represent three rather distinct cultural groups. Findings therefore provide strong support for perspectives that emphasize the significance of the cultural element in the dynamics of alienation.

Notes

1. Cf. Clifford R. Shaw and Henry D. McKay, *Delinquent Areas* (Chicago: The University of Chicago Press, 1929); and Clifford R. Shaw and Henry D. McKay et al., *Juvenile Delinquency and Urban Areas* (Chicago: The University of Chicago Press, 1942; Solomon Kobrin, "The Conflict of Values in Delinquency Areas," *American Sociological Review*, XVI (December 1951), 653-61; and Walter B. Miller, "Lower Class Culture as a Generating Milieu of Gang Delinquency," in Rose Giallombardo, ed., *Juvenile Delinquency: A Book of Readings* (New York: John Wiley & Sons, Inc., 1966), pp. 137-50.

2. For an alternative conceptualization of cultural commitment or assimilation and normlessness, see Allen E. Liska, "Comment on 'Class and Culture in Social Structure and Anomie,' " *American Journal of Sociology*, LXXVII (May 1972), 1213-17. See Rushing's response in William A. Rushing, "The Author Replies," *American Journal of Sociology*, LXXVII (May 1972), 1217-24.

3. See Joseph A. Kahl, *The Measurement of Modernism: A Study of Values in Brazil and Mexico* (Austin: The University of Texas Press, 1968); see also Joan Moore, *Mexican Americans* (Englewood Cliffs, N.J.: Prentice-Hall, Inc., 1970), pp. 128-29.

4. Miles E. Simpson, "Social Mobility, Normlessness and Powerlessness in Two Cultural Contexts," *American Sociological Review*, XXXV (December 1970), 1002-13.

Appendix A: Samples

The samples consist of 1,029 farm workers from six counties in east and central Washington, and 240 farm owners and operators from one county in east Washington.

In all counties in which farm workers were sampled, agricultural production is a major aspect of the local economy, and sizable numbers of farm workers can be found in all six counties at some period during the year. In some areas fruit production predominates, in others vegetable production, and in some areas there is a mixture. In one county hops production is extensive. Fruits grown are apples, peaches, pears, and cherries, and vegetables include potatoes, sugar beets, beans, tomatoes, peas, and onions. Wheat and peas predominate in the county from which farmers were selected.

The period of study is from March, 1966, to September, 1967. The period between March and November, 1966, was spent making observations of communities in the six counties, talking to persons in these communities and throughout the state, and conducting exploratory observations of and interviews with farm workers. The bulk of the data on farm workers, however, is based on interviews that were conducted from January to July, 1967. Most interviews with farmers were conducted in December, 1966. Different procedures were used in selecting the two samples.

Farmers

A list of farm owners and operators in the one county was obtained from the Agricultural Stabilization and Conservation Service, and a systematic probability sample of 300 names was drawn. Of these, eighteen were inapplicable (e.g., the respondent had moved) and eight could not be located. For thirty-four of the remaining 275, or approximately 12%, either the farmer refused to be interviewed or an appointment convenient to both farmer and interviewer could not be arranged. Hence, 88% of all farmers contacted were interviewed. Most interviews with farmers were conducted in December (1966) because this is a period of inclement weather when farmers are most likely to be available for interviewing.

The median age of growers is 50.9 years, almost identical to the 50.4 years for all Washington farmers and farm managers. All but 4% were married, widowed, or divorced. The median total reported *family* income for 1965 is $10,212, which is considerably higher than the median of $3,600 *personal* income for all Washington farmers in 1960.[1] Less than 5% reported an income below $4,000 and only 18% below $6,000. Exactly 50% earned in excess of $10,000 and 29% earned more than $16,000. The sample is obviously not representative of all Washington farmers, but it is probably representative of persons who operate big fruit, vegetable, and wheat "ranches" in the state.

Farm Workers

Extensive interviewing operations for farm workers were limited to the January-July period to assure as much as possible that only "hard-core" farm workers would be included in the study. Late summer is the peak season for the fruit harvest, and students, retired persons, and vacationers arrive in fruit areas at this time to work. In order to exclude these persons, interviewing operations were terminated before the fruit harvest season began. (An exception was made for cherry pickers because the harvest season for cherries is June.)

The sampling procedure imposed several additional restrictions on sample selection. To make the sample as homogeneous as possible, only male family heads were included. In addition, steps were taken to assure that both residents and migrants were included (a resident was considered anyone who had lived in Washington for at least six months at the time of the interview), as well as anglo-Americans, bilinguals, and non-English speakers. (Ethnicity was determined by physical characteristics, surname, and ability to speak English. The use of surnames was essential for screening out several American Indians who could pass for English-speaking Mexican-Americans.) Thus, within farm workers, we have six cultural-resident groups. The number from each group is given below, with percentages of total sample in parentheses.[2]

	Residents	Migrants
Anglo-Americans	282 (27)	259 (25)
Bilinguals	192 (19)	109 (11)
Non-English Speakers	72 (7)	115 (11)

Since the major aims were to examine differences between farmers and farm workers, and differences between groups among the latter, the principle concern was to avoid biasing factors rather than to attempt to draw a probability sample.[3] The general procedure was as follows:

First, counties were surveyed to locate areas (isolated communities and clusters of dwelling units, parts of a town, or rural sectors) where low-income and slum-like housing prevailed.[4] The general rule then was for interviewing teams to canvass the area for adult male farm workers (interviewers polled all houses to see if the male head was engaged in farm work). Some 55-60 workers, mostly Anglo-Americans, representing approximately 5% of all known farm workers contacted,[5] refused to be interviewed. When interviewers encountered a worker who could not speak English, they gave his name and address to a

Spanish-speaking interviewer. Although most Mexican-Americans would have preferred to be interviewed in Spanish, only those who spoke little or no English were interviewed in Spanish.[6]

Locating concentrations of most groups was relatively easy after the early stages of the research. Most communities were small and both resident and migrant residential areas were conspicuous once interviewers had learned how to recognize them.[7] Locating migrants was somewhat easier than locating residents, however. Most migrants lived in housing used almost exclusively by farm workers, including private and public labor camps, run-down motels, clusters of inexpensive and deteriorating cabins, apartment houses, and trailer camps. Since these are vacant most of the year, a number of areas were identified while they were still vacant and were watched until occupants began to move in. Once an area appeared to have reached its capacity, or when occupancy began to stabilize, an interviewing team canvassed the area.

Representativeness of Samples

The sample and subsamples obviously are not random samples of farm workers from Washington, or even representative samples. For example, the median personal income of $2,436 for the sample is higher than the $1,568 which the census reports for all Washington farm workers in 1960.[8] Wages for farm workers, as for all occupations, may have been higher at the time of the study than in 1960. Probably more important is that young single males who are temporary farm workers with very low incomes are excluded from the study: 38% of farm workers in the census are below 25 years of age in comparison with only 17% in the sample; corresponding median ages are 32.0 and 39.5 years. Also, the sample probably contains a disproportionate number of anglo-Americans whose median personal income of $2,644 is somewhat higher than for the total sample.[9] With these exceptions, however, the sample would appear to be representative of more or less full-time Washington male farm workers who are family heads.[10]

Notes

1. Farmers were asked to report only their family income. Since the census does not report data for family income, our figure would be expected to be somewhat higher than the census figure.

2. An original quota of 1,000 respondents was set, with the sample to be evenly divided between residents and migrants, and anglo-Americans and Mexican-Americans, with the latter divided equally between bilinguals and non-English speakers. In general, deviation from the original quotas was

determined by differences in availability of the different populations during the study period as well as the availability of Spanish-speaking interviewers. However, the higher proportion of anglo-American residents results from special efforts to assure that the quota for this group would be reached in order to be able to compare workers and farmers with ethnicity and residence controlled.

3. Original plans were to draw random samples from labor camps and farms where workers were employed, from which systematic samples of workers were to be selected. Investigation revealed, however, that no master list of labor camps from which a sample could be drawn existed. Also, many migratory workers live in areas not technically classified as "labor camps," such as privately owned, run-down shacks that are advertised as "cabins," usually located on the outskirts of town away from the main flow of traffic, or in isolated areas on back roads; no list of such places existed. Sampling farms was problematical because of the farmers' sensitivity to the publicity being given to farm workers by various federal agencies and groups in the state. Much of the publicity stemmed from newly enacted Office of Economic Opportunity programs. However, the living conditions of farm workers have also been the topic of discussion and the target of programs for several groups and agencies in Washington. And, in 1960, a Seattle television station made and showed a film, "Bitter Harvest," depicting the living conditions of farm workers in Washington, which many growers still vividly recalled at the time of the study.

4. Since none of the counties was densely populated, there were relatively few concentrations of residential dwellings. This made the identification of low-income housing much easier than it would have been in more populated areas. Actually, only three counties were surveyed intensively; the other three were almost exclusively fruit areas and so did not contain many workers during the study period.

5. The low refusal rate may be due to the fact that respondents were paid $1.50 for the interview.

6. Although all Mexican-Americans who were interviewed in English were classified as bilingual, it is possible that a few were unable to speak Spanish. It would have been desirable, of course, to separate these from the bilingual Mexican-Americans. However, since so many of the English speaking Mexican-Americans would have preferred to be interviewed in Spanish, the problem of including true bilinguals in the non-English speaking category was much more serious than including only English speakers in the bilingual category. Consequently, interview procedures were adopted to distinguish between English and non-English speaking Mexican-Americans, rather than to identify those Mexican-Americans who could not speak Spanish.

In translating questionnaire items into Spanish, an effort was made to produce a translation that was not so much correct in the formal sense as to be meaningful in the vernacular of Mexican-American farm workers. The original translation was made by an individual who had lived in Mexico for several years and was familiar with the vernacular of Mexican peasants; he had conducted interviews and made translations in connection with other surveys in Mexico and southwestern United States. In addition, the translation was assessed by one of the study interviewers, a Mexican-American sociology graduate student who grew up in a farm worker family in the west. There is always the problem, of course, of whether questions still have the same meaning for persons with different cultural backgrounds.

7. Surprisingly, however, little help could be obtained from permanent residents of the communities; the residents were not unwilling to cooperate but usually did not know where farm workers lived. This is discussed in Chapter 3.

8. U.S. Bureau of the Census, *U.S. Census of Population: 1960. Detailed Characteristics. Washington*, Final Report PC (1)-49D (Washington, D.C.: U.S. Government Printing Office, 1962), Table 124, pp. 325-26. Also, in three of the five states represented ten or more times among migrants (Arkansas, Oregon, and Texas), farm workers' income is below that for all occupations except "private household workers"; and in the other two states, only one other category has a lower median income ("other service workers, excluding private household workers" in Arizona, and "wholesale and retail laborers" in California).

9. The proportions of Washington farm workers who are anglo-American and Mexican-American cannot be obtained from census materials.

10. Ninety percent report being married; others were family heads, although the wife-mother was absent because the respondent was divorced, widowed, or separated. In addition, five workers reported being single. Probably, these subjects were not legally married nor legally responsible for the families with whom they were living and apparently supporting.

Appendix B: Index of
Cultural Assimilation

Because assimilation is such a slow, gradual process, and because it involves changes in so many different cultural elements (values, ideals, customs, norms, language, beliefs, speech, attitudes), it is difficult to measure all of its aspects. It seems clear, however, that despite the fact that all three cultural groups studied are composed of U.S. residents, they are not equally assimilated to U.S. culture. Mexican-Americans are particularly prone to retain their cultural heritage and to resist assimilation to the anglo-American culture.[1] Moreover, since language is the one most important determinant of cultural participation—symbolic and overt—it is a good index of the degree to which members of cultural minorities are assimilated into the dominant culture of a society. Only when one speaks the language of a society can he truly understand many of the beliefs, values, attitudes, and norms of that society, and hence only then can be adopt them as his own. In short, the ability to speak the language of a society is a necessary condition to being assimilated in the culture of that society.[2] By this criterion, anglo-Americans would be the most assimilated, and non-English speakers the least. Although bilinguals do not lack facility with the English language, the retention of their native language reflects their continued participation in and identification with a non-anglo culture. In addition, other correlates of cultural assimilation distinguish between the three groups.

It is generally assumed that children are valued more in Mexican society than in anglo society (and the same is generally true for ascriptive societies in comparison to achievement-oriented societies). Consequently, we would expect differences between our three groups in number of children. Results are reported separately for respondents with income below and above $4,000. For those below $4,000, the average number of children (with N in parentheses) is 2.71 (298) for anglo-Americans, 3.62 (167) for bilinguals, and 4.08 (127) for non-English speakers;[3] for those above $4,000, averages are 2.78 (190), 4.43 (93), and 5.96 (25). These differences exist despite the fact that anglo-Americans as a group are older; median ages of fathers are 45, 33, and 38.

Although education is frequently used as an index of socioeconomic status, it is also an index of cultural assimilation when we compare cultural groups.[4] It is through formal education that many of the norms and values, and beliefs and knowledges which characterize a particular culture become assimilated. Results show that for farm workers below $4,000 (N in parentheses) median years of education are 6.72 (297), 4.31 (166), and 2.43 (128), and for those above $4,000 medians are 8.29 (190), 4.75 (91), and 2.28 (25). Regardless of income level, education is inversely related to cultural assimilation as indexed by national origin and language.

Surprisingly, Mexican-Americans are more apt to report some form of voluntary association membership than anglo-Americans (54% to 32% report at least one such membership). Analysis of type of membership, however, produces results consistent with the above.[5] For Mexican-Americans, church membership is by far the most frequent type of membership reported. (Virtually all Mexican-Americans reporting church membership are affiliated with the Catholic Church.) Given that church congregations are probably patterned along ethnic lines, the ratio of church memberships to all other memberships may be taken as an index of assimilation. Ratios for the three groups are 0.79, 2.44, and 10.25. It is probable, therefore, that the higher social participation rate for Mexican-Americans reflects a participation in cultural activities that is different from those of the dominant culture.[6]

Whether we consider cultural values about children, education, or associational membership, the level of assimilation in anglo culture is inversely associated with the degree of cultural differences, as reflected in the differences in national origin and language. Differences in the three groups, therefore, reflect real cultural differences, not just differences in class and socioeconomic factors. The distinction between anglo-Americans, bilinguals, and non-English speakers would appear to be a reasonably valid index of cultural assimilation.

Notes

1. See John H. Burma, ed., *Mexican-Americans in the United States* (Cambridge, Mass.: Schenkman Publishing Co., 1970), p. 105. See also Clark S. Knowlton, "Petron-Peon Pattern among the Spanish Americans of New Mexico," *Social Forces*, LXI (October 1962), 12; and Ozzie G. Simmons, "The Mutual Images and Expectations of Anglo-Americans and Mexican-Americans," in Staten W. Webster, ed., *Knowing the Disadvantaged* (San Francisco: Chandler Publishing Company, 1966), pp. 134, 137-38.

2. Park and Burgess state: "The competition and survival of languages afford interesting material for the study of conditions that determine assimilation." Robert E. Park and Ernest W. Burgess, *Introduction to the Science of Sociology* (Chicago: The University of Chicago Press, 1921), p. 771.

3. In the following discussion, results will be presented for anglo-Americans, bilinguals, and non-English speakers in that order.

4. See Prodipto Roy, "The Measurement of Assimilation: The Spokane Indians," *American Journal of Sociology*, LXVII (March 1962), 541-51.

5. Over 90% of all three groups report less than two memberships.

6. We are unable to control for income since type of associational membership is recorded only by ethnic group identity and not for specific individuals.

Index

Aberle, David F., 123.
Achieved status, *see* Status.
Acquiescence,
  and anomia, 80, 103-04.
  and goal orientation, 125.
  and social class, 64, 80, 83-85.
  the problem of, 83-85.
Adams, Richard N., 38, 103, 142.
Agricultural economy, 60-63.
Alienation
  and aspiration, 152.
  and causal homogeneity, 156.
  and culture, 89-102, 151, 171-75.
  and fatalism, 81.
  and false consciousness, 155.
  and relative deprivation, 4, 11-14, 29,
    41-53, 69-70, 79, 82-83, 85-86, 89-102,
    152, 156, 171-73.
  and social class, 69-70, 82-83, 85-86,
    171-72.
  and societal integration, 174.
  class and cultural contexts of, 11-14,
    31-32.
  concept of, 3-9.
  as attribute of social structure, 5-6.
  as attribute of individual, 6.
  in the present study, 29-32, 152.
  Marx's concept of, 7, 59, 60, 61-62, 72,
    73, 75.
  specific meanings of, 6-9.
  technology and, 11.
      See Also: Anomia, Cultural assimila-
      tion, Culture, Farmers, Farm workers,
      Normlessness, Opportunity theory,
      Perceived opportunity, Powerlessness,
      Relative deprivation.
Allen, Steve, 21, 34, 35, 36, 37.
Altus, William, 37.
Analgesic subculture, 159-60.
Anderson, Nels, 21, 22, 34.
Anglo-Americans,
  number in sample, 30.
  state residence of, 30.
    See also: Cultural assimilation, Culture,
    Farm workers.
Anomia,
  and aspirations, 153.
  and culture, 89, 93, 95, 98-102, 152, 171,
    172.
  and fatalism, 81.
  and social class, 79-83, 85-86, 153, 171,
    175.
  concept of, 8-9.
  defined, 9, 82.

measure of, 80-83, 84-85.
  Srole's definition of, 79.
  Srole's scale of, 78.
  correlates of, 81.
    See also: Acquiescence, Cultural
    assimilation, Farmers, Farm workers,
    Opportunity theory, Poor, the, Rela-
    tive deprivation.
Anomie,
  Durkheim's concept of, 8.
  Merton's concept of, 12.
    See also: Normlessness.
Ascribed status, *see* Status.
Aspirations, 145-50, 159.
    See also: Cultural assimilation,
    Culture, Farmers, Farm workers,
    Perceived opportunity, Social class.

Backman, Carl W., 57.
Bacon, Margaret K., 12, 17.
Bagdikian, Ben H., 56, 57.
Baker, George C., 37.
Ball, Richard, 159, 160, 168.
Banton, Michael P., 57.
Barry, Herbert, III, 12, 17.
Beck, Bernard, 38.
Bell, Daniel, 5, 14, 73.
Bell, Wendell, 16, 87, 141, 152.
Bendix, Reinhard, 16, 44, 53, 55, 58, 120,
    122, 141, 142.
Bennett, William S., Jr., 120.
Benson, Joseph, 121-22.
Bentham, Jeremy, 15.
Bilingual Mexican-Americans,
  number in sample, 30.
  state residence of, 30.
    See also: Cultural assimilation, Culture.
Blake, Judith, 140.
Blau, Peter M., 34.
Blauner, Robert, 11, 17.
Blum, Zahava D., 14, 20, 33, 34, 124, 139,
    143.
Bonjean, Charles M., 87.
Braceroes
  as farm laborers, 25.
  defined, 34.
Broom, Leonard, 38.
Buckley, Walter, 32, 34.
Bureaucracy,
  and powerlessness, 65-67, 70, 166.
  as condition of work, 72.
  farmers and, 74.
Burgess, Ernest W., 103, 184.
Burgess, M. Elaine, 169.

184